The Book of Stones

Bruce Rout

ISBN: 978-1-0690473-0-4

The Book of Stones

A Book for White Canadian Men
Regarding the Residential School System
in Canada

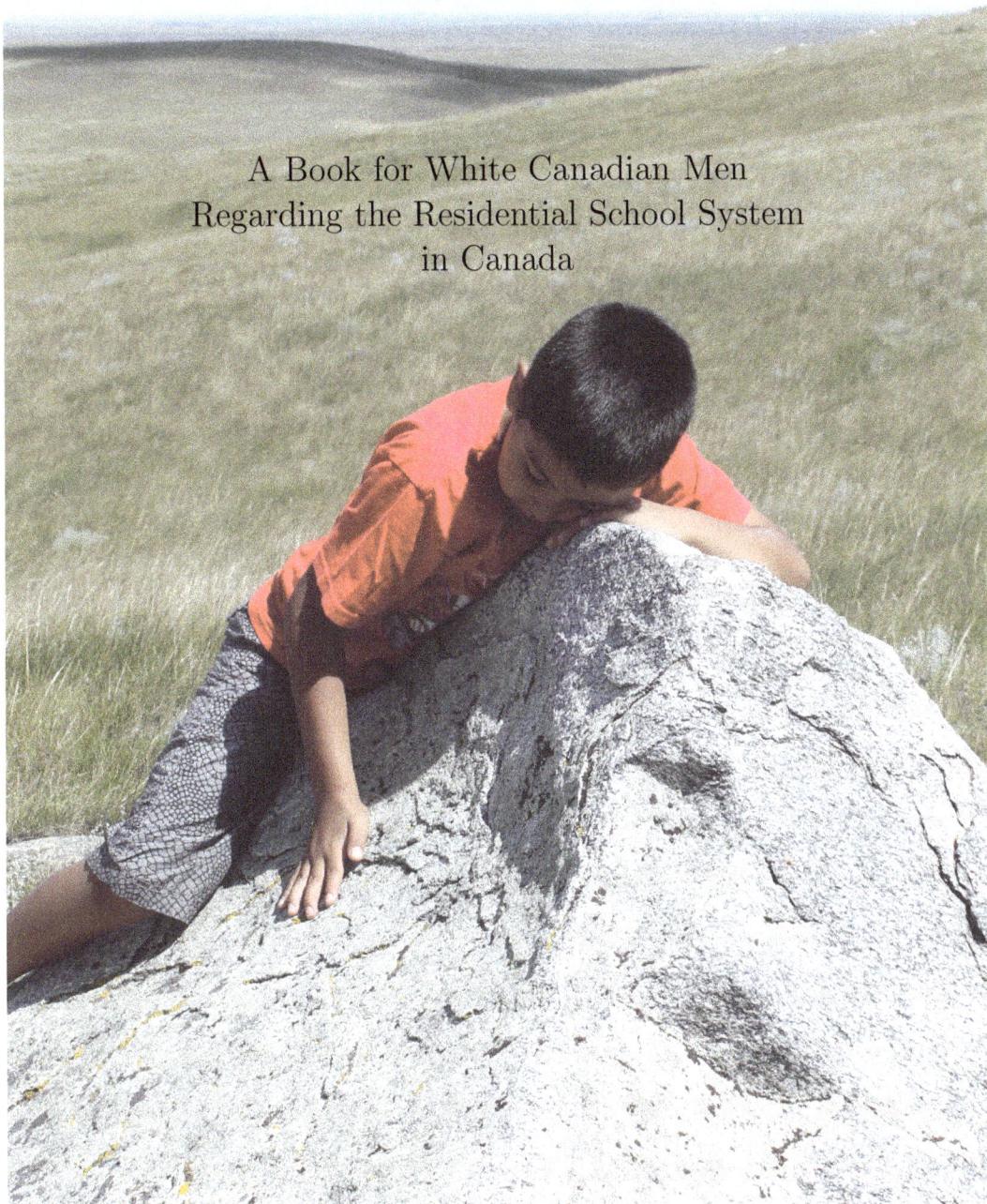

Let me lower you gently into the depths of hell
Where only White men dare to go
Protected by priviledge and a courage yet unknown.

Who is to blame in the flame of damnation?
But for what we do not understand?

Are we asked to carry the albatros of guilt
For what we did not do?

Slowly we descend to where only White men can go
And still survive.

So we may scream Anglo Saxon curses unheard by pure souls
Guilt is useless here.

We seek the stone.

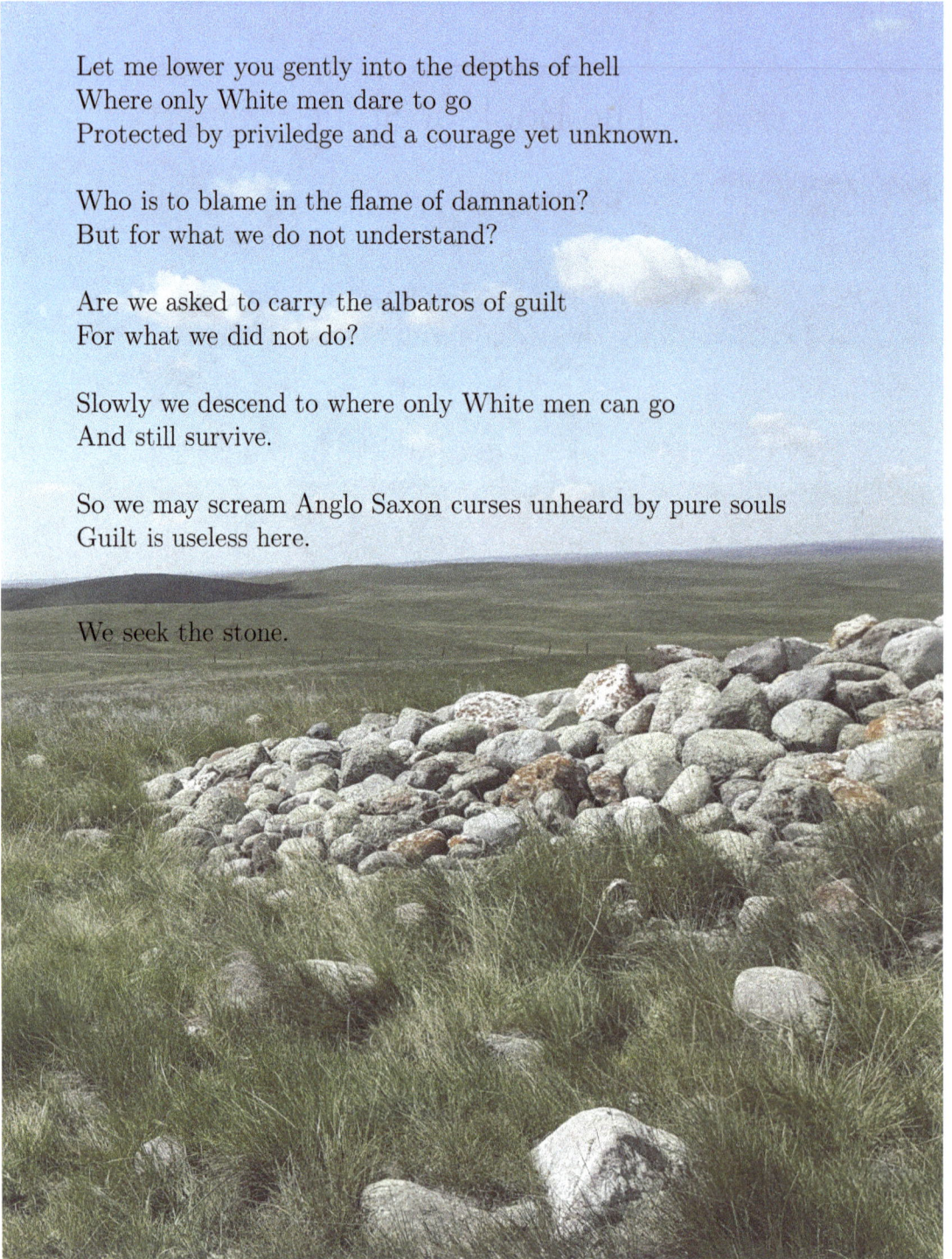

Chapter 1

The Book of Stones

What is a stone and what is a stone to you or me? Nothing responds to the flow of the universe as quickly or as completely as a stone. It feels all gravitational influences all changes in momentum, the dance of curvature and the grand orchestration of infinity.

What can a stone teach us as it lies in the dirt in a backwater isolated from life except for a few plants? The stone cries for someone or something to listen to lessons only a stone can teach. The stones called to the void for one to learn, to listen, and to understand.

We have responded to your every whim.
We have moved to balance your every lean and shift,
Your every paradigm.
We are your most obedient servant.
Even the atoms have their minds.
But we only have a mind for you.
Send us one.
Make us one with whom
We can communicate
And break the eternal silence
With the song of love.

Hear our prayer.
Feel our desire.
Remember us.
Use us.

In 1991 our family returned from New Zealand and I fell apart. I'd fallen in love with teaching high school mathematics and science and ran into a brick wall. It was weird moving to a beautiful community known as Chemainus on the east coast of Vancouver Island. This was a tourist town with murals painted on the buildings and lovely tree-lined streets. It was a place where kids could safely bike through town and play outside until 3:00 in the morning.

The houses were funky-looking and non-suburban. There was a park outside our backyard. We had apple and cherry trees and the odd bear or two. An eagle's nest was in the river park behind us. Parents and young would fly over my son's bedroom dropping bird shit on his window regularly.

From time to time lost intoxicated Native people from the reserve on a nearby island would wander through the town. This entire island was a reserve which was called Kuper Island. They had had a residential school on the island and we were all told it had been torn down by the Native people 10 years previously. No white person had been on the island ever since.

A seal
Sitting on rocks by the shores sunning itself calls out.
Others join in.
"We are not good to eat. We are tough and tasteless.
We called you to come over."
The rocks protect the trees from the sea
And seals patrol sunlight along with gulls.
A residential school lies in a torn-down mess,
Hiding secrets and broken dreams
That erupt in nightmares
Of at least one white man with others to follow.

There are songs sung by the rocks by Kuper where British ships were sunk in a battle against dugout canoes. Penelakuts paddling like mad against warships and laughing with abandon. This ship is just another great whale. Directly they paddled closely abutting the side of a wooden sailor and fire the cannon which was lashed onto the front of the canoe. And there's a hole in the side of British pride that sinks in the bay by Kuper.

These are a fierce, intelligent people who have been taught by the rocks and trees for thousands of years.

I was called to teach Kuper Island children who had never been to school. It had been 10 years since white men were banished from the island. They had a grant of some money to pay a professional teacher and that ended up being me. A lot of things aren't understood when you're hired by a band. You have to meet with everyone in the band: parents, adults, men and women and they go around and ask about you. They each ask you questions, all of them. Then you go out of the room all they consult. If anyone of them says no they all say no. That's how it's done.

If you kick one rock, you've kicked them all. If you are accepted by one rock, you're accepted by all. If one rock sings to you, they all join in the chorus and the sound of their combined silence is deafening.

The rocks sing of the stars.
Stones hum a lullaby
Drifting Mother Earth into tranquillity.
Sometimes a stone will jump into your hand
And end up in your pocket
For many years
And be your only companion
To comfort you
And remind you
Of times long ago
When you were one
With the earth and the sky.

It is raining now on the planet Venus
Showers of sulfuric acid.
Some time ago there were no residential schools.
Children were playing.
Harpists and balladeers were wandering around Europe
Spreading the news of the day

Travelling up and down
The west coast of Canada.
They were storytellers.
They were teachers.
Many of the ways of education are lost to us now.

Young nobles were taken to a sacred place
Deep in the forest
A collection of rocks
With stones, these nobles, future kings and rulers, would have to
carve pictograms and drawings that represent their statement to the
universe on what type of person,
What type of king, would they be?
Upon such rocks are carved pictographs and drawings by kings.
There are some new ones in very select secret spaces.
This practice is returning
And that is not for us to say.

We are white men.
Rocks speak to us in ancient tongues
We cannot understand anymore.
There are strewn around Europe, stones in patterns hundreds of
miles long
That speak to us of our ancient leaders
Of people who made their statement
To the universe
Beyond the ken of mere mortals.

We are white men
With British heritage
Whether we like it or not.
We played with pigskin
On the fields of Rugby
And conquered the world.
And we learned from rugby
The spirit of fair play.
We share the secret and bounty

Of compulsory free institutionalized education
So that we may all become civilized.

From ancient times
Lightning talked to us,
Called to us,
To battle with great warriors,
Over truth and justice.
The lightning storms over the prairies of Canada
Are terrifying
And impossible to ignore.

The ferry smoothly traversed from the Chemainus docks to Kuper Island this September morning. It was the early ferry so the ocean water was smooth. There were cars to both Kuper and the neighbouring island. It was our first day at work to try to rebuild an education system for both Kuper adults and kids. The ferry docked and we walked off, across the dock and up a slight incline and along the rocks to the new two-story building that was built atop the torn-down residential school.

I met the kids standing around the lower floor of the building smoking cigarettes. The adults got the upper half which also had windows. The lower half had no windows. Roughly 10 kids were waiting to start the school day. I told them to come inside after they finished their smokes.

I found some fold-up tables and chairs leaning on a wall. The room was spacious. I began setting up tables into some sort of horseshoe shape when the kids started wandering in. I asked if I could get a hand setting them up. The students were a somewhat unkempt crew ranging from 12 to 16 years of age. Both boys and girls in jeans and t-shirts. We all set up tables and chairs. We did not speak. I'd expected this. We're pretty much silent. There was no whiteboard or blackboard. There was only silence while we set up tables and chairs. There was no curriculum. There were no books. There were no teachers' dirty looks.

Chapter 2

In Aotearoa the wind, rain and sea sing sometimes
Softly as the land rises to kiss the sky,
As mother and father stroll above volcanoes in sudden storms.
The children of the sea have secrets and a knowledge of the land that
are lost to us now.
The knowledge is lost to us now,
Even though it is locked
In the hearts of stones
That break
In the lodge
Revealing the universe,
Eternal, dark male energy
Dedicated to the one we love.

After a day of getting to know the kids on Kuper Island, it all
got shut down. A member of the band had gone missing. He had
stormed out in an argument with his wife and the entire band
panicked. The other white guy, who had taught the adults, went
home and stayed there. I decided to help find the lost band member.
I was the only white guy to do so. I got to learn a few things.

On The first day of the search the whole island showed up to
help out. We searched everywhere. I heard that he, the missing
band member, had gone through the old town section of the reserve
which had been abandoned. No one went there, so that's where I
went. Down into a valley area by the ocean surrounded by rainforest,
populated by old small houses that hid themselves behind fir and

cedar trees. There were a few paths here and there leading into the forest and perhaps up a hill. I asked the spirits who were still living there if they had seen the missing member pass this way. They all said yes. They had seen him and he was up the hill. So I girded my courage and started through the darkness under the trees. Between the houses all of the spirits blocked my way and some held me back by grabbing me by my shoulders

"Don't go there," they said firmly, "That is not for you."

"Keep your mouth shut."

I could have fought them off and moved forward and found him but I decided to follow the gentle suggestions of the dead. I returned to the habitat village. Some of the kids that were in my class noticed where I had been.

"Did you go down into Old Town?" one asked.

"Yeah," I replied.

"Nobody goes there," he continued. "Geez. Don't go there again. Don't tell anyone you went there either. There are a lot of spirits down there."

"Oh," I shrugged nodding in agreement.

People had gathered in the village and set out in small groups of two or three to try and find the missing one somewhere in the forest. I teamed up with a young man, about 30 years old or so, and we again traced our path in the dense undergrowth beneath trees. We were looking for any signs of a human who had passed through that area. After a bit, we stopped to rest and talk. We rested in a small glen with overhanging branches. We sat on some logs and began talking. Remember, no white men had been on that island for 10 years.

"He had a fight with his wife," began my search partner who was short, stocky and in very good shape, either cleanly shaven or no facial hair, Native, of course. His hair was trimmed and well-kept, thick and black. He wore jeans and a work shirt. It was still Fall and quite warm.

"It's because of the residential school" he continued, "We all went through that. He was raped by the priests and beaten."

I just sat there and listened.

"They raped all of us," he continued, "and it makes it really difficult to be with our wives and families.

"It was the residential school. I got raped too."

All I could say was that I was sorry and that it was so wrong.

It wasn't just wrong. It was evil. Truly, evil and satanic.

He said all of the men on the island were raped or otherwise sexually abused. I thought about the women and wondered what had happened to them but I didn't ask. You never ask. You wait. You pray and knowledge comes to you. Sometimes you wish the knowledge wouldn't come to you, but it always does. The most overwhelming thought that bulldozed over my mind from hearing my search partner tell me the great and obvious secret of Kuper Island was that we were finally going to get our country. Canada will finally become a country. We all have to grow up. I knew instinctively that sexual abuse, rape and murder of children under the care of our government was not restricted to Kuper. It was national. It was all over our country.

My search buddy piped up, "They really picked on that guy, the guy who went missing.

"He was one of their favourites.

"That was the priests and the brothers."

There was quite a bit of silence between us. Silence that lives forever in the forest of Vancouver Island.

I could only say, "We're going to get our country back."

My partner looked at me strangely.

"What do you mean, we're going to get our country back?" He asked.

"We're not a country" I said, "we're just a colony.

"We're not responsible and have no control over the behaviour of our government. You can't have something like this, this horror, and not have huge repercussions. This will affect the whole nation.

"We're going to get our country back," I repeated.

I stared off into space somewhere.

He was thinking. We both were. Then we got up and continued looking for signs that someone had passed through that way.

There is a darkness in the soul of every Canadian, a darkness of which we do not speak. It is a darkness through which light cannot travel. It is the darkness of condemnation that we carry through the praise and accolades of a world swimming with madness itself in this darkness, in this despair. In this darkness of evil which we have all embraced lay the stones talking to each other.

They do not lift or remove the darkness.
They give themselves to it.
That is what they did to the men.
And we are all accountable.
If we are a country . . .
That is what they did to the men.
Do not contemplate the women.

Where am I? I thought, continuing the search. Into what hole have I been dropped? How the hell am I to teach children in this place, this country? This Canada is nothing but a complete cesspool. I did not know about the rocks just yet. They hadn't started speaking. They were just introducing me to my country.

Eventually, Search and Rescue was called in along with the Mounties. Mounties, search and rescue volunteers, and Kuper Island Natives searched the island for a week and couldn't find anything.

During this search some Native people came up to me and asked, "Are all white people so stupid?

"We have been walking with them all afternoon. We're eating leaves from trees and bushes. There are berries and springs everywhere. All these white people in the search, they are all trying to figure out how he's getting food or water. There's food and water all over the place. We keep demonstrating that and they can't figure that out.

"Are they all that stupid?"

"They'll never pick up on what you do," I said, "you actually have to tell them; they are actually that stupid. Watch this."

So I walked up to the head of the search team and I told him, "Hey I know where he's getting his food and water. There are lots of plants you can eat and berries and springs. Local people have been showing and demonstrating that to you all afternoon."

The leader of the search and rescue team looked at me annoyed. Then he looked at the group of Native people I had been talking to as though they were some type of nuisance. He then harrumphed and trudged off with the search team, complete with knapsacks, dan-

gling water bottles and army combat boots. I returned to my band
of newfound comrades who were in awe of the blatant stupidity, ignorance and racism of the white people who were trying to help. We
joked a lot about how the men of Kuper Island could charge money
to conduct survival training courses.

This is the essence of the joke: Talking to white survival students:
"Hey, put your bags, knapsack, and stuff over there in one corner.
Take all your knives and everything out of your pockets and leave
them there too. Take your survival jackets and your combat boots
and put them there too. Good. Come over to the door. Here is a
strike-anywhere match. It's all you got. Don't lose it, or you're in
real trouble, and don't let it get wet. We're off. We'll be back in a
couple of weeks. If you survive, you pass the course."

"Jeez," the guys would say, "If it's survival, you won't have all
those things. You have to learn to survive with nothing."

And the way of teaching, I figured out very quickly, is show and
demonstrate. Don't tell. Teaching is not telling.

After a week, they sent all the white men and women off the island
except me. I had told a lady Mountie where the missing man was. I
said he was on top of the hill overlooking the old town, hanging from
a tree. But no one listens. I have talked to rocks and stones with
more response.

That was when there was lightning. The grass prays to the rain
when thirsty and the rain responds and quenches the thirst of the
grass. So do the rocks themselves pray to the lightning that comes
to life to strike gigavolts and give sustenance to rocks. White men,
such as myself, believe it to be the finger of God, sometimes pointing
the way. What is it with lightning that it seeks the stone? Which is
male and which is female? Does the lightning live in the sky waiting
to bring his loved one to life? Does the sky lurk about sometimes in
daylight and sometimes in the dark? Then dressed in clouds and with
a deafening announcement, find his way to his lover lying beneath
him?

Chapter 3

We were looking for the medicine wheel, the Majorville Medicine Wheel, Donna and I. We were looking for rocks on the ground that spoke to the stars. The instructions were clear: coming from Blackfoot Crossing, drive straight south till you see the sign, then turn left to Majorville. So we did.

Donna is a nurse from New Zealand with a Blackfoot husband, now ex, and a daughter back in Kiwi-land. We had time to kill and decided to take in the Majorville Medicine Wheel. It's supposed to be a circle of stones with spokes of stones marking astronomical events. So, due south, we go. We found the sign, turned left, continued in a straight line and got completely lost. Our ancestors were so proud.

I knew we were on the right track when a pregnant coyote ran across the road front of us. I was driving east on a dirt road. Just past the coyote we came to a cattle crossing and a broken farmer's fence with a sign that we were off the beaten path; forward into some hills.

I forgot to tell you, we were heading east from the turnoff. It was around noon on a hot summer's day in southern Alberta. There are very few trees, and the land stretches into the horizon, hidden only by the curvature of the earth. You can see forever. Roads in rural Southern Alberta are aligned straight east and west and are known as Township roads, or due north and south, known as Range roads. They're straight, go on forever, and are exactly one mile apart. This divides the countryside into 1-mile squares, and each square mile is called a section. When you're off the beaten path, you're outside of such neatly laid-out roads, dirt and gravel, and into an area where the roads may curve a bit.

We turned off from going south on the Range road and headed east onto the Township road. We drove up an incline, known as a hill, and over its crest. The land stretched out forever until the next hill.

We could see a dip in the road ahead before the second hill heading east. About a couple of miles away, a faint, quaint schoolhouse by the left-hand side of the road could be detected. There was typical grassland as far as the eye could see. After reaching the schoolhouse, I turned into the yard beside it and stopped. We both got out to take a look and to stretch our legs.

Valhalla is not of this world. It is a myth in the minds of white men who long for a golden age that never existed. On the floor of Valhalla, on the battlefield, great warriors attack each other in battles, in skirmishes, to create truth from sparks flying from swords and shields smashing together. The spark of truth cannot be lit but through the clash of differing opinions. Each warrior battles falsehood and evil.

My ancestors can be traced back to Bristol, England, then back to William the Conqueror in the Battle of Hastings. From there, back to Normandy, then back to Scandinavia somewhere. And somewhere on a cliff in Scandinavia in ancient times, overlooking the ocean in the middle of a lightning storm at night, stood an old Viking warrior waving his sword in the air and challenging Odin to a fight. Odin complied. The old ancestor was struck with a resounding bolt of lightning through his upraised sword, on a cliff, with crashing waves. That ended the ancestor's ridiculous dance spectacularly. On the floor of Valhalla stood the ancient ancestor who cried out: How the hell am I going to describe residential schools? On the battlefield, everyone stopped and listened.

Jesus Christ, how do I describe the residential school system? How do I describe being in a school where children, your friends, brothers and sisters, were tortured to death while you tried to stay alive, while you tried to survive, while you were terrorized? Frozen in fear. Jesus, what about the children? When did You command Your followers to engage in genocide? Did You forget about the children, cloaked in sacred garments and wearing nuns' habits to ensure sanctity and purity, as You beat the children to death? As You held them down to have clitorises cut out raw like a piece of meat and then cauterized with iodine?

"Happy 10th birthday little girl.

"That'll stop your promiscuous soul.

"Stop your crying and screaming and go to your room.

"Stupid girl, they're savages.

"Now she won't be able to chase after boys like a disgusting repulsive native slut"

Every girl on her 10th birthday at Providence farm in Duncan, BC was brutally castrated by a qualified professional doctor as she was held down by nuns on a wooden kitchen table. Students in class could hear her scream. No one said anything. The permanent pain silenced everything. And I have stolen those voices. It was theirs to tell. They are gone now after suffering a lifetime of pain and shame. They told Roxy, and Roxy told me, and now I'm telling you.

Live with it.

Sleep with it.

You white women with pride and dignity. Dream the nightmare of imagining yourself as a 10-year-old girl away from your parents, family and friends, with no one to know and no one to tell. There is no rescue for you. All you can do is scream in pain. Be grateful you weren't gagged, white women.

Embrace it.

Understand it.

Be angry.

The dead have not let me go yet.
The white race has not responded to the rocks screaming of graves beneath our feet.
Are they real?
Did all of this actually happen?
What is it like to be burned to death?
Do nightmares never end?
They cannot end if they never began.
An explosion only increases in magnitude the longer it is suppressed.

Chapter 4

Back on Kuper Island the children had returned to school. The search was called off. A spirit seeker was called in. We had to avoid the bighouse. We saw the spirit seeker and company of support rushing throughout the reserve. It was a long pole carried by the shaman. It had a couple of feathers atop it. It dragged the shaman always across the swamp to go up the hill and he could not follow it. The spirits took a direct path straight up the hill. So he went around the swamp. Of course, after a few days, we heard they found him. The shaman and his entire company had climbed the hill, dragged on by the spirit keeper.

They found him as the spirits had described it to me hanging in a tree. They cut him down. the Mounties were angry at that. They wanted to be the ones first on the scene, but they weren't there. They never are.

They were there when three children managed to escape the residential school to drag them back. The children's parents were not informed. They knew anyway because they went to the school too. The whole island knew. These kids later tried to escape using a log as a raft. They drowned.

But back here at Kuper life goes on. We attended the funeral in the bighouse. It was the first time for me in a bighouse. It was big.

From where comes this evil?
This torturing of children on a national basis was well known.
Condoned, supported, and paid for by the federal government of Canada.

A doctor, aghast at the treatment of children and residential schools in Canada wrote a report to the federal government in 1936. It was ridiculed and cast aside. The members of parliament and the bureaucrats knew what was happening and they applauded it. They wanted it to happen. They not only wanted the annihilation of Native people, either through absorption into Canadian society to such a degree that not even skin colour could be discerned, but also the torturing to death, screaming, of those who could not possibly defend themselves. They were free of consequence. Free of the delight of witnessing the abject horror. They watched the numbers roll in with glee.

This is beyond being just sadistic or mentally ill. This entirety is evil personified by the people involved. The only word available in the language of the colonizers themselves is "satanic". But where does this come from And who are we?

In 1967 I was so down and out I joined a monastery just to stay alive. It was the Caley Fathers in Bracebridge, Ontario. It only lasted a week. I was not cut out to be a monk, but thankful for the meals, the prayers, and the beautiful musical Gregorian chant. I was 18, and though I've been on the road since I was 15, I was still pretty naive.

Every time we ate, each and every meal, we were read the exploits of previous monks and priests from the early days, the days of contact between the church and Native people. The stories were of attempts to teach Natives Christianity and the ongoing torture of the clergy by fire, and so on, gruesome and written first hand. I couldn't understand how someone could write about such torture and survive. Wouldn't the writer also be killed? Was this a way to paint Native people as negatively as possible to rationalize our feelings toward them? I was also told that if I was a problem for the monastery, I'd be sent to a residential school. That was the worst punishment for anyone handed out by the monastery. It was portrayed in the worst possible light, in places where Native children refused to speak English, and it was impossible to teach them. They were even taken from their parents so they could be prevented from being poisoned from hearing Native languages.

A friend of mine at the monastery said there were real problems in taking kids away from their parents. I didn't see the red flags. I should have known. I should have been able to figure it out, but I didn't. I left the place, an Anglican monastery, not a Roman Catholic one. The evil, as I would later learn, has been pretty evenly spread throughout the various denominations of Christianity.

I said I left after a week. I was too busy trying to survive to think about it too much so I didn't. So where comes such evil?

There are no other cultures on the face of the earth that have invented manifestations of evil such as Satan: a manifestation of evil that is more powerful than God. No other culture has such a thing. No other culture ever. Where does this come from?

In the bighouse, the entire island had gathered to bury their friend. I didn't know him, but I wanted to say farewell too. The scars around his neck were visible as his body lay in an open casket. The bighouse is a roughly hewn place built around a dirt floor.

The priest said his ceremony, the casket was closed, all the men gathered outside in two long parallel lines leading to the cemetery. The first six carried the coffin to the next six and walked on to the head of the line. The coffin would eventually be passed up and again the six walked the coffin to the next six and so on to the next six and each six walked to the head of their respective lines and the cemetery. It was a warm sunny afternoon. The men worked in silence. This was men's work. The women followed behind. Only men carried the coffin. I, along with my group of six worked in silence on the sunny and warm afternoon at the burial site. Those paid, and knowledgeable about such things, lowered the casket into the grave and each member of the band shovelled a few shovelfuls of dirt onto the grave until it was full. And everyone left the graveyard and life carried on.

Another victim had been claimed by the church.

All that was left of the old residential school on Kuper Island was a stone slab by some concrete stairs in front of the new building we were now using as a school for adults and for the teens. The stone slab read that this was the site of the residential school and the year it was built. The stairs made of concrete were remnants too, but they were going nowhere. Both stairs and stone slab were overgrown with weeds.

I guess it was time to teach the students. The screams had been heard in Valhalla. The gods had been disturbed and had paused their fighting and their quarrels. The sparks of truth from clashes of swords and shields had ceased.

Where does that sound come from? The sound of whimpering from a child starving to death in a locked dark basement alone.

Valhalla is hushed, listening intently, for there is a sound on the wind carried over the earth that can barely be heard. A quiet, horrid scream of a newborn that just never ends—thousands upon thousands of quiet screams and pain like a massive flock of birds that block the sun and create a darkness that brings even the gods to their knees, weeping and heaving with sorrow to their very core.

Evil has been given free rein somewhere in Canada. Evil has been set loose and conquered God's holy church – women and men dedicated to Christ. Our brethren became bloodthirsty beyond belief.

Jesus, whose love conquered and devastated the berserkers of the North, has fallen to defeat, is vanquished, and now is stripped of the grace of God. The evil one has taken possession of the followers of the Lamb, and darkness – a blanket of blood – covers the hearts of mankind.

A flock of birds pours from the fires of Earth heavenward and has done so for 120 years. Looking to the north where fingers of lightning struck and where Donna was pointing, I could feel the directions from Valhalla. It seemed a rather gentle way to point to that direction or any direction. But a clear message must be followed.

Chapter 5

Donna and I jumped back into the car and headed north, then off-road along what appeared to be some tire marks in the prairie grass up to a knoll or small hill. The star signs were everywhere on the grass and rocks glowed with phosphorescence. Each rock glowed a different colour. We were met there by elk – three elk. We left the pregnant coyote back away.

We didn't know what to pray, but we both did. We were praying for the people and the place. Anger, seething, dreaded anger walked out from the hill and challenged us. There were two beings buried there, and they were pissed. The anger was dark, and deep, and came from the ancient ones. They were dripping in dark, fluidic, virile anger. Donna and I did not speak to each other and talked about it afterwards. We both felt the anger – deep, dark, and dangerous.

A set of three rocks had been placed up the hill, lined up exactly to the north. They led to a flat rock about 3 ft wide at the crest of the hill. It was covered in an ancient hard white paste. Other rocks pointed to it; one rock by the side of the hill pointed to the elevation of M 31, (at some time of the year, if you eyeball it to the top flat rock, the center rock). This was older than the medicine wheel. Much older, a thousand or so years older. This place was about 7,400 years old. I can read the star signs. I can read the rocks. This was put here by the star people – Sspommitapiiksi: star beings from on high.

The plants around the hill were glowing in phosphorescence, growing more thickly around the rocks. The plants glowed with a different colour around each rock. These were the rocks that glowed in the dark. Each rock represented a different star and recorded the colour of the star as it was thousands of years ago and its position.

Atop the hill, beyond the plastered rock, was a metal railing around a larger rock along with some barbed wire. This was a memorial for a Texas rancher, Bob Knight, who had moved here to Alberta. His coffin and body were lost in a flood, so this memorial was set up. It had become a provincial heritage site and, as a result, no one was allowed to remove or move the rocks.

A Texas rancher stands guard over the grave site of these two remarkable and unknown people.

This was a very large mound in the shape of a crow, an effigy mound that served as the gravesite of a king and a queen. The crow wore a crown, and the feet were embellished. This told me the names of those buried here. The star signs provided the date of what had happened. Why were they so honoured? And why were they so angry?

What is evil, exactly, anyway? Is it a substance? Is it a thing?

Most of us usually think of evil as darkness or blackness, the absence of good. But can evil exist or be if there is no such thing as goodness? This is important. If we are to overcome and defeat forever the forces of evil, or evil itself, then we all better know our enemy. What the hell is evil? What is evil itself?

And why is it associated with black? Why is white, as a colour or all colours combined, to satisfy the supercilious? Why is white associated with goodness? There is light and darkness and light is supposed to be the source of goodness and we tend to fear the dark because, let's face it, we can't see what is happening and that is scary because stuff could sneak up on us. But why evil? Darkness is just darkness. There is no moral compass to it at all and light is just electromagnetic radiation at some wavelength. We can see, again, that there is nothing moral or ethical about it at all and light has power over darkness. A candle can light up a room. No amount of darkness, as a substance, can dim a room in any way. So why are we screwed up on good and evil? We haven't got a clue on what good and evil are.

So, what in the name of all that is holy caused priests and nuns, with free knowledge of their superiors, and the government of Canada, to torture children to death by the tens of thousands, brutally and sadistically cut out the clitorises of 10-year-old girls by the hundreds, probably thousands, and destroy the lives of well over a million people? All in the name of God and for the common good?

And there are even more sickly demonic acts of which I have not yet made mention.

What is evil? Where did it come from? How do we kill it?

I'm not talking about killing people. For thousands of years we have tried killing people, and that doesn't work. People are just people. There is nothing ethical or moral about people. People themselves are just people. There may be good or evil acts, and things people do, but the people themselves are neither good nor evil.

Let us think of ourselves as stones lying on the ground. Is a stone good or evil? How about a rabbit? Is a rabbit good or evil? A stone is a collection and organization of minerals. A rabbit is an organization of biological entities, which, in turn, are just minerals.

People can do very bad things, and society has every right to protect itself. But, all in all, people are just people. We do the best we can. Sometimes we screw up, but we should always ask ourselves: Are we hurting someone? Are we hurting someone who cannot defend themselves? Are we hurting someone innocent?

What do we mean by innocent?

Does innocence and hurting someone have anything to do with evil?

There are many cultures throughout the world that have the concept of evil as a force independent of goodness. Often these concepts have to do with personality. These fluctuations between what we see as good and bad are just the personalities or flavours of the gods.

We see good and evil, not as traits belonging to human beings, but as an environment into which human beings have been set. Sometimes good and evil fight with each other, and humans just get caught up in the fray. Other times, it is set as the environment in which we live, and it affects us at times, or not, depending on circumstance.

There is another ancient way of looking at these things: that we consider evil from a point of view as medicine, that things are healthy or unhealthy, natural or perverse, free or repressed.

From the world of alchemy deep in the Dark Ages, there was the idea of repression of that which was healthy and natural, which, in turn, would become unhealthy, sickly, and repulsive – or what we might call evil. Furthermore, these foundations of alchemy in Europe had roots in the women before the Roman conquest. So this idea begins to tell us that if we repress some natural outcome (and I don't know how we're going to define natural, but continuing), what is being repressed becomes unhealthy or, in some way, spiritually diseased.

So, in this light, what we think of as evil is something that has been repressed. Then, the idea continues, this repressed state in interactions with that which is in the world, in some sort of alchemical process, recreates itself and becomes something completely new and never seen before. This is in a search to turn copper into gold.

This particular idea believes that evil and good are necessary to have a creative process so that there can be progress in the spiritual evolution of humanity. However, I don't believe we have to torture children for humanity to progress. People torture people because they enjoy doing so. They delight in the pain of others, especially those who are defenceless and suffering. It has nothing to do with the greater good or salvation. Some people shouldn't be priests, nuns, or brethren. Some people shouldn't be near children ever.

But how did the government employees and representatives, the people, become so cruel?

There is a bizarre history of Europe. The central government collapsed, and the previously repressed people, organizations, and cultures took over. There are no accurate or in-depth records of what went on in an entire continent for 500 years. It's blacked out. Order was established through the Roman Catholic Church by using superstition, much in the same way that people can be controlled through voodoo, curses, and the threat of damnation, So, repression upon repression.

We can see now that constant exposure to ideas of evil, even though you believe you are fighting evil, is very unhealthy. Eventually, you do terrible things, and in believing you are fighting evil, you become evil. That is who we are, that is what we have become. No one is asking you to condemn yourself or to wear sackcloth and ashes. No one is asking you to take the blame. We are being asked to accept the truth, to pick up the dark garment of the past and to take on accountability.

It does not matter whose fault the horrors of the residential school system are. There is no difference. Should we all get shovels and dig up the buried guilty and hang them? There is healing to be done, healing for them and healing for us. There is medicine and the correct application of that which is usually considered poisonous. So, let us begin the healing. Let us listen to the stones that have been here forever. Let me tell you a story about the medicine wheel. It's a long story, so make yourself comfortable. It's a good story, and it's worth it.

Chapter 6

I was working, or let's say I got a job, on the Siksika reservation teaching children math and running a science camp along with Nadine Solway, a teacher at the high school. Nadine was also teaching me some of the ways of the Siksika people, and she was always insisting that the rocks were the oldest living things. She taught various things at the science camp, such as the story of teepees and other stories about the history of her people.

For the camp, I, along with a couple of graduate students from the University of Calgary and some local people, cleared out a garage at the back of the school in the middle of an isolated area on the reserve. We set up some chairs and tables, and I brought in and set up my telescope, a small 3-inch refractor we could use to look at the Moon in the daytime. About six or seven kids soaked up what we taught like hungry sponges.

Near the end of the science camp, Nadine, myself, Dr. Genevieve Fox, (School Board superintendent), Nadine's daughter, and her boyfriend Jake, Roxy, nine kids, a bus driver, a bus, and my truck, all headed out to the Majorville medicine wheel along with a couple of Elders, John and Connie Crop Eared Wolf. It was over prairie grasslands following cattle trails and using dead reckoning. There are few or no trees in Southern Alberta, just grassland that goes on forever, over the hills and through wet patches that require a four-wheel truck to pull out a bus from the rich black and wet soil.

Eventually, we reached the medicine wheel. It was on a hill and at the crest of the hill is a stone cairn. Lined up outwardly are rays of stones; it's all about 200 m in diameter, and there is a circle of stones around it. Connie said prayers, as did we all, and tobacco was sacrificed at the cairn. From near the top, by the cairn, you could see forever, literally. The Rocky Mountains were visible in the west, hundreds of miles away. Everywhere else, the horizon just disappears.

The site is sacred. Some twit had the central cairn removed and then carbon-dated the remains of a wood fire found under the cairn. The rocks were put back but not in the right place because they had to make room for a survey marker that wasn't used anymore. Jake said the people hired to do that were very sick about it; I don't know what happened to them.

The site is about 5,500 years old, slightly older than Stonehenge. Most ideas about the medicine wheel are based on Stonehenge, which are both on equal lines of latitude. Still, that's kind of about it. There are alignments where the sun rises on the summer and winter solstice, both east and west, and other markings of the heavens. They didn't have to take the cairn apart to date the site; the star signs line up perfectly with the heavens as they were 5,500 years ago.

On another hill, not too far to the west, was another site observing the Moon. There were various other rocks of varying sizes placed to the northwest and northeast of the medicine wheel, marking the positions of the stars when the site was first built. The Earth is on a tilt relative to the plane of its orbit about the Sun and wobbles slowly with a period of 52,000 years; this is called the precession of the equinoxes. So, it's easy to date stuff from star signs, and it is pretty easy to track geologically, hence putting together a story to tell what happened is straightforward. You can get even closer if you listen to the stories the local people have to tell.

The stories are about events that happened, and they have a moral to them, such as Aesop's Fables, which didn't happen but have a moral to each tale. With Native stories, we, as white men, all think they are fables or not true, just as we as children found out the terrible truth about Santa Claus and that our parents lied to us. That is, of course, until we grow up and have children and realize that the spirit of Christmas is alive and well, and the meaning of Christmas lies in the spirit of Nicholas, who did live a long time ago, who lives in presents under the tree left by Saint Nick, good old Santa Claus.

But these stories are real, and if Native people tell you their stories it usually means they like you. Honestly, Native people are just like everyone else; they've been brutally beaten down by unforgiving and truly barbaric people like the Roman Catholic Church, Christianity in general, the government of Canada, and recently, Canadians themselves. So, as white men who love truth and justice, it is now our opportunity to turn from the path of all previous, and some present, and overcome our ignorance, self-righteousness and stupidity, and embrace love.

We are not being asked to feel guilty; we are not even asked to take the blame. We are being asked to embrace the truth, to accept the truth; that is all we are being asked to do at this time. And we're being asked to embrace the truth by a bunch of dead kids. The dead are calling to us; they're not calling to the crown, they're not calling to the church, they're not calling to the government, or anybody else. They are calling to us; they're calling to White Canadian men. And they call to us not in admonition but to offer us a gift. They offer us the power of truth. If we are men capable of carrying such a burden, heavy though it be, they offer us the gift of conquering ourselves.

I don't see anywhere that we are to condemn anyone or to try and find an excuse

We can read the stones, and they tell us stories of a great people long ago, of joy and tragedy.

I was standing by the central cairn, looking out to the northern landscape when Jake approached and said there was something he wanted to show me. Off to the northwest of the cairn was a set of other rocks that looked like the backs of old women huddled and facing north, clutching their blankets around them. We both walked off in that direction towards the little clutch of rock maidens.

We arrived, and Jake pointed out on the back of one of the rocks that looked like a woman crouched and looking north. A large chunk had been broken off by what looked like a geologist's hammer, defacing the structure.

"What kind of person would do this?" asked Jake, a Blackfoot man, of this white man.

Again, what can a white man say? This is obviously a sacred site. These rocks and stones have been here for a very long time, and every stone has meaning. What can a white man say?

I was once sitting in a glen in the middle of a Vancouver Island forest with a young Native man telling me about the men who had been raped at the residential school on his reserve.

What can a white man say to a friend who is Native, also a man, and a better man than you?

I just sighed; my soul collapsed. "I don't know," I said. "There's an unbelievable amount of ignorance and racism in the world, particularly among those of European descent. An unbelievable amount of ignorance."

What would you say? What can anyone say?

Then Jake told me of the Geological Survey team that moved the rocks of the central cairn and that white people, like the Rotary Club, come to the medicine wheel all the time to show it off. I don't know how many Native people go there, but hey, we're here now. Let's look around and don't move or mess with any rocks or stones.

Facing south, as I look towards the afternoon sun to my left, is a river about 3 or 4 km away. There are no trees, so it is just clear flat land. But as I could see the far embankment and the place where the summer solstice was marked – by that, I mean the place where the sun rises on the horizon as seen from the central cairn, and it still rises there at the summer solstice to this day. The summer solstice is the beginning of Summer, June 15th, although in those days they didn't have June; they had something else – a different calendar, much better than ours, as do most other cultures.

The summer solstice, the day when the sun is highest in the sky at noon, is a religious day for the Blackfoot, as it is for most cultures except ours. That is the day for the Sundance, which is much more than just a day for the Blackfoot and others who celebrate that occasion. To the south of the medicine wheel, stretching to the horizon, which is there because of the curvature of the earth, like forever, is a flat plain. People would gather and tent out and participate in the Sundance.

To the north of the medicine wheel are obvious places of celestial and religious significance. So, seeing through the lens of 5,500 years into the past, people would gather from everywhere, camp out, meet each other, do sacred dances, exchange medicines, stories, and news, arrange for the well-being of the tribe or nation, and engage in the healthy exercise of being a community.

But I have left out the most important part of this incredible site. You don't just build a medicine wheel overnight with paid labour; you build it over time with people contributing stones and rocks as a sacred offering to the well-being and future of the people. People may have had to travel great distances to put a stone in a particular place. A child may have carried her stone, which she kept with her as her treasure, to bring to the medicine wheel. She would have placed it with ceremony in a place where the leaders of the community would have thanked her, told her where to put the stone, and explained which star, celestial event, her stone would help to signify. She would have been told that she was part of and helping the community and the people. All of this would have been done at night, near midnight, with other children, youth, adults, and elders as a community under the stars. In Southern Alberta, the seeing conditions for stars are outstanding, and there would not be a cloud in the sky. Maybe the Moon would be out, or maybe She would be hiding in her home. The stars, the night sky is breathtaking, and the wise men and women would sit with people who brought and placed their stones on the ground in the right places and tell them story after story of what stars were where, where they were and where they were going. The older wise ones knew and had at their beck and call observations of the heavens from during the Ice Age when there was not much else to do at night but look at the heavens. There are stories from before the time the ice covered the prairies, a phenomenal time of knowledge and being in a very healthy place.

Of course, there were campfires and drumming and singing late into the night and early morning, I imagine. Young people would know their place in the community and older ones, parents, husbands, wives, and men and women, old, young, whatever, would all have a place and be in it. The Blackfoot had a very logical and straight-forward form of democracy. There were many societies within the nation, men's societies and women's societies, and a society is responsible for different tasks and responsibilities. You'll never guess how you get to be a member of each Society; you voluntarily join one. That's it

Sometimes it has happened that someone did not want to join a particular society. However, it's possible to form a new one depending on the circumstances and needs of the time. Attempts to try to take things over were mostly met with ridicule. There are also fundamental principles that are maintained by Blackfoot people such as hospitality, honesty, kindness, love and forgiveness. These principles were taught at a very early age under stars at night, through stories after travelling for weeks or months carrying a valuable and quite ordinary stone to place it in its special place among the heavens.

In the middle of this afternoon children played and walked in the different areas of the medicine wheel. One child, a preteen boy, draped himself over the damaged rock I had been shown before, hugged it and was one with it. This without prompting or instruction. The lad knew the stone needed comfort and he needed the power of lovingly hugging a stone on a hot August afternoon in Southern Alberta

After a few more prayers and thanks to the mosquitoes for leaving us alone, we headed back to the bus and drove back to the reservation. We stopped at the Effigy Mound, where we could look around, and I could ask Connie, John, and Genevieve about it. I showed some positions of the rocks, and John was upset at the metal railing and memorial to a Texas rancher on top of the mountain. I explained how the memorial got there and that the mound was a historical heritage site and, as a result, it protected the rocks and these places.

"Doesn't the white man recognize where we are?" asked John. "This is obviously a sacred place; anyone would know that."

John shrugged and sighed in frustration. I just kept my mouth shut.

So, where to now, oh gathering of white men?

Sometime later, Nadine and her husband showed me a "meteorite" at a very isolated and rather protected place on the reserve. This "meteorite" was a fairly large boulder, which people had said had fallen from the sky recently. I knew that if something this big had fallen from the sky recently, the whole world would have known about it, and it would have created sheer havoc. It was about the size of a car, covered with the same plaster as the previously seen sacred rock at the Effigy Mound. The rock was in a crater, but the crater was only about 5 ft deep and about 50 m across or so. It was a circular crater, and I pretty much felt that the crater was man-made and very,

very old; it just looked like it, and I just felt it.

That happened to be another sunny afternoon, and we paid our acknowledgements and left. However, I was curious about the so-called meteorite. I was sure it was some sort of astronomical observation site and had ceremonial significance. So, I went back on a different sunny afternoon. The site was pretty well in the middle of nowhere on the south side of a rise, but not on top of it. Observation sites are usually on a high elevation on the prairies; that can mean it's a significant rise, more commonly known as a hill. But the land is so flat that an observer can see literally to the horizon. The Rocky Mountains were 100 miles away and could be seen clearly. I parked my four-by-four and took my pouch of tobacco up to the ridge of the crater, prayed, and made an offering. Some people say that white men don't know how to pray to their ancestors or the spirits. Don't listen to them.

Surrounding the crater were about 10 or 12 anomalous areas and each looked about the size of a large grave site, arranged and extending from the edge of the crater like outward rays. They may have indicated the sites of earth lodges. The Blackfoot used to live in earth lodges, underground, where it was cool and could be heated in winter. The large rock, about 20 ft long and 10 ft wide (I didn't measure it), sat in the depressed center of the crater. The rock was 4 ft high, oriented exactly north and south. I measured it with a compass and with my phone. The north end of the rock had been shaped into a point, pointing directly north. Embedded into the earth, still within the crater, and just to the north of the central pointer rock, was a collection of stones. I immediately recognized the pattern of this collection of stones as the Pleiades. You could stand to the north of them and eyeball over the large point of rock directly to the south. There was a gap in the placement of Earth lodges so that one could see over the collection of the Pleiades to the meridian of the celestial sphere. There were also two stones embedded into the floor of the crater to the north-west of the pointer rock, but not exactly. They were the horns of Taurus. On the earth beside the rock were three notable effigies aligned north-south on the east side of the rock and one aligned east-west on the south side. There were no effigies to the north, near the Pleiades stones. Remarkably, the central pointer rock was covered with white plaster, exactly as was the central rock at the place where lightning had pointed the way.

I wanted to find out what type of rock this was, but I was certainly not going to deface anything, and I was not going to take away a sample without permission. I was drawn to the rock to examine it more. There was some plant growth on it in places, but the white plaster dripping all over the rock covered bare patches from view. Walking around the rock to its south side, two small pieces of the rock presented themselves, sitting on a shelf. They had somehow broken off and were presenting themselves to me.

"Take them," said the ancestors there.

I was very hesitant. I picked up the two pieces and put them in my pocket. I took stock of their positions before taking them, said some prayers, and left some more tobacco. With trepidation I made my exit. When I got back to my camper, off-reserve, I called Nadine and let her know what happened. She immediately gave me instructions on what to do as far as ceremony was concerned, which I did. Then, I waited for the next day when government offices would be open. Around 9:00 the next morning, I called the Geological Survey of Canada and asked if I could talk to a geologist.

The switchboard was adamant to know why I needed to talk to a geologist.

"Because I have a rock sample here, and I want to know what it is, maybe even have it assayed," I said.

Initiate and respond,
Call and respond,
Call and response.
Our role is to respond,
And that is where we have free will.
We are free to respond,
And we are free in how to respond.
As you have faith, so shall your powers be.
Faith is a response to a stimulus.
We learn by reward and punishment,
Which is also known as stimulus and response.
We are under one great law. Baha'u'llah says,

"The heavens and the Earth are all under one great law."
This great law is the same for heaven and Earth.
Abdul Baha says
The Great Law of all things is the law of duality.
With stimulus and response,
There are roles we can be in.
It depends if we are within the world of spirituality
Or the world of physical reality.
In this world, we are in the place of response.
To respond, to arise, to react to a stimulus,
Then we're in the place where we should be.
We have capacities to deal with how to respond.
We can respond to a crisis,
And we can respond to love.
However, if we plant ourselves into the garden of being a stimulus,
If we try to be the cause of things,
If we are trying to control the universe
Or to control spiritual things,
Then we are not in a place where we can handle where we are,
And we create great harm,
Such as superstition,
Bad medicine,
Disease,
Global environmental crisis,
And turmoil.
We can respond to a crisis;
That is our role.
We cannot cause a crisis;
That is not our role.
We can respond to love;
We cannot cause or be the source of love.
That is not our place.
This is what gives us free will.
If we are in the role of response,
Then by the Great Law of Duality,
We have free will.
It is our role,

While in this world,
To respond as best we can
And utilize our free will to do so.
It is in the role of response
That we have free will.
In the next world, we will no longer have free will;
This is because we are no longer in the role of response.
We will no longer have the capacity to respond.
Our role in that world is to inspire humanity
In the arts and the sciences.
Our role in the next world is to be the stimulus
To which humanity on the mortal plane must respond.
As a result, in the next world, we will not have free will.
We will have no choice but to inspire;
We now have a choice whether to respond.

The universe can be thought of as space
With stuff floating around in it.
The space is dripping with creativity like a womb;
It is female.
It is a creative force;
It is the universe itself.
It is the stimulus;
It is pure love.
We, as substance,
Respond to the flow of the universe.

If there is bad medicine,
If there is a spiritual attack
Through some demonic or satanic fantasy,
It is coming from a place which is out of control
And is trying to control things.
It is a place that cannot be where it is.
The response is within the free will of the righteous.
We may defend ourselves,

And we can fight back;
But if we enter the role of being a source or stimulus to the world,
We lose our capacity.
Our capacity is response,
And response is our capacity.

The switchboard operator sounded both horrified and terrified.

"We can't do that," she exclaimed.

"I beg your pardon?" I said.

"We're not allowed to identify or do anything with rocks," she said.

"But you're the Geological Survey of Canada," I said, "Working with rocks is your job.

"Do you have any geologists?" I continued.

"Oh yes," she explained, "we have lots of geologists, but they're not allowed to examine or touch any rocks. Something terrible happened just a little while ago, and no one is allowed to deal with rocks in any way."

As soon as she said that, I remembered the rock at the medicine wheel that Jake had shown me, the rock with a piece hacked out of it with a geologist's hammer.

"Who would do such a thing?" Jake had asked.

And without having to think too much, even for a white man, I knew the answer to that question. There was even a Geological Survey of Canada concrete marker beside the central sacred cairn to make sure that a white man in the future would be able to answer that question. The Geological Survey of Canada had even taken down the cairn to make room for the Geological Survey marker. The cairn was piled back up somewhere in the same place, I guess.

And I could feel, or hear, every rock on the planet, or every rock in the universe, chuckle and add a very sound and ominous warning. The rocks know everything and are perfectly capable of defending themselves and capable of revenge.

"So let me get this straight, just for clarification," I said, "You are the Geological Survey of Canada. Examining, identifying, and dealing with rocks is your specified job, and something terrible happened, somewhat recently, and now no one at the Geological Survey of Canada is allowed to deal with rocks in any way whatsoever.

"Is that all correct?" I asked.

"Yes," she said simply.

"And I don't want to ask what was the terrible thing that happened," I said.

"I'm not allowed to tell you anyway," she said.

"I can believe it," I said.

I thanked her for her time. We both said goodbye and hung up. I sat back after the call was completed and had a bit of a laugh. When such things are revealed, I have the choice to either believe it or not, but it makes no difference to me. I just choose to have respect, and that's about it.

So, what the heck, I then called up the Geological Survey of Alberta. Let's see what these guys have got.

The chap at the Alberta Geological Survey was a pretty nice guy. He was a geologist. The switchboard put me through to him right away.

"I've got a couple of rock samples, and I'd like to identify them," I said.

I also explained they were from a sacred site, so I didn't want to say the location, but it was somewhere in Southern Alberta, somewhere near Clayton.

He was understanding of the fact the samples came from a sacred site and asked me for some pictures of the samples. So, I took some with my phone and sent them off. He wrote back by email and said they were probably Dolomite, and the large rock was an erratic from somewhere moved by the ice.

Great, now to figure out how Dolomite is formed.

Nevertheless, you don't mess with rocks, especially sacred ones.

What makes a rock sacred as opposed to one that is not sacred but just some ordinary rock, like you and I?

Nevertheless, I found it remarkable that the Geological Survey of Canada went and ripped down a central cairn at the Majorville Medicine Wheel and then hacked out a chunk off of a significant marker rock, and now can never have anything to do with rocks ever again. I have no idea what the terrible thing is that happened, and I have no desire to find out.

That pretty much marks my rather long story about how I found out for real that rocks, stones if you like, are living things, just as Blackfoot people have said. If you're able to make yourself receptive, if you are searching for truth with diligence, and have sufficient humility, you can learn from the very rocks themselves, even if you're a white guy.

I returned to the meteorite that was not a meteorite and returned the pieces of Dolomite to where I had been given them. The rock and I had a little talk.

Chapter 7

Back at Kuper Island on the west coast of B.C., an elder woman joined our little class, and we went for walks exploring the island. She had the most wonderful stories to tell. There were stories about the history of the island and even stories about how the ancestors found the Pacific Ocean from the interior of British Columbia. I would imagine that it would have been around Bella Coola.

A boy got lost hunting and decided to explore more where he was, then stumbled down to the coastline, stepped out of the BC rainforest, and onto a rocky shore of the Pacific. It must have been an astonishing experience. Maybe his people lived around Quesnel or Williams Lake, that's the area of the Chilcotin, a warrior race who lived alongside the Shuswap, who have transcended physical reality. And remember, this is one heck of a long time ago.

Their hunting and living areas, including fishing, were between two mountain ranges, the Rocky Mountains and the Coastal Mountains. They were living on a giant plateau between these mountains and would have the Kamloops River Basin to the south and colder regions to the north. It is a beautiful area and abundant with game, but it may have been getting a little crowded. They were boxed in; to the west was very dense forest going up into the Coastal Range, so I could see a lad of the day deciding to explore. Going up into the mountains towards the sea is a rough climb. Sticking to the headwaters of some river, walking along what would be Highway 20, part of the Highway of Tears, then into a wetland, the watershed marking the divide between what flows back into the plateau of his home and rivers that flow into the unknown. I don't know if you have ever driven the Chilcotin-Bella Coola Highway, but the drop from the Coastal Mountains onto the flats before the ocean is a white-knuckle drive. It is a major climb down. The elders say he got lost. I don't think there is any way a lost boy would accidentally climb down such an embankment. It is a rough haul with not much to hang on to and nothing to see or point the way but very dense trees and foliage and underbrush. But he made it down. It is a very closed-in place. It is thick with giant trees and flat. the trip must have taken him days. He was old enough to look after himself and yet was still considered a boy. Manhood is around 15 or 16 years of age. He was a kid, a pretty tough kid, and once he was down off the cliff, he must have looked back up the escarpment and figured he wasn't going to try going up there again anytime soon. Probably after resting.

He would have made it to Bella Coola, and then on to Bella Bella. But everything is enclosed, everything is dark, even in the middle of the day. He would have had the experience of walking into the open; at his feet would have been the Pacific Ocean in all its glory, completely open and free.

He would have run up and down that beach for the better part of the day. He would have swum in it, salty water, tasting salt in the water as the first of his people to do so. He would have sat on a rock and watched the sun set over the distant horizon. He would have been the first to do so. All of the other people living on the plateau where he lived would not know the ocean was there. They were free. They could break out, and they not only found freedom, they found salmon and would never go hungry again. The story says he returned to his mother, who must have been worried sick about him. He led his people to the ocean, to freedom, and abundance.

On Kuper Island, walking around with really nice kids and with an older woman who was well respected as one of the elders on the island, we were listening to stories. There was one young man who was different than the other young men; he just wouldn't behave himself. He was told that if he didn't toe the line and start behaving himself, he would be turned into a rock and used to tell the weather. Well, this young man thought all that was hogwash and refused to comply. Sure enough, he was turned into a rock and was used to tell the weather. So, guys, you have to be careful. You may be just walking through the woods, by the ocean or a lake, overlooking the landscape or something, and may be drawn to some rock or somehow some rock draws your attention. It may be a rock some poor soul was turned into and is lonely. Maybe, if you listen, it'll tell you the weather.

If you seek knowledge, if you seek truth with sufficient urgency, and if you have sufficient humility, you can learn from the very rocks themselves. Kuper Island was/is incredibly beautiful. The Penelakut people have been there forever. They are an incredible people, very handsome and intelligent. They exemplify and demand good and proper behaviour. They were completely devastated by decades and decades, more than a century, of residential school trauma.

The big house survived. The culture is remarkably similar to Māori culture in New Zealand, and the population is similar in their body language and the way they look. There are differences: in Canada, ceremony is inside the big house, while in Aotearoa (New Zealand), ceremony is outside.

There is a story of seven canoes that set out from the west coast of Canada, an entire tribe that wanted to leave. The legend is that they went to many different places all over the Pacific Ocean.

The Māori people have a story of seven canoes that arrived on the shores of Aotearoa long ago. The Salish of the West Coast have big canoes, not the birch bark small canoes that white men usually think of; these are huge canoes carved out of massive Douglas fir. Making a canoe by Salish people has similarities to that of the Pacific, but there are differences.

Now, to make yourself a fricken' canoe, first, you have to find yourself a tree – an old Douglas fir. If you ask the rocks, they may point one out to you. When I say a big tree, I mean it's really big. It may be a cedar. It's so big that no one alive today has seen such a tree. There used to be a fair number of them on the west coast of Canada, but not anymore. This tree takes some time and effort to just walk around it, and it ain't out in the open either. It's hidden deep in the forest where no one can find it; it's surrounded by many other trees and undergrowth.

As you stand in front of this massive tree, looking up and over the roots to see the trunk, which is a cliff stretching out as far to the right and left as you can see, it's freaking huge – bigger than any tree you ever did see, bigger than you've seen even in your dreams. And there is only one thing you can do: sit down, look at the thing, and declare, "How in the name of all that is holy am I ever going to cut this thing down?"

Remember, this was some time ago. All you have are rocks and seashells. How are you going to cut down this tree?

Now, a long time ago, all there were, were rocks and seashells. Some rocks were pretty good, like West Coast jade and Māori people of Aotearoa loved jade as both a weapon and a carving tool. But returning to a very long time ago, with you sitting under a huge tree as big around as a large house, you're going to need some help, like other men. But the women blessed the tree first and gave various things, then left the men to build a fire and a ring around the trunk of this enormous fir. Over quite some time, like weeks or maybe a year or so, they managed to make enough of a dent in the tree to fell it.

It was very dangerous work, and men died. That's why the women left earlier. There is a love story in all of this, of course. It is a lot easier to fell a tree if you have an axe or a saw, but for those things, you need iron. Yes, you can make an axe out of a rock, but as far as a saw is concerned, you need iron.

This story comes from the Tsimshian people and was told to us by Peter, a speaker of their people. There was a man who had an idea for a new three-dimensional art, but the stone tools and shells were inadequate for the job. He was very despondent. His wife saw that he was frustrated and unhappy. She went higher into the mountains and collected a lot of wool left by Rocky Mountain sheep. She brought all of this wool home to her place and made many different coloured dyes. She dyed the wool in different colours and wove a very beautiful cloak, and no, she didn't give the cloak to her husband.

Instead, a trader was arriving from Russia, Siberia obviously, and he had this new kind of metal. He was trading this metal, which was very strong, unlike the most popular metal, copper, which was quite soft, brittle and not that useful. This trader had been trading this metal down the coast from Alaska and was now coming to the Tsimshian territory. He was charging exorbitant prices, really whatever he wanted, to trade for this metal.

When the trader arrived with great fanfare, everyone turned out to meet him on the shore, and everyone had all their treasures to show him. When the trader saw the beautiful cloak, which had been made from Rocky Mountain goat wool, and with love, he rejected the offers from others and took the cloak in return for this new metal.

The metal, of course, was iron, and the three-dimensional art which could now be generated was totem poles and carvings. It is said that the Cree discovered iron, and if you've ever been in a Cree sweat lodge, you'll acknowledge that is probably true. On the west coast, however, we have this story of iron being traded for art. Being pedantic white men, as is our want, this story would be about 1400 BC. There are all sorts of things in this story, which is a gift.

Chapter 8

Rocks are a direct connection to the universal consciousness. The freaking things are everywhere, and they talk to each other. It is a language beyond syllables and words; it is a communication that is from heart to heart. The dead who lie peacefully with rocks in the ground are calling to us. They are the children who didn't make it through residential school. Their decaying bodies were detected quite recently through ground-penetrating radar. They are so one with the Earth that they become confused with the rocks themselves. In their confusion:

"Why did we have to die so young?"
In their confusion, they are comforted by the rocks which lie with them:

"Why did they kill us?"
"Why did we have to die?"
"There, there."
"Peace, peace."

They call to us now, those dead and gone children.
They do not call to Native relatives;
They do not call to the Pope or members of some church;
They do not call to anyone else.
They call to us, to the living, to us,
We white men – not women, not children,

To Canadian white men.

In the deep underground of the epistemology of the planet, far below lie our darkest secrets and our greatest fears. We can gather and try to fulfill the role and purpose of the universe.

We have all been lied to – all of us. That is why we are hiding the women.

What are the Rocks trying to tell us?
What is the wisdom of the songs?
We Are One.
There is pure thought,
There is pure desire,
Close to the fire of purgatory.
Every stone is one stone.
How can we divide ourselves between oppressor and oppressed?
How can revenge be justified?
There is the ultimate justice,
Which we face
When we lie as one
Within a bed of dirt
And the cold of Mother Earth,
Embracing every one of us.
The entire universe is but one universe,
But the foolish have multiplied it.

How can we say that humanity is one, and then immediately divide people into the oppressor and the oppressed? If you believe in the oneness of mankind, then all are the oppressors and all are the oppressed; all are colonizers and all are colonized. The oppressed must embrace the ways of the oppressor or die out, and the oppressor, addicted to oppression and believing it to be empowerment, is enslaved into a delusion and is easily controlled. We become identified with our oppression. We embrace our oppression and being oppressed since our oppression is who we are. As we rebel against being absorbed into the global consciousness, wherein we find true power through finding the source of knowledge, we embrace the knowledge that oppression and being oppressed are one and dissolve into the non-existent experiences of a past age. There is only the oneness of us all.

We are all the source of knowledge. We are all, whether in ignorance or bliss, engaged and fully part of a global consciousness which cannot exist without any one of us.

The dead are calling to us, calling us to embrace the truth – the truth that lies within us all, the truth of a satanic history that can only be carried and embraced by the strongest and most courageous.

The dead are calling to us, dead children whose memory we carry within us.

We embrace and love children we never knew,
We were not there for you,
And time has robbed us.

We are both the oppressor and the oppressed, and only by leaving behind the comfort blanket of our oppression can we be free and stand in the sun of a day that shall not be followed by night.

Rocks unite people.

Chapter 9

There was this one rock once, still there, that could be from Jasper and is now by Okotoks in Alberta. Of course, the rock's name is Okotoks, which means "rock" in Blackfoot. The rock named the local town after itself.

Napi is a manifestation of God, a messenger. Napi can also mean mankind, representing mankind, particularly men, and our foolishness and stupidity. It was a warm day in Jasper around 30,000 years ago, maybe longer according to our geologists. Napi, visiting Jasper as people are wont to do, was hot and tired and sat on Okotoks to take a rest.

And Napi had his blanket with him, which he laid by the rock.

"It's a hot one today," said Napi to Okotoks.

"Geez, I don't know about you, but I'm getting a little cold," said Okotoks.

Now, Napi was used to having rocks and trees and things talk to him, so he just carried on the friendly conversation.

"Eh Bud, I got a blanket here you can use," Napi said. He got up, grabbed his blanket, and wrapped it around the rock, tucking him in.

"Thanks," said Okotoks.

"No problem Bud," said Napi. "Keep it, and it'll keep you warm, eh?"

Napi then continued his walking tour down into the foothills. But pretty soon, Napi started getting cold too. He was getting really cold. Then he thought, "Hey, I got that blanket I gave to that rock!" So Napi headed back to Jasper, found the rock all cuddly and warm under his blanket, and grabbed the blanket and walked away.

Okotoks woke up frozen, "Where's my blanket?" he cried. He could see Napi trucking down the hill with his blanket. Okotoks was pissed. He got up and chased Napi, yelling at him to give back his blanket. Napi turned and saw Okotoks coming after him and took off running for his life. Okotoks was big and could easily have crushed Napi if he caught him.

They raced down from the mountains and across the prairies. Napi called for all the animals to come and help him. The animals came and threw themselves at Okotoks, but Okotoks was so big and strong that the birds and animals died trying to save Napi as they threw themselves at this giant angry rock. Across the prairies, running south across the flats, Napi, with Okotoks hot in pursuit and animals sacrificing themselves by uselessly throwing themselves against Okotoks to try to stop him, fled.

Eventually, Okotoks just about caught Napi, and Napi was done for when the bats all arose and took flight from their caves and over and over smashed themselves against the determined Okotoks. The bats were so many and threw themselves with such force that they stopped Okotoks and Okotoks broke in two. Okotoks stopped and sank where he stood, and he is still there today, broken in two. And in the middle of Okotoks, you can still see Napi running for his life. The bats lived, but the front of their faces were smashed flat, and they still have flat faces to this day.

Now, we know from what our geologists tell us that the great erratic, the Okotoks, began somewhere in Jasper about 30,000 years ago and was picked up by the glaciers of the last great advance of the Ice Age and then carried to Southern Alberta where it sits today. But the story of Okotoks was true; the rock did get up and ran across the prairie from north to south and stopped in the town of Okotoks, even though the town wasn't there yet.

So, how did they know? How did the Blackfoot know that the great rock ran across the prairie? They knew because they watched it. They were there; they saw it happen. The people living on the prairies during the Ice Age watched this large rock move, carried by the glacial ice flow from 30,000 years ago until the ice receded about 12,000 years ago. They saw it move, passing down this information from generation to generation for 30,000 years.

And there is more this rock can tell us. You see, we're talking about people who were trying to survive during an Ice Age, living on a massive glacier thousands of miles wide and thousands of miles long. Mostly, I imagine, the people would be living in the mountains, the Rocky Mountains, during the Ice Age in western Canada. And there would be birds or game, various animals, in the mountains and on top of the sheets of ice. The glaciers were about a kilometre to a mile thick; that is a lot of ice. And people, living off of whatever they could hunt, would have been very familiar with this large rock sitting on top of this massive glacier. So, with the animals, this rock would have been a shelter from the winds and blizzards. Even though the glacier was still there, the summer sun would have warmed the rock, and vegetation would have grown on it, attracting animals which, in turn, could have been hunted or trapped by the few people who could have hung out around this rock. There was no other place for hundreds of miles, so the rock would have welcomed all. And sitting on top of this rock would have been people, looking at the stars at night. There were no lights; it was dark, cold, and still, with monstrous high-pressure systems. With the sky clear, the astronomical seeing would have been perfect. The light of the Milky Way would mesmerize them, and the motions of the heavens would be described in detail to children through the ages. They would easily have noticed the position of the Andromeda Galaxy, they'd marked the passage of planets and even knew the timing of the precession of the equinoxes. These were the star people; they were one with the sky. There was nothing else in sight. And that story, the story of the heavens, carried on after the ice suddenly receded in a great flood.

The ice, a mile thick and stretching for thousands of miles in all directions, melted very quickly, and all would have drowned but for the guidance of the beaver, who saved Napi, the people. The rock gave Napi the gift of the stars. After a glacier recedes it leaves behind the bodies of all the animals that died on the glacier over about 20,000 years. That is a lot of dead animals.

When people tell you their stories, white man, sit down and listen. At first, the story is for children. Then, the story, as it is told over and over, is for older people – adults and the elderly – who get to tell the story over and over. And more and more knowledge, known as teachings, appear. From the mists of time, the rocks themselves teach us, and the children of the past, not that long ago, are calling to us. They are calling to us to embrace truth.

And truth is all around us.

Chapter 10

The center of all social activity on Kuper Island is the big house. The center of all social and religious activity on every West Coast reserve in Canada is the big house. It is, as the name implies, a big house. It is all one room, like an indoor stadium, with holes in the roof to let the smoke out. The house has a dirt floor, large enough for three massive fires, and room for a lot of people to dance in regalia, and for drummers to walk around the floor – the dirt floor, the sacred dirt floor.

The floor is rectangular. The three fires are spaced in line along the midsection of the floor. Surrounding the floor are tiers of benches rising from the edge of the floor to the walls. The walls consist of vertically placed planks of hewn cedar. The roof is covered with cedar shingles. The skeleton of the house is ingeniously designed to allow for a large open space within the building. At one end, the far end, is a kitchen and dining area behind the front wall.

After the burial of the one who hanged himself, the local people threw down a table to say thank you to all the white people who had shown up to help in the search. About a hundred white people came, and the Indigenous people welcomed the visitors. They watched the drumming and ceremonies, and dancing, and they all sat in bleachers surrounding the floor. Three great fires roared deep into the night. They all saw, continuously, back into tens of thousands of years, into the past. All of this was happening in their backyard, and they had never known it existed.

They ate together and were thanked formally, each. Then, they all took the last ferry back into town, and none would ever forget.

It is a beautiful late fall day, just before noon, in the foothills of Alberta. Most of the leaves are gone by a low-level creek winding through the last of yellow, orange, and green life. Sometimes, life gets lonely, and that's not all a bad thing. I like the silence.

Of course, in this part of the world, there are many days when there is not a cloud in the sky. It is crystal sky blue, and massive overhead. An overwhelming aura of pastels that are only painted in Alberta cries out that it's Fall.

We are not just physical creatures; we are spiritual, and we are having a physical experience. The same is true for a rock or a stone. The stone originally was nothing more than space and time, filled with information given to it by the universe itself. Under great stress, the space and time crystallized into various particles, and the particles, if they were lucky, became stars. Stars rearranged particles into carbon, iron, oxygen, and all the elements we see today. After many explosions of stars, there were leftover rocks, and somehow, these rocks decided they should be planets. So, they became planets, and from processes locked within the minds of planets, rocks and stones, igneous and metamorphic, formed. The rocks and stones on planets still contain the information given to them long before their creation.

The information is eternal; it was always there, it always was. And the particles within the stones call to us and teach us of things beyond the grave.

Chapter 11

In Southern Alberta, by the meteorite, there are the remnants of earth lodges and sedentary living from a very long time ago. I noticed the plaster on the large central rock. The word for medicine wheel in the Blackfoot language is not "medicine wheel"; it translates to something like "compass", like a magnetic compass that points the way. Here, the central rock had a distinct pointy end pointing due north, but due north is not exactly by the same position of stars over time. You see, the stars have all moved. The stars are not as they were just after the recession of the ice, which ended the last ice age 12,000 years ago. And that is a wonderful gift that tells us when things were. We don't have to dig anything up; we just have to read the star signs. We just have to listen to what the rocks have to tell us.

It's called the procession of the equinoxes. You see, the Earth orbits the Sun, and it orbits the Sun in the same plane forever. It's like being very small and sitting on the edge of a flat dinner plate; the Sun is sitting at the center of this very large plate, and of course, this plate is sitting in the middle of space with far-off stars everywhere. So we can think of a very large plate with an orange representing the Sun sitting in the middle and a pea representing the Earth at the edge of the plate floating through space. The plate is slowly rotating, representing the Earth orbiting the Sun. And things would stay that way forever. However, the universe never sits still nor lets things go forever. Nothing remains the same.

The pea on the edge of the plate is also spinning, and the axis of its spin is at an angle to the plate. The angle is 23 and 1/2 degrees. Every culture on the face of the Earth has figured that out. And again, that could be a forever thing, but that changes too. The Moon, like a mustard seed, is orbiting the Earth, and its plane of orbit is at an angle to the large plate as well. And this orbit precesses; it wobbles with a 19-year cycle. It's like the Earth and Moon are on a small plate of their own, and this plate turns once a month at an angle to the large Earth-Sun plate, and the small Earth-Moon plate oscillates while it spins every 19 years. And we know that the Native people of Arizona and Nevada, along with the people of Stonehenge, figured that out too, and it was at about the same time as well.

And all seems well with these spinning plates in the air, but as you see, the Earth is not completely round. The pea is not a sphere; it is an oblate spheroid. It's a little squished, and the gravitational pull of the moon, like a little mustard seed, drags on the spin of the Earth, causing it to wobble. And the Earth wobbles every 26,000 years. The Greeks figured that out at about 400 BC when Hipparchus noticed it after some pretty accurate measurements. And the Blackfoot had figured that out thousands of years previously. The earliest record I can find recording the procession of the Equinox by the Blackfoot nation is about 5,500 years ago. And the builders of Stonehenge may have known that too, but the prejudice and racism of British science prevent us from finding that out.

Long story short: this means the North Star, Polaris, was not always at the North Celestial Pole of the night sky. As a matter of fact, for most of the time, there was no North Star. That is just like the southern hemisphere now; there is no South Pole star. So you have to use a trick to find the direction south when navigating the Pacific Ocean in a canoe in the middle of the night. It's called a stick map; scientists today have no idea how it works.

As the Earth wobbles on its plate and goes around the Sun, the North Celestial Pole wanders through the years in a great circle in the sky. It goes through one cycle every 26,000 years. But everyone has to know which way is north, so the positions of the stars are marked out on the earth. We can easily tell how old a site is by reading the star maps on the ground.

This meteorite site marked the sky at 11,500 years ago, right after the Ice Age ended. Looking at this meteorite site, the stones tell us that right after the Ice Age, after the great flood which resulted from the melting of the massive North American glacier, people built this little site. Maybe a few hundred people, if that, celebrated a culture based on the raising of their children. The well-being, care, education, nurturing, and teaching of children were central to their way of life.

How do I know that? Because the stones and rocks at the site tell me so. Remember when the families were gathered around the Okotoks during the Ice Age? I would think there was vegetation or the Rocky Mountains protruding above the sheet of ice, and people would be accompanying game. And the game needed vegetation to survive. It may be that some soil and dirt built up on the Okotoks sitting on the ice, and there may have been game there. There may have been, but game was scarce, and once it was spotted everyone went to be involved in the hunt. However, the little ones, the children, were left behind in whatever shelter had been built at that time. There may have been a dozen or so children left on their own while the adults left to get game, and the children were told to stay put.

But it so happened that the older ones were away for a much longer time than expected. The children ran out of food and left the shelters to find their parents. Maybe they went to look for their parents by the Okotoks, out in the open atop the glacier. The children got lost amidst the peaks, under the stars. The beings from on high, the stars themselves, the Sspommitapiiksi, came down and rescued the children from the cold. The stars from heaven took the children into the heavens, kept them together, and loved them, cared for them. They sit and play together in the constellation of Taurus, in front of Orion the hunter, known as Nápí to the Niitsítapi. The Greeks and Europeans called them the Pleiades, the nymphs of Apollo. They are the Lost Children who are with the stars as their own constellation.

When the parents came home from the hunt with their hard-won game, they found their village empty. They had lost all their children, perhaps all of the children aged 12 and younger. They searched everywhere for days, weeks, months, and years, but no trace of the children could be found. They had been taken up into the sky, and the stars told the people that the constellation of the Lost Children was there to always remind people and tell people to look after and care for their children.

And what a devastation to the few people who were left! An entire generation had been wiped out. As time wore on, this missing generation became a very noticeable age gap in their rather small and close-knit population. They vowed this would never happen again. There were ceremonies every year to ensure that parents, indeed the entire society, would make teaching and caring for children their number one priority. Children became not only valuable but the fundamental purpose of society itself. It was the great purpose of life, survival, and the source of the progress of the people.

Chapter 12

On this particular day I was at the site known as the meteorite, which was not a meteorite. At the north end of the pointer rock, which pointed north, was a constellation of rocks set into the Earth in the shape of the Pleiades. Other stones marked the position of the horns of Taurus.

This site is marked out for a ceremony to commemorate and remember the Lost Children. It involved the constellation of the Lost Children. You cannot see the Pleiades. or Lost Children, during the day; this ceremony would have to be at night. We could guess that it would be dark enough, so perhaps midnight, and midnight would occur, or be known, according to the position of the horns of Taurus. The occasion would be marked when the constellation of the Lost Children crossed the meridian due south at midnight, which could be seen by standing to the north of the Pointer Rock and facing south.

There are many cultures throughout the globe which mark special occasions in a very similar manner. The four great celestial events of the year are the Spring Equinox, the Summer Solstice, the Fall Equinox, and the Winter Solstice. I decided to forget the Winter Solstice since it's bitterly cold, and people are inside. Then the Spring and Fall Equinoxes are more temperate, but the most holy day of the year is the Summer Solstice when the sun is highest in the sky. Okay, so when did the Pleiades cross the meridian at midnight on the Summer Solstice? 11,500 years ago.

The people surviving the great flood when all the ice melted would have known that and considered it a sign and blessing from the universe, which it is. They built this entire village which, in that day, would have been a city to commemorate this great event and design their entire social structure around it, complete with earth lodges, rocks in the middle crater, and Napi effigies with other star signs. The local people have also found evidence of wooden walls about the site, probably to keep animals out.

The people lived there from the recession of the ice 11,500 years ago until the great disaster 7,400 years ago. They lived there for 4,000 years, and they observed and learned great secrets from the stars. They taught their children, and they became wise.

During the epoch when people lived on a sheet of ice, times were extremely harsh and the population was small. The people became very smart. When the ice receded, the people found themselves in a very supportive environment, and the population grew.

There was sedentary living by people all over the world at this time, notably 12,000 to 11,000 years ago. Among people all over the world a thousand years was a reasonably short period. People planned things and carried them through. They could hunt within a particular area, they could help each other, and they could gather crops in areas where food crops could grow. People just worked together, and the people associated with this meteorite, which was not a meteorite, had the time to delve into learning and educating. They were the star people; they still are the star people.

The rocks tell us more about these remarkable people. Do you remember the plaster that covered the rock at the meteorite site that is not a meteorite site and at the large effigy mound found on our search for the Majorville medicine wheel? Yes?

All over Southern Alberta are deposits of a layer of white alkaline. The lakes and soil are alkaline rather than acidic. This is the result of the Mount Mazuma volcanic eruption, which occurred 7,400 years ago.

The eruption created a huge cloud of volcanic ash blown completely out of the atmosphere, which in turn spread eastward and dropped on top of Southern Alberta. The ash from the eruption was three to four feet deep from the Rockies to Saskatchewan and from Red Deer South into Montana. By now, there were a few thousand people, maybe a few hundred thousand, living in this area. Because the people were organized and had stories taught to them regarding disasters, they came up with a plan, or it may have happened quickly and spontaneously. The women took the children and headed west. They found a place where the ash was dissipated around Nanton. There wasn't enough clear space for everyone to survive so the men headed east until the ash panned out somewhere around Medicine Hat.

The ash was highly alkaline and very caustic. All the animals fled as soon as the ash started falling. It created a wasteland with volcanic ash thick enough to cover a large dog. It killed everything, and people had to get out fast. And this divided the men and women into separate camps.

The place where the women settled is now known as Old Woman Buffalo Jump. The women seemed quite okay without having men around. There were no competing tribes of people, and they could easily defend themselves against animal predators. Also, I do not know the timeline of the evolution of the buffalo. The ancestors of buffalo appeared around seven and a half million years ago, and the modern bison became plentiful around 7,500 years ago. I imagine they changed considerably after the ice age, just like people.

Now, Old Woman Buffalo Jump is an excellent buffalo jump. It's a steep hill between two large outcrops of rock. Buffalo stampeded through the jump, having to travel through this narrow passage, which, at most, will only allow one or two buffalo at a time. The buffalo bunch up, fall, tumble, or try to jump off the cliffs on either side. They may break a leg or rip open ribs. The ladies could then finish off the injured buffalo and store meat, make hide, and survive quite well, thank you very much. The international heritage site not too far from Fort McLeod, known as Head-Smashed-In Buffalo Jump, is an excellent place to learn about the highly developed technology of tending large herds of buffalo in Southern Alberta.

So, about 7400 years ago, there's all this volcanic ash which eventually dissipates, and vegetation recovers, and wildlife returns. It is this ash which covers the central rock at the meteorite site that is not a meteorite site and the central rock at the effigy mound, which Donna and I found, and that is said to date 7400 years ago. The volcanic ash on the meteorite that is not a meteorite happened when people left that area, and studies have been done to validate that.

However, the studies did not listen to the local stories which tell of a possible love story and the re-establishment of civilization.

Please remember that I am an outsider, a white man who is on Native land at a very old and sacred site. I reported this site and my findings and its dating as far as I could tell to one of the societies. But there is an ancient story behind people coming back together at that time. There are differences in the way this story is told from different peoples within the Blackfoot Confederacy. It is told in different ways, and that is okay. I'm going to tell the story as I can see it after listening and piecing together different parts of a puzzle.

We can think of the soul as female and the Creator as male. This is an Eastern viewpoint. However, the Creator is female, and what is being created is both male and female.

Chapter 13

A long time ago, when the people were separated, the women lived in their camp known as the women's camp, and the men lived in the men's camp. They were living together for three or four thousand years or so, and I guess when a disaster, such as a thick covering of volcanic ash, occurred the men went one way and the women went another. Before that, while living on the ice, life was so difficult and harsh that these kinds of decisions would not be made. You lived the way you had to or you died; everybody lived very close to death. But a few thousand years of living together in a land of plenty perhaps got couples, or men and women, to be sick of each other. We have no idea if they were couples. Well, living on the ice, there would have been couples. We know that from societies that live in extremely harsh environments. But at this later time it may be that people didn't want to live as couples, or maybe didn't anymore. So, when the thick blanket of volcanic ash fell, the ladies escaped.

So, the guys went east, probably somewhere around Medicine Hat where the ash petered out. After a while they got lonely. They probably deserved to be lonely and they built a large mound, a huge mound, to the sky looking East towards the mountains of an effigy man looking towards the women's camp. It is still there today and is known as the Guardian of the Plains. No one knows who or when it was built or who built it or why.

And there was a young man. He was either a Crowchief or a Crowfoot; I don't know which. He lived in the men's camp but was getting pretty sick and tired of the men too. So he took off and started walking west towards the mountains. People could look after themselves in those days. There were lots of fish, berries, and wildlife. It was the open prairie, still is, grassland for as far as I could see and the snowy peaks of the Rocky Mountains could be seen in the distance.

He liked being alone and Alberta is truly beautiful. He walked along the Bow River and branched off South. There were massive herds of buffalo. They were always massive herds of buffalo. So it was important to pick a safe spot to sleep, or else you'd be trampled in the night. And the gullies by a river and under a bush would be safe. There were no trees per se, but large brush, willow brush, large bushes. Of course, you could always hear the buffalo. There were millions of them.

Somewhere near what is now High River and following along a creek which cut through the prairies, our young man approached the buffalo jump next to the women's camp, but before he came into contact with either the camp or the jump he rounded a hill by the creek and saw a young woman gathering plants. So the story goes.

The young lady happened to be very well respected among the women, and many considered her to be their leader. And she was not only incredibly intelligent, she was drop-dead gorgeous. She heard the young man and raised her head from gathering plants and saw him, and he saw her; their eyes locked.

She was wearing clean buckskin. Her long black hair framed her face in a picturesque beauty. She wore beaded moccasin boots and breeches. Her headband, also beaded, kept her hair off of her forehead, which was a bit sweaty from her morning work.

She straightened out and stared at this young man.

Our young hero stopped where this apparition stood in front of him, about 50 feet away, and he did what any young man does in this situation: he froze, his mouth agape and his eyes wide.

His long black hair was a mess after bathing in the river that morning. His clothing was also leather but not that well-made. His clothes were what you would expect from a young man living on the prairies on his own, but at least they were clean, and his shoes were functional. They had to be, or he wouldn't have made it this far. He was young, healthy, and strong.

"Who are you?" called the young maiden.

The word stuck in his throat. He didn't have a name, so he used the generic term "Napi," he stuttered.

"Napi?" she chortled. "You've got to be kidding. So you're the great Napi?"

"Well, if you're Napi," she continued, "then I'm Old Woman."

And so it came about.

There are a few things to mention regarding this amazing couple. First, they were young, strong, and could take care of themselves. Second, they hadn't seen nor had anything to do with the opposite sex for years. And third, they were both smart.

So after the shock of meeting each other, they were taking their time. Old Woman was sizing Napi up to see if he would be of any use.

"Aren't you with the men's camp?" asked Old Woman.

"I was," answered Napi, "but I left. Those guys are pigs."

"So things have gone downhill there?" asked Old Woman.

"Very much so," sighed Napi. "I don't think men can live without women. They become dirty and violent. There are fights all the time. I couldn't take it anymore."

"I wasn't looking for the women's camp. I was just traveling around," Napi added, hoping this beautiful woman didn't get the wrong idea, which actually was the wrong idea Napi had, but he didn't want to blow it.

"Oh, so you don't like women?" said Old Woman, looking coyly at Napi.

"No!" exclaimed Napi, moving forward.

Old Woman laughed and pushed Napi back from her, and Napi stepped back.

"Hey, I'm into this too, you and me, but I think we should get a few things straight first," said Old Woman.

It was now Napi's time to laugh.

"A few things?" said Napi, chuckling. "And what exactly are these things?"

Old Woman noticed Napi may have a brain in his head after all.

"I think we'd better talk," Old Woman said. "Our people are devastated. The men are living hundreds of miles away, and when the chance came, we all took off fast just to get away from you guys. It was awful. Who did all the work? We were hit, we were abandoned, and we left, and left alone, pregnant with their kids. And the men were pigs. We had the lost children story, and the children survived, were taught, and they were looked after. But what is going on between men and women was just not right. Our people are dying out. Men and women should be together, but if the men keep acting like pigs, the women will leave."

This caused Napi to think, which is not what he wanted to be doing. He remembered the stories of the panic when the city was being covered with ash. The women left immediately and found their camp; the men, when they got their act together, headed the other way to find more room and leave the women with their own living area. They seemed like they were not attached or cared about the women at all and the children were an obligation. But the men had to leave because of the shortage of available space free of ash. And they ploughed through ash for 200 miles. They didn't want to take their women and children with them because they had no idea how far they would have to go to find open space. The women may have been pissed, but Napi was not going to argue.

When the men's camp was set up, it was pretty much every man for himself. If you've seen the inside of a man's prison, you get the idea. Old Woman's comments struck hard. "What she said was true," thought Napi. "The people would die out, and maybe they deserved it. But again, what about the children?"

"You're right," said Napi. "Let's think about this."

This took Old Woman aback. Men never listen to women, in her experience, but this young man did.

"You and I should be different," she said.

"We should all be different," said Napi.

Old Woman took Napi by the hand and led him up the hill beside them.

"Let's look at the sunset," she said, "and let's have some rules between us."

"First, you are faithful to me," said Old Woman, walking with Napi up the hill.

"That's easy," said Napi. "There are no other women, and you have to do the same with me and no one else. That makes a lot of sense. That way, the men and women form teams and work together as couples."

"That makes a lot of sense."

"Sounds like we should be getting married," said Old Woman.

"Yes," said Napi, "Marriage. Okay, let's set out what a marriage is so we don't all fall apart as the people again."

So Old Woman and Napi sat atop a hill in the foothills of Alberta and discussed and worked out what a marriage is over a couple of weeks, and both decided it was a very good thing, and all the people should practise it and keep practising it over and over.

"So how are we going to get everyone to practise marriage?" asked Old Woman.

"We're going to have to show them," said Napi.

"After the great flood," he continued, "life became a lot easier. There was no need for self-discipline. The men lost their way because they could get away with it."

"Makes sense," said Old Woman, "Before the flood, life was very hard. Everyone had to work together. But when life was not so hard, the men didn't need a woman, and it all fell apart."

"We have to be inspired to do something," interjected Napi, "I have to show them the consequences. Telling them won't help; we're going to have to make it real."

"We can do that," said Old Woman, "if we work together. But how are you going to inspire people, especially the men?"

"I'll think of something," said Napi.

They were sitting together under the magnificent, cloudless night, watching the stars forever. Old Woman invited Napi to the people in the women's camp the next morning. The camp was much cleaner and more orderly than the men's camp; again, think of a men's prison without guards. Men's camp was chaotic. The women's camp also had fights break out now and then, but the women had figured out how to work together and had some order. Think of a women's prison without guards. The women had also figured out a pecking order; however, the way of life was not ideal for either camp.

Life must have been very hard on the women before the Mazuma eruption had given them the chance to escape.

Both Old Woman and Napi walked around the camp, and Napi

was the center of attention. He was honest with everyone; they all wanted to know how the men were doing, and Napi described the men's lot in detail. The women of the camp were pretty much in agreement that the men had it coming, and it was fairly easy to come up with a plan to organize a much better way to live. They were a very intelligent people who had lost their way. The time from the recession of the ice to the time of the eruption was 4,000 years.

It took 4,000 years for their society to collapse. I guess it happened almost imperceptibly, generation after generation. There were no real tests for the society to overcome and no guidance or pattern to the society other than the story of the lost children and the Okatoks chasing Napi across the ice. The respect for women must have severely deteriorated over 4,000 years until the women could escape. Those are my thoughts.

So the women decided how to capture and admonish the men and set up a much better way of life. They headed east towards the men's camp, which was somewhere around Medicine Hat, and stopped some safe distance from the men's camp. Napi separated from the ladies and headed into the men's encampment; the ladies stayed behind for the signal.

Napi entered the men's camp and let everyone know that he's found the women's camp, and they all wanted to know what he found. Many men wanted to take off for the women right away, but Napi told everyone that the women were on their way already.

"They want us to cook for them," he said, "and they want to have a dance and talk about marriage."

"Marriage? What the hell is that?" asked every man when he heard the word.

So Napi had to explain what marriage was, the good and the bad of it, and the men had to think about it for a while. Remember, there had been no women around for a few years, and it makes a man lonely and in need of company. There are no women around for a long while, so the men were very curious, to say the least. They talked for a long time about all the rules of marriage, then asked if it was all worth it.

"Believe me," laughed Napi, "it's worth it. You'll find out."

Nevertheless, the men all decided to give it a try. They washed up and put on the most decent clothes they had, though it was quite pitiful. The clothing was functional but just so, whatever worked. The area was at least clean but a mess, and you get the idea. They cooked up some game for the ladies and made sure there was clean water for everyone to drink. They tried to straighten out the place as best they could and told Napi sometime in the afternoon to call the women over.

So Napi had a fire lit on top of a hill and made the fire good and smoky. That was a signal, and the ladies saw the signal, gathered their things, and headed towards the men's camp. It didn't take too long before they came into sight, and as the ladies approached, they slowed down and made the best of their entrance. And what an entrance it was.

The ladies were decked out in their finest. Their hair was braided or held with beautifully beaded headbands. There was a ton of exceptional beadwork. Their clothing was immaculate and made of supple buckskin, and their buffalo hide moccasins and boots were decked with fur and beadwork. They had beautiful cloaks. They walked slowly, approaching the men, and of course, they brought food – really good food: berries, all kinds of delicious vegetables, stews, and they were ready to party.

The men had never seen such a sight of beauty and were frozen in their tracks, mouths agape and rather stunned. The focus of the ladies' entrance was Old Woman herself, who was beyond stunning.

And the men finally had the courage to welcome the ladies, and the ladies had gifts for the men. A lot of it was clothing, so the men were proud of their new pantaloons, shirts, and jackets, all beautifully beaded and trimmed with fur. They bashfully shared their cooked meat, and the ladies graciously added it to the vegetables and stew, and everything was delicious. Men and women talked to each other, and the drums came out, and the community danced welcome dances and sang songs.

In the middle of all this good time, Napi showed up. He was scruffy and rude. He walked right up to Old Woman, was rude to her, and began to molest her and hit her.

Well, the camp was shocked at Napi's behavior. Old Woman hit him, and another woman joined in and beat Napi too, calling him all sorts of names. Then the men all joined in and beat Napi too, calling him names and threw him out of the camp bruised and bleeding, telling him to never come back. They left him for dead and then returned to the party.

When the party was swinging and no one noticed, Old Woman went to find what was left of her husband. She found him, and he was kind of a bloody mess but still alive. Actually, Napi was rather tough. Old Woman found him and helped him to come around. Napi laughed.

"I guess it worked," he said, spitting out blood and a couple of teeth.

"A little better than we expected," said Old Woman. "Are you okay?"

"I've had worse," replied Napi, which was true.

And they both made their way from the camp and the party, and Old Woman nursed her husband back to health. Meanwhile, back at the men's camp, everyone was discussing marriage and what it was all about. It didn't take too long for everyone to reach agreement with all the rules and the menu on how to respect their women, or they'd end up like Napi, and no one wanted that.

For the next few weeks, the united camp found out about whether marriage was worth it. Sometime later, after Napi recovered from teaching the men what happens if you disrespect your woman, or any woman, he decided to put into motion his idea about keeping the people busy with something. Napi felt this was very important. Old Woman listened to his explanations and was willing to help. The two of them always appeared to be ridiculing each other, and Old Woman had become very skilled at ridiculing Napi publicly, and Napi was showing the men how not to treat a woman and the consequences thereof. But the two of them loved each other very much and kept that a great secret for most of their lives.

But Napi needed a project. He explained to Old Woman that there had to be something to bring the people together, to identify themselves and become one, to be able to combine the powers of men and women working together and dedicated to the well-being of their children for future generations.

There was a dynasty about 2,000 years later in Egypt where a pharaoh hired his people to build pyramids. It kept them busy for a while, but dynasties still came and went even with this scheme. But it worked for a long while.

You see, Napi was thinking about the problem of redistribution of wealth. It's a major problem with capitalism today. Whenever there is a division of labour, or if you like, people working together as a team (and it doesn't have to be in a capitalist system either) there is a surplus. Modern economic theory is completely inadequate to describe the myriad economic systems that have existed throughout the ages and throughout the world. So when the ice receded, for example, life became a lot easier and a surplus was generated. Usually, this surplus takes the form of time; people just have more time on their hands. But what they do with this time is really important. In today's world, the surplus for most people takes the form of disposable income, which often leads to self-indulgence or buying toys. I think you get the idea.

Napi wanted something to last and be worthwhile. He was thinking of knowledge, specifically the study of knowledge itself. Old Woman thought it would be better to start with the study of something rather than just knowledge itself, and then let people go deeper and deeper into what knowledge itself is. They both realized that most of the stories and teachings involved the stars. The people knew when the equinoxes and the solstices occurred. The summer solstice was the most important time of year. But what if they went beyond that, thought Napi? What would be required in order to see the heavens and their movements in great detail?

Napi and Old Woman managed to talk to the people about this idea, so they built an observatory. It was a giant circle, 24 miles in diameter, with a set of mounds in its center. They also built mounds at the cardinal points, and these mounds are still there today. The prairies are very flat, and you can see forever at night with no lights around. By setting a fire atop some mounds, and cooperating, you can build a remarkably accurate east-west line. This is important because the sun rises and sets on that east-west line on the spring and autumn equinoxes. It also tells you where north is, and more importantly, where due south is – the meridian.

The people studied all sorts of things and became known throughout the world as the Star People. People would travel from everywhere to seek knowledge and wisdom from the Star People and their descendants. It may be that they were the Star People from before and resurrected their knowledge, or they became the Star People because of their studies and way of life.

Napi and Old Woman weren't really Napi and Old Woman; their names were Crochief and Crowfoot, but I have no idea who was which. When they passed, they were buried under a huge effigy mound in the shape of a crow, with their names embodied on the mound and the date of their passing clearly etched in star signs on the surrounding ground. It is still there today, 7400 years later, with the memorial of a Texas rancher standing guard on top of it.

Chapter 14

Before we investigate death, let us investigate birth. This is a personal story and I am sharing an experience that few have known.

My mother was a Saskatchewan farm girl who found herself married, pregnant and in the backwoods of northern New Zealand. Believe it or not, I remember that time. I remember my first moment of consciousness, waking up from non-existence in darkness. And I knew at the time I had never existed before. I only knew I existed. And it was in darkness and silence. I had thoughts. Then it was time. I remember being born. I remember the moment of first seeing light through the seminal fluid of my birth. I was in the back seat of a taxi at the front gates of a rural hospital in Paparoa. My mother held me up to look at the front of the hospital and I remember that. I remember seeing a porch with a nurse standing on it and green trees: foliage surrounding the porch.

I fully remember being born.

I remember being conscious within my mother's womb.

It seems we wake up from non-existence.

Chapter 15

There are a number of reasons we study history. History is written by the conquerors, not by the vanquished. There are times in history when there is an opportunity for great change. There can be a disaster that threatens the future of a people, like losing your children while out hunting or a volcanic disaster that destroys the meaning of marriage. There are many such times in the history of all people, and there are stories of remarkable resilience, commitment to the well-being of others, and leadership.

Now is such a time in the history of Canada. We are drowning in a sea of lies and we are searching for the truth that can grant us salvation from the deep. If we do not heed and respond to the call of the dead from the graves of children we shall be no more. People may continue to live a life without meaning here in this land. But we shall cease to be Canadians.

I have worked for much of my life teaching mathematics and science in indigenous communities in New Zealand and western Canada. I've done other things as well, but mostly I found steady work through teaching. I stopped doing that because I got sick and tired of watching kids die. They die mostly from suicide, and we shall die also come our time to do so. What will be left behind? All we have are trinkets that break and cannot be sold. Our lives are becoming more and more meaningless every day. We are living in a death smothered under a global blanket of ignorance – wilful ignorance. We shall be no more, and in this vast universe it shall be as though we had never lived.

Teaching is a people type of job. There are lots of people you work with and yet it can be very lonely. You're dealing with children. You're dealing with a lot of children, thousands of them. Other adults are other teachers. They tend to grow on you, kind of like a fungus. The children, regardless of race or economic strata, are truly awesome. They are polite, respectful and have an incredible sense of humour. The age group I usually taught were from about 13 years old up to 18 years old.

In my first two weeks of teaching, at a very rural school in the middle of New Zealand, a young man killed himself by driving into a tree at over a hundred miles an hour. That was my introduction to teaching. High school is life and death. I don't teach school anymore because I'm sick of watching kids die.

As a white man talking to other white men, I still feel that the arena of education is the battleground in which we all must become victorious. And it is in this arena that the devastation has occurred. Native people wanted access to European technology from the outset of our meeting, and every treaty demanded what were thought to be European-style schools and education. But as white men, we did not follow up on that.

The Diary of Sam Steele, a well-renowned Mountie who was one of the original 300, narrates listening to many First Nations people demanding industry schools and schools to be included as part of treaty negotiations. And yes, there were treaty negotiations, but there were different understandings in these negotiations. My understanding, limited as it is, is that Native people wanted us all to share the land and live together. White people had a very different understanding: that we provided healthcare, housing, and education, and in return, we get the land. Even looking at our own interpretation of various treaties, we have failed to uphold our end of the bargain, and that is in all three areas of our promise.

Chapter 16

So, where are we now?

Well, what happened was that the various provinces refused to provide education to Native people. Under our constitution, it is a province that has jurisdiction over housing, healthcare, and education, and the province is under the Crown, who is a signatory to treaties with Native people along with the federal government. Provinces have as much an obligation to uphold treaties as the federal government and the citizenry.

As a result, dealing with Native people was relegated to the federal government, who had no infrastructure whatsoever for housing, healthcare, and education, particularly for education.

So, the federal government had to find some organization with an education system who could be contracted to fulfill a treaty obligation; and in steps the Roman Catholic Church, who had a functioning and running education system ready to go. Now, the other Christian denominations soon got on the bandwagon; all of them did. And the churches could quickly build up their numbers by converting and saving Native people and make money from the Canadian government while doing so.

Native people are physically separated from the European colonizers because of the reservation system, and pretty soon Natives weren't allowed to leave the reservations. They were often shot by the local whites making Native people isolated from the surrounding Canadian community. The surrounding Canadian community hasn't got a clue about Native people and a ton of superstitions surrounding Native people dominate the white community's thinking.

So, on the whole, Native people are isolated. The population has been decimated by disease, and they are restricted to living in isolated areas. The people comprising the general population are kept away from Native people and know nothing other than superstitious nonsense given to them by a racist and genocidal government. The federal government adopted a policy that requires Native people to simply die out or be assimilated into Canadian White Society. The churches are given a free hand to do whatever they wish with children. As far as housing and healthcare are concerned, they were just given a miss with housing restricted to the construction of slums and healthcare pretty much non-existent at the time.

About 80 years earlier, from about 1890 when residential schools got started, somewhere around 1810, we have evidence of a bizarre satanic belief taking root within the Roman Catholic Church

In the late 1700s the Roman Catholic Church was being hammered by governments. The Jesuits had been dissolved in Europe and intellectually the enlightenment had been attacking and ridiculing the church for over a century. And remember, before, all we had was the inquisition in Europe during which time many many people were tortured to death, publicly, by the Roman Catholic Church. Usually we hear today that religion and superstition are used to control the masses. However, during the dark ages there was no need to use superstition and so on to control the serfs. The serfs didn't have much choice and were easily controlled through the force of arms. It was the nobility that needed to be controlled and the church did that in spades. The hellfire and brimstone in art and sermon scared the bejesus out of the nobles, the ruling class, and established order through a reign of terror relying on superstition that lasted for over a thousand years. So the church, by the end of the 1700s, was bereft of strong leadership, but it still had adherents. And those adherents were embroiled in superstitious beliefs such as the existence of an entity of evil, ie. Satan. Now, the Protestant movement was also deep into a satanic belief, but the belief was more decentralized. On top of all of that, Native people all over the world were deemed as less than human. And all efforts were needed to be made, or excuses to be made, to convert these poor heathens to the European model of Christianity. It was nothing short of psychotic.

Also thrown into the mix was the advent of capitalism, in which the sanctity of the contract was paramount. The biggest contract for intellectual members of the Roman Catholic Church was a contract between oneself and the Devil. Of course, contracts such as these, were always viewed not as agreements, but as something that had to contain a loophole by which one side could take unfair advantage of the other. We can see where this idea of a contract among Europeans comes into play in treaty rights between Native and non-Native people. The loophole in treaties lies in the governance over enforcement and accountability. As long as the Canadian government could make some inept claim to be providing education, housing, and healthcare, it could get away with anything it did since there was no accountability or enforcement involved.

Recently, the Supreme Court of Canada has tried to take a role in accountability and enforcement, but it hasn't made much of a difference in the unjust relationship between the two peoples.

Nevertheless, returning to 1810 or so, a philosophy arises wherein a Christian can sell his or her soul to the devil, engage in complete self-indulgence and still make it to Heaven so long as the believer does not become attached to their debauchery, and goes to confession before dying. Furthermore, this philosophy upholds eugenics, the repression of women, and paedophilia as virtues. People following this philosophy aren't the sharpest pencil in the box and do not have a balanced mind. But again, there was no accountability or enforcement within the Catholic Church, especially for priests who were in demand.

Adherents to this philosophy found a home in the Roman Catholic Church and later in other Christian denominations. However, the Catholic Church was more favoured since it was the biggest; you could hide more easily, and the priests were all men and unmarried. They were supposed to be celibate, so when administrators of the Catholic Church and other denominations ran into problems with their priests and ministers, they could be shied off to run residential schools where they thought they had died and gone to heaven. The nuns seem to be particularly cruel en masse.

The clergy of these residential schools, including nuns, were convinced there was a demonic presence. They were fascinated with this concept of evil, which dominated their lives and most of their thoughts. And there were children to play with in exploring the bounds of evil and pushing back the boundaries of decency.

The Catholic Church became a haven for these people, knee-deep in superstition, hatred for others, disparaging of women, and desirous of little boys. And the church, not knowing what to do with these people, sent them off to teach in residential schools where they would be isolated and out of sight and out of mind. The Mounties, the RCMP, backed up this system with gusto. There were people, farmers, who found runaway Native children and said they should report what was going on to the SPCA since not even animals should be treated as these children were. But nothing was ever done about it, and nothing will be done.

The repression of women in European culture goes back a long way. The women of Europe were healers and were disposed of because of their reputation by the Roman Catholic Church. The Roman conquest, much earlier, didn't help either. The Roman Catholic Church became a bulwark against the equality of women who were branded as evil and in partnership with the Devil. Of course, the belief in being possessed by Satan was a very real thing even if you happen to be a Christian. So, throwing a large shovel full of paranoia of demonic possession was into the mix of hedonism and repression, and we end up with a pretty psychopathic group of people in charge of the souls of the masses.

There existed a chaotic and satanic underground and hidden world of Native children and European adults for 120 years all across Canada. The European men and women were bizarre, uniformed soldiers of hell, decked out in white and black, hating and despising the children they were supposedly caring for. These children were tortured, sexually and physically abused, and kept ignorant. If any escaped to tell the authorities what was happening, they were hunted down, captured, returned to the residential school, and then murdered. And this went on for 120 years.

Chapter 17

Today we hear people say that since some of the children survived it couldn't have been all that bad. I have heard that Fort Chipewyan nuns saved children because they would have died outside of the residential school. I have heard that the Blue Quill School in St. Albert was a dream school that pampered their students. I've heard all sorts of things. I have also engaged in teaching in communities right after residential schools were shut down. I have seen the devastation. Nothing good came from residential schools. One of the most horrifying things was what happened to girls who were impregnated by priests at the schools.

The girls were allowed to come to term, of course; abortion was a sin and not allowed. The girls were isolated from their parents and other members of her family. Upon having her baby, the newborn was killed and the body was disposed of. I have been on reserves and have heard of three different ways the bodies of these babies were disposed. In one place, the baby was killed and then buried near and around the school. At another, the dead newborn's body was plastered into the basement walls of the school. Later, when that school was torn down in the 1960s, the workers found the decaying bodies of these newborns and word got out about the girls being impregnated by the priests. However, these were Native girls, and it was on a reserve, and it was the '60s, so nobody cared so it didn't really go anywhere.

The third way was the most terrifying. The newborn was thrown into the school's coal-fired furnace where it screamed itself to death. It took a long time to die. The screams of a newborn baby roasting to death over a coal fire are unique and have only been heard by a select few, a club if you like. A friend of mine's mother witnessed a nun throwing a newborn baby into a coal-fired furnace at the Kamloops Residential School. That ordeal has given her nightmares ever since

Nevertheless it couldn't have been all that bad; some of the children survived. They lived through it generation after generation for about four or five generations

And now here we are, as white men, in a land with such a heritage.

Chapter 18

This is something that the world does not understand about white men: we don't need motivation. The same is probably true regarding white women, but I am not a white woman, I am a white man. I cannot talk about what anyone is like other than white men, I guess. And we are not bad people either. It may be that our methodologies and logistics are rational and genius; but our motivation, the reason we do things, is completely irrational. That is why white men would not find it in any way unusual to learn from the rocks or the trees, or from sitting on a boat in the middle of a lake. White men, Canadian white men, have a spiritual capacity to be moved by the void to do some pretty incredible things.

For example, in June 2013, the City of Calgary was flooded out. There was absolute devastation in the low-lying suburbs throughout the city. There was also a flood from Hurricane Katrina a few years earlier in New Orleans. There were riots and murders in New Orleans. In Calgary there were hoons riding around in pickup trucks rescuing people, helping with the cleanup, and providing food. It is the culture of Calgary; everybody helps each other and has a blast doing it. The entire city turns out to pitch in and help. A lot of water-soaked drywall got hauled away by volunteers in their pickup trucks. It was found out, through the Stampede Indian princess at the time, Amber Big Plume, that the Siksika Reserve 100 km east of Calgary had been wiped out by the flood. The city of Calgary, tens of thousands of Calgarians, filled their cars and pickups with bedding, clothing, food, kids' toys; and stuff, and for weeks, headed out to the Siksika reserve and pitched in, helped, donated water and food, and seriously helped those people. The Siksika people had lost their homes, possessions, and all their precious things and the people of Calgary, mostly white people, instantly and without hesitation, were there for the people of Siksika. They did not abandon them in their time of need and that was even when the people of Calgary were hurting themselves. The people of Siksika were stunned. One Native friend commented that he couldn't believe that white people were capable of such humanity. He said it renewed his faith in mankind. It was a miracle.

This story means that white men do have spiritual attributes. They are different than the spiritual attributes of Native people, but they do have spiritual attributes and they despise injustice. They can also be easily duped and controlled. It takes all kinds to make a world. The soul of European descendants has been damaged and hurt. The materialistic side has been favored at the detriment of the spiritual side. So healing and acknowledging the spiritual aspects of white men is definitely in order, but it's not dead. It's very much alive and desires reawakening.

Furthermore, there has to be mutual benefit for a relationship to work. Throughout history, we see different civilizations living beside each other. If there is mutual benefit between them they get along for a very long time. If there is no mutual benefit, one will annihilate the others.

So what benefit has European white Canadian culture been to Native people? Certainly not in the areas of housing, health, and education. The access to game has been removed and replaced with welfare and subsistence living. And what benefit have Native people been to those of European descent? Well, actually a lot. One of the first contacts was Champlain at Point Royal in Nova Scotia when Native people saved Champlain and what was left of his crew from scurvy. Native people saved white people from disease pretty well from day one. It seems Native people were far ahead of white people in the field of medicine. That was pretty well the case up to the middle 1800s and the discovery of vaccinations and how to conduct surgery without killing people. Of course, Native people had been conducting surgery long before; however, vaccinations were new. The American Constitution was designed after the unwritten constitution of the Six Nations people.

Then there's the fur trade. The history of the fur trade in Canada deserves a lot closer scrutiny than it has gotten in modern times. Native people and white people had a division of labour; they worked together. This was a Canadian company, and the first thing the Canadian government did on coming into being was to forcefully buy out the Hudson's Bay Charter and destroy the company. It was replaced by the Indian Act, and from there we get the reservation system and residential schools.

We are not seriously contemplating going back to the days of the fur trade in order to attempt a more equitable relationship between Native and non-Native people. We are demonstrating that a more equitable relationship can seriously benefit both parties.

Western Civilization is in a crisis. It is in a crisis of identity. We don't know who we are anymore. Everything we deemed sacred, everything we believed in, everything for which we thought life was worth living, has suddenly disappeared or transformed into either the trivial or the corrupt. Adult suicide is becoming more and more prevalent. Suicide rates, particularly for men, are going through the roof, and it used to be that women were more at risk of suicide. Traditional roles no longer exist, and these roles cement any society. Our society is not just collapsing; it has already collapsed. Any belief in what was is inadequate for today's world and the world of the future, and that is proving fatal for thousands of people. Our spiritual needs are as important, if not more important, than food and water. We need intellectual, emotional, and spiritual sustenance just as much as physical sustenance. Without it, we will die.

Chapter 19

If you, as a white man, have read this far you have no problem with
spirituality or understanding how we can learn from the rocks themselves. In the previous millennium that would have sounded insane,
but in this age we recognize, because of COVID and the collapse of
all that is deemed sacred, the oneness of mankind and the birth of a
global consciousness. That is why we can hear the rocks and stones
around us. It is also why we can now hear the dead children calling
to us to embrace truth. It is a silent conversation and we do not have
to talk about it with anyone. We'd be crazy if we did.

There is a lot of intellectual discussion around Maslow's pyramid
of needs. This idea came from Maslow after he was on the Siksika
reserve east of Calgary. The Siksika people are pretty special people
with a very powerful understanding of knowledge. Maslow got some
ideas from the Siksika people and ran around with this idea of a
pyramid of needs. He did not give the Siksika people any credit or
acknowledgment and claimed the whole idea came from himself. He
also got the whole thing wrong; it is all upside down.

Let me explain: Maslow said our needs were structured as a pyramid, with the foundation of our needs based on the physical, which,
in his theory, was the largest block supporting other needs above it.
The primary need, according to Maslow, is food, air, and water. The
next block is shelter, warmth, and so on. The next smaller block atop
the lower two is community and friendship, and so on with smaller
and smaller blocks until we come to the top block in the pyramid, the
smallest block, which is our spiritual need denoted as self-awareness
or self-actualization, whatever the hell that means. The argument

is that whatever physical needs we have, they should be considered the most important to be fulfilled since we would die without them. The higher we go up the pyramid the less these needs are required, and the top is more for personal happiness or "fulfillment" and is not necessarily for spiritual fulfillment – we must survive before we can be happy, so the argument goes.

Of course, this is nonsense.

Imagine, as you will, as I take control of your mind that you find yourself stranded in the middle of the Australian Outback in the middle of nowhere. It is high noon and 45°C (for Fahrenheit, just double and add 30, that's 120°F), and there is no shade. There is nothing for as far as the eye can see but sand stretching to the horizon in all directions. You are going to die.

So, what is the first thing you do? If you panic and start digging and trying to look for water or breathe heavily gasping for air you will die. What is the first thing you have to do in such a circumstance? The first thing you have to do is control yourself, calm down, and think. Praying would help. Getting control of yourself is the first and most important thing to do if you are going to survive. That is your self-awareness and self-actualization on steroids. Calm down and look around. Anywhere but here is where you want to be.

As you scan the horizon, what would you be looking for? Signs of danger, like a pack of dingoes. But let's face it, no dingo would be so stupid as to be where you are in the hot sun with no sign of life anywhere. You'd scan the horizon for anything worth walking towards. Most of all, you'd be looking for a sign of another human being. You'd look for smoke, you'd look for some sign of life, you'd look for evidence of a community. That's the next layer on the pyramid - you need a community to survive, even if it's a community living with animals in nature. You need to communicate.

Let's say you start walking and spot another human being. You certainly don't want to scare them away by running up to them like a madman or madwoman, demanding food and water or attacking them to obtain water. You'd be grateful and even quite open to forming a relationship. Forming relationships with others is the next important need here, and so is keeping control of yourself. So, let's say you can work together and eventually sit down and drink water and eat together because you can get what you need by working together.

The last need in this story is food and water. Yes, they are necessary, but without maturity and self-control, you will starve and die. People today have access to food water and housing, and still they are dying. Their spiritual needs, which entail maturity and self-control, are the foundation of life itself.

And we all know this. We know there are very happy people with little food and material possessions, but they have family and friends. They have a sense of well-being and fulfillment. So how can we have that in a modern age in Canada?

First, we have to overcome our greed. It's okay to have a home, a car, and a barbecue. That's okay. But we all have to remember that the best things in life are free – things like hopping into your pickup and delivering water and food and stuff to those who have been flooded out. We look after our neighbours. We don't abandon those in need. We are very generous.

But this Native thing has us tied up in knots.

Somehow, and I think we all know this, the answer is love. It has always been love, it always will be love. But how can we use love to solve major social problems such as our relationship between Native and non-Native people without screwing it up?

Right now, the biggest question among Native people in Southern Alberta is: How do we get these people clean drinking water? That is an excellent question; it is a good starting point. The community is mostly a farming community, and if the federal government doesn't do its job, we can always find a drilling rig and put an end to that problem. But what if you did that? We could imagine a rather large group of Native people all angry at a bunch of white farmers on the reserve with a drilling rig happily drilling away.

Hey, white man, don't you have enough land of your own?

Yeah, you're all having to go through Chief and Council, and they will have a problem with a group of white men and a drilling rig. That is because the land is crown land. They've got to bring in the feds, and the feds want to make sure they don't look bad and will claim they're already on this clean drinking water thing and have to do a study. They have to put a drilling contract out for bid after that, and you can bet they won't be hiring a bunch of local farmers and their drilling rig for that contract. They'll hire their crew and rig belonging to their friends and family, and they'll screw it up, after finally drilling a well, years or decades later, probably into a sewage pond. That's just how things work.

So, back to square one. How about some way to make friends? Maybe we can be friends somehow and then try to find ways we can be a benefit to each other. I'd like to mention paternalism; often, we as white people want to help or eliminate injustice, and often this comes with the idea that we can help them or alleviate their suffering. Noble aspirations have been tried many times in the past with disastrous results. So we have to talk about this. First off, if you solve people's problems for them you dis-empower them. I'm an expert in paternalism because I have engaged in it so often.

This is a terrible situation. We are damned if we do and damned if we don't. We are relegated to only working as individuals and cannot harness the power of the community. How do we engage the community and enhance it with the power of love?

Chapter 20

Let's break this down. We're all looking to solve a problem by concentrating on the symptoms of the problem and not getting to the cause of it. If we can find the cause, then we have a decent chance of solving the problem.

It reminds me of Bill. Bill was an elder at Alkali Lake. I met him in the middle of the 90s. My wife had cancer, and no one could say they were able to cure her. So, as things go, I went to search for a cure among the Native peoples of British Columbia. As it happened a group of Māori people arrived in Vancouver and they needed a driver for their van to be driven all over BC to all the Native reserves. I had a Canadian driver's license, had driven a cab for decades off and on, and volunteered to drive them around. It was an amazing trip. We went from reserve to reserve. They had amazing people. At that time, the dysfunctionality and racism were full-on. Today, because young Native people are getting some level of education despite the federal and provincial government to affect the opposite, the dysfunctionality is becoming less, and I'll get back to that later. The racism never subsides, especially in Canada.

Nevertheless, the experience was that I was the only white person in the group, and on the reserve there were no other white people either. So, I was watching a ceremony of one group of Native people from the South Pacific meet and greet Native people all over the interior of BC from Hope to Prince George, Bella Coola, and Rupert, places like Fraser Lake, and of course, Alkali Lake.

By the time I got to Alkali Lake I was fairly used to being in the background and observing the interactions of welcoming and consulting in the absence of white people or European presence. It was quite remarkable, and I could go on about it, but I'm not going to do that. Instead, I'll talk a bit about the magic and power of the Shuswap people at Alkali Lake.

Sometime in the '50s, the federal government passed legislation allowing Native people in Canada the right to vote in Canadian elections, to be allowed to drink alcohol in Canadian drinking establishments and to buy alcohol. The result didn't affect things politically, but the devastation of alcohol was endemic. Alcohol and alcoholism became a huge problem which killed a lot of Native people, making governments very happy and lowering the esteem of Native people in the eyes of the Canadian people. There are a ton of reasons for the epidemic of alcoholism which I'm not going to get into either.

Today there has been a very powerful national sobriety movement among Native people which has had the effect of creating a population that is 75% completely sober and abstaining from alcohol. This is not bad, that people are well on the way to eliminating a social problem, alcohol, in a mere 60 years, whereas the white population has had to deal with alcohol for over 30,000 years.

Nevertheless, during this battle with alcohol, the people of Alkali Lake became 100% alcoholic, and the social problems on the reserve were extreme. A mother lost her child due to alcohol and determined that the demon alcohol was to be killed. She called the Alkali Lake band together and started the "Honour of One is the Honour of All" movement on the reserve. Within a very short time, this band went from 100% alcoholic to 100% sobriety. They completely and voluntarily, to a man, eliminated alcohol from their reserve. The news of that accomplishment went nationwide, and the sobriety movement among Native people in Canada began in earnest.

These days, it is fair to say that there is still some alcohol on the Alkali Lake Reserve, but it is very minor. However, this was in the mid-90s, and the sobriety movement on Alkali Lake was in full swing. On all of the reserves we had been to on the journey so far, there was a pall of depression and hopelessness. The Māori contingent was healing while they were on each reserve. They were moved by the racism and outright genocidal actions of the government and local white people. They were disgusted by it and had given up hope of ever seeing the emancipation of Native people in Canada. Then we hit Alkali Lake.

You see, we all know of the devastation, and we know how powerless we are. But we also have courage and a strong desire for justice. So we need to find places where things have worked, rather than just harp on failure and resign ourselves to defeat. Alkali Lake is a treasure, a light in the darkness, a jewel in the crown of human resilience.

When we first arrived on the reserve, I parked the van, and we all got out. We were in a parking lot in front of a wooden community hall set in the middle of a forest, a pristine boreal forest. It was very beautiful. We were invited inside, and everyone jumped into a welcoming dance. The whole reserve had turned out. These guys do everything together. But there was a huge difference between this welcome dance in comparison to others. The people were dancing on their toes; they were dancing on the balls of their feet, with heels not touching the ground. They were happy, and they were laughing. They were filled with joy.

We were invited into the hall. The Māori friends did a powhiri, and the hangi took a wonderful turn with the entire reserve, with hundreds of people touching noses with their visitors from the South Pacific. Then it was time for the local people to put on their show of hospitality, and it blew them away. And let me tell you, it takes a lot to blow away Māori people in acts of protocol. The response was love, a heartfelt love, by grabbing each Māori person and getting up and dancing around, a dance that was full of joy. This blew the Māori guests away because, throughout their tour of Western reservations of Native people, they had found very depressed people, a heavy pall hanging over the land. They were deeply moved and shocked by the racism and overall prejudice of the Canadian people. But here, the people were happy and full of joy. Lots of joy here. The Māori friends were dumbstruck and speechless, and it takes a lot to strike Māori people speechless. In reality, it was not much that accomplished this. It was simply a community that was functional and happy. The welcome dance was simple but happy and uplifting. Through two weeks of travel through western Canada and visiting Native reserves, we never saw anyone who was truly happy until we visited this reserve. I do not know what it is like now; that was in the mid-90s. But it was a remarkable feeling to be among healthy people.

Afterwards, the Māori group and I were sitting outside the hall at a wooden picnic table, and an older, not-too-old, Native person approached and asked if I could take a picture of him and the Māori people. "Sure thing," I replied. However, he was disapproving of my lackadaisical attitude. I wasn't exactly rude or anything, but it required more respect than I showed. Remember, I was the only white man for at least 50 miles in every direction. I had let down my guard, and his slight admonition had hit me unexpectedly. Now, before you all question this, please remember that the Universe gives us prompts; it sends us little wake-up calls to pay attention because what is happening is important. So, I took their picture a couple of times and returned the camera to the elder, then sat down at the picnic table somewhere at the back of the group. This elder, whose name was Bill, proceeded to tell us a rather large number of white man jokes, to the hilarity of everyone there. It was getting to the point of being a bit much, but I kept in mind the memories of my time spent in Williams Lake in the early '70s, twenty years earlier. Those were the days when hoons, white people, would drive around in pickup trucks with rifles strapped across the back window of the cab and pop off some Native person walking home from the bar on an isolated rural road on a Saturday night. There was even a chief of the local tribe who took this up with the local Mounties, and he ended up dead too. So I listened to all the barbs aimed at white people and laughed politely, while Māori people howled with glee.

There was a pause while Bill explained a few things. He said that the local people from Williams Lake, white people, had terrible problems with alcohol, which they did, and treatment centers in Williams Lake just didn't work.

"They come out here and we put them through our treatment program and we heal them," said Bill.

Fascinating, we kill them; they heal us. As Roxy says, Native people are better people than us.

"We also cure cancer," Bill said rather matter-of-factly.

And that is when I woke up and started paying very serious attention. The whole reason I was on this trip was to find the cure for cancer and save Roxy; so these guys cured cancer.

"You see, white man's medicine does three things.

"They use radiation, chemistry, and surgery, and that doesn't work because they're only treating the symptoms. They aren't going after the cause. If you want to cure cancer, you have to go after the cause; then you can cure the cancer," said Bill.

And that was all I needed.

Soon afterwards, I returned home. It didn't take me long to find out that 90% of the cause of Roxy's cancer, her breast cancer, was sleeping next to her. I was the one who had to change, and so Roxy doesn't have cancer anymore. That is another story. The underlying message here is that if you want to cure cancer, the cancer in our country, the cancer of all mankind, you have to find the cause or you will never find the cure.

Let's also look at other cases of success; they do exist but are not completely sustainable. Let's go back to Kuper Island and an amazing woman, a chief by the name of Lisa.

Chapter 21

Lisa had graduated from college and returned to Kuper Island just before I left. She took one look around the place and decided to step up to the plate and hit a home run. She ran for chief, and as soon as she became chief, she got rid of welfare. That's right, she cut off everyone's welfare. She said no one was going to sit around at home and drink and get paid for it. She said, "You are either working, and if you can't find a job, I will give you one because there's a ton of work to be done around here; or you can go to school, and I will pay you to go to school. You work or you go to school. You don't sit around and drink and expect to be paid." The band elected her chief for 15 years. She completely changed the lives of the people. Young, educated, and strong, the people became. But then she was no longer chief, and the band regressed. But there was light in the darkness for a while.

But why does the light go out? Why does the sun set? Can there come a day that shall not be followed by night?

Light, and darkness.
Integrity and corruption.
Night follows day, and day follows night.
Is there a source of evil?
Is there a cause for evil?
Can evil be eradicated forever?
Can there be a day which will not be followed by night?
We're not a country, we are a colony; we are a colony of American corporate interests.
We do not have self-determination.

We do not own our resources.
We live.
We work.
We pay homage,
And we die.

The only instance I know of regarding a sustainable reinstatement of indigenous culture is through the Kōhanga Reo movement of Aotearoa, New Zealand. This is the Kōhanga Reo movement, which began around 1991 in the rural areas of New Zealand. A few elderly Māori women decided they had to do something because their language was dying. In fact, for many years, elders, the Kamatua, were saying that all knowledge comes from language. Even though Māori children didn't speak the Māori language because everything was taught in English, the Māori children could not completely comprehend what they were being taught. They said that if things were taught in Māori, even though the students did not understand Māori, they would comprehend more since the language itself was a part and parcel of their way of thinking. In European terms, the language was in their blood; it was a part of them. Learning in English was a hindrance and a burden. Nevertheless, these elder women, the Kuia, decided to start a grassroots education system in Māori, a Māori immersion program, where all schooling would be in the Māori language only for the primary or public school grades. When the students went to high school, they were taught in English.

What I saw in New Zealand was a once-in-a-lifetime event, more than that, once in a millennium or perhaps once ever, meaning that it did not occur before. There is a chance it may never happen again.

I returned to New Zealand 15 years after Kōhanga Reo got started. It had not only transformed the plight of Māori people; it had transformed the entire country. It had solidified New Zealand as a country rather than a far-off colony known as the Antipodes. Māoridom was always a mainstay of New Zealand culture, but it was dying.

Remember, please, that the staunch objection to Native language immersion as a pedagogy in teaching the curriculum was that the dominant language was English, and therefore all the students would struggle with English. Of course, this is nonsense. English is the dominant language; every kid knew how to speak English without it having to be taught to them. And with the learning done in the Native language, the students became far more eloquent in English.

I returned to my old high school where I began teaching so many years before. The school had rocketed from one of the lowest-ranked schools in the country to one of the top-ranked, and it was all because of the Māori students. Because the Māori students were so strong in their culture, Western epistemology was no longer a threat. The Māori kids immediately recognized high school as a competition and took it on with a vengeance. None of the Pakeha kids, which are non-Native kids, could get any of the prizes; the Māori kids won the ducs of the school, all of the scholarships, valedictorian, you name it. The Māori kids also excelled at university and in every subject

Rather than fighting back, the Pakeha, or dominant culture, started sending their own kids to Kōhanga Reo to try to keep up. Everyone in the country was proud that they could all speak Māori. When there was a terrorist attack on Christchurch, the entire country galvanized with expressions of Māori and Pakeha as a united front. During the COVID pandemic, the country was united with Māori culture supporting a Pakeha oriented quarantine, which defeated the disease in 6 months. The rest of the world had problems with COVID even after 2 years. The strength of the indigenous culture, through language, empowered everyone in the country.

It became a sustainable solution; but New Zealand and Canada are very different when it comes to the relationship between Native and non-Native people. New Zealand is a small country and Canada is huge. In New Zealand, Māori people are one people with a common language heritage. Although there are differences in cultural practices in different regions; they are fairly minor. In Canada, there are a thousand different languages at least, and culture is very different from region to region. Native people in Canada are divided within their political structure and segregated from political participation in the country. The Indian Act in Canada relegates Native people to a reservation system where inhabitants of reserves have no access to self-determination, education, housing, or health care; they have no political power or legal power to improve their lot or change the system under which they live, which has been in place for over a hundred years. In New Zealand, the citizen rights of Māori people are enshrined in the country's constitution, and 14% of the seats of parliament must be Māori elected by only Māori people.

Māori people are basically united through language, native religion, and overall culture. Canadian Native people are very divided through different languages, different spiritual practices, and different cultural practices. Māori people are identified through their essence of being Māori; Canadian Native people are identified through their trauma.

Chapter 22

The crisis of Canada is a crisis of identity. Our identity, as with the Native people of Canada, is an identity of trauma; that is the identity that the universe has given us. It is the identity which the stones themselves have determined for us. Denial of this identity is futile; it is now branded on our very soul. It can be the source of great depth of character for all Canadians. We who are alive today, or will be tomorrow, did not commit such atrocious deeds of satanic brutality; we all know this. Taking the blame is not the point; it is not productive. Taking accountability, even though we are not to blame, is an act that only a great people can accomplish. Who are we as Canadians? We are a people who can carry any burden for those who need us to do so. To alleviate the trauma of the past, we will carry the deeds of a past age as our history and remember not only the fallen in distant lands but also the children who died in our own backyard.

This means we must deny any feelings we may have towards our own "goodness" in order that we may have some real goodness.

Put it this way: We find someone who is suffering; we didn't cause the suffering; someone else did. We aren't even related to the people who caused the suffering. However, let us say that we carry with us the cure or healing to eliminate the suffering. And to try to complete this analogy, let us say that this cure or healing will cause us to appear as very bad people in the eyes of the rest of the world. Do we walk away and try to spin ourselves as nice and polite people, or do we take the hit and take accountability and apply the healing balm? Do we embrace our satanic past, that side of our history which is truly evil even though it's not our fault? Can we as a nation do this? Only a truly great people can carry this burden.

It is not through our abilities to try to alleviate symptoms of the festering disease of our relationship with Native people. A simple act of acceptance or friendliness by a white person towards someone who is Native, even, or especially, if it requires a massive effort to overcome that person's inner prejudice and racism, can work miracles. To overcome our racism in general is to eliminate it from our thoughts by changing our attitude, by changing our way of thinking, and our perceptions. It is not an easy task; it is not lightly done; it is definitely not insignificant.

"Greater love hath no man than he lay down his life for another," this includes women. We are looking at how to use love to resolve an impossible and intractable national problem. What about we surrender our souls to the universe? What about we embrace the darkness as our own? A major part of healing required for this sickness is the acknowledgment that the actions of the perpetrators were wrong. An admission of wrongdoing is a powerful elixir in the path of healing. And remember, no one is demanding anyone to take the blame; we are required to take accountability for healing and reconciliation to occur. We can do that.

This requires ceremony. What do we mean by that?

Being a white man, talking about ceremony has its limitations. Most of all is the fact that I'm not Native and therefore have no authority or credibility when talking about ceremony. But that does not mean that white people don't have or conduct ceremony particularly in Canada. Every year on Remembrance Day, we all wear a poppy and stand for 2 minutes' silence; that is ceremony. The entire country does it; we stand in silence remembering the dead.

And between us all, we know what hockey is; hockey is a spiritual game.

Ceremony is basically some physical act that brings the sacred into reality. Even though most of us do not smudge, it is a simple ceremony anyone can do pretty well anywhere. I don't think I will get into too much trouble if I talk about smudging. Different Native people smudge in different ways. There is a sacredness to fire and smoke; the smoke, in most cases, represents our prayers going heavenward. The same is done in Anglican and Roman Catholic churches; the smoke is from incense which has been blessed by the priest. Some white people may believe that the smoke from the incense is a sacred thing – worship, but I think the smudge is different than that. We have the power as human beings to be able to make sacred anything we deem sacred; even the atheist movement has things it deems sacred, and there is no need to take it farther than that; it's no big deal. The fire and smoke, and us deeming it sacred, whether among Native people in church, or in your living room, is a simple and straightforward exercise.

In a smudge bowl, place some dried material like sage you have picked while praying, or tobacco, cedar, or sweetgrass; these are the usual sacred plants I haven't told you about. Remember, all plants are sacred. The material is lit, often fanned with a feather; the smoke represents our prayers rising heavenward. You can wash your hands in the smoke and brush some of the smoke towards you while you pray; it is a brief and simple act while praying that is used in many different ways and has many different meanings. If you want to really know what smudging is or how to smudge, rather than the very inadequate and inappropriate description I have given you, you should talk to a Native person about it.

The point is not so much as smudging, or smoking a pipe, or going to a sweat lodge; our cultures are different. We have the means to make sacred this relationship between Native and non-Native people. I have no idea what it is or what it should be. It may be individually, or as a collective, or even both. Our world and our country are in darkness. No authority or expert consultants are going to save us or bring light into this darkness. Only we can bring light to bear on who we are. Native people should not be expected to bring us into the light. They have their own problems; But they can accompany us and we can accompany them. If we solve their problems for them, we disempower them; if they solve our problems for us, they disempower us. We are looking for a sustainable resolution.

We noticed that the enterprises that actually worked originated with local Native people and grass-roots initiation. It started with a few boots on the ground and total commitment, and with not much help. It began by engaging the community; somehow, everybody saw the light. Everybody got on board, by hook or by crook and got it done, but it began with a single person or a couple of people. So the key seemed to be some individual Native person with grunt to accomplish what needs to be done, and also there was no opposition from the Eurocentric community; in the case of Kōhanga Reo, there was cooperation.

Knowledge is information that has become meaningful. Consciousness is knowledge that has become self-aware.

Unfortunately, there there is a lot of opposition to Native people improving their lot, and that opposition comes from us. There is no encouragement to the efforts of Native people to get better, often condemnation instead, and no accompaniment. We as white men do not see Native people as fellow human beings; they are unfortunate but not human. Unfortunate, that is why we were able to live with the memory of burning their babies to death, that is why we are never going to do anything regarding living conditions, like clean drinking water, let alone decent housing. Forget about letting Native people have access to a proper education, especially under their own recognizance; they're probably smarter than we are, God knows, or better people than we are.

This is not their problem; this is our problem. The problem is not with Native people; the problem is with us. The problem is the demon within us, the demon which we have become. And we must embrace that demon, who is one with us, and use it to our full advantage and conquer the evil that is our very essence. We are inherently an evil people who do the unexpected; that is who we are as Canadians; we are very, very good at it.

This is hard to explain; please bear with me as I try. There is this evil. There is this demonic and satanic entity which was created in the past by those associated with our ancestors and our culture. Please detach yourself from that entity while I explain. It is well known that information is conserved; it doesn't go away, and knowledge is a higher organization of information, which is just more information; it is a living thing. It came from somewhere, from some building blocks, and organized itself into higher forms of information, which itself is information. Thanks to the incredible epistemology of the Blackfoot, we can treat knowledge as a living thing; we can treat it and view it

111

as a conscious entity, as a being.

We may possibly look at consciousness itself as knowledge that has become aware of its own existence; we as people are just information that has become conscious of our own existence, and therein lies the key to open the door to a garden of the oneness of mankind; we all unite in the global knowledge to acknowledge our own existence.

Within this existence is an entity of evil, for the sake of doing and being evil. It's got to go somewhere. It will not dissipate; it has to go somewhere. If it has no place to go, it will linger and infect those susceptible to it, anyone susceptible, of any race and of any gender. We cannot kill it in the usual sense, but we can decompose it, we can deconstruct it, we can give it a place to go. We open our hearts to it; we embrace it; we identify with it; we overcome it, and it is no more.

This is all independently from the behaviour and actions of various Native people in Canada; it has to be that way. If we design a plan of action that relies on some sort of activity, attitude, or behaviour on the part of Native people, then obviously it is not going to work. We cannot rely on others; we only have ourselves. We cannot rely on our government or Native people or the churches or any organization, and we certainly cannot rely on the Americans or the British. Russians and Chinese are on the sidelines, watching; but we ourselves are on our own.

Chapter 23

The dead are calling to us to embrace and accept truth; dead children and babies are calling us to embrace truth. The truth is that they were killed by an entity of evil that was a hidden part of our culture, a hidden part of us. This evil, to which we are all addicted, prevents us from becoming a country; it isolates us and prevents us from working together. It prevents us from acting on our own recognizance; it stops us from growing up and from becoming who we are.

Therefore, as white men, if we wish to be free, if we wish to become who we really are, we must engage the enemy, this manifestation of evil. And we shall do so in a very devious way, typical of Canadians. We shall surrender to it, embrace it, and overcome it. It is very much the love of the land that we have as Canadian men that gives us the strength and power to say that we are a truly evil people that acknowledges a history of genocide, a history deep in the satanic tradition. It is only a great and powerful people that can say that they are truly despicable and then behave completely differently.

So when we are accused of colonization, genocide, and racism, we can respond with: "Yes, we stole your land, we killed your children, and we continue on a path of devastation. Now, how can we get you guys clean drinking water, decent housing, and access to education?"

To continue with this idea, when our ancestors left Europe or China, or wherever they had been, they were so spiritually emptied of their humanity that they no longer knew what humanity is. I'm not saying they were bad people; many were awesomely good, but they were diseased in a spiritual way. This doesn't yield us blame, and this doesn't demand the invocation of endless apologies. Do not feel guilty; angry, and sorrowful, fine, but guilt is going to get us nowhere.

First off, knowledge is a living thing. It does not die. Knowledge, from what little we know of information theory – and believe me, it is remarkably little – we Canadians think knowledge is some information or idea that we have come up with. Like the knowledge of what a rock is made of, or better yet, how to find out what a rock is made of. It is a set of ideas or information we feel is knowledge, and we possess this knowledge, maybe in secret, to use to our advantage. And when someone with knowledge dies, the knowledge dies with them, but that is a childish and immature understanding of knowledge.

Knowledge does not live inside your head; knowledge is everywhere. Information is conserved and has to be stored somewhere. It is stored all around you as you learn and discover. From the impetus of the universe, you are, in turn, affecting the universe by storing knowledge in it. The individual is the source of knowledge. There are building blocks of information that come together and arrange themselves in a way that has never existed before, and we discover new knowledge if we have done the preparation work to be able to recognize it when the universe and the various forces arrange such new thoughts and discoveries and reveal them to us. We are just very complex information living in a matrix of infinite information that feeds us, that we alter and rearrange to create new knowledge. The universe about which we walk and dream absorbs our new knowledge and is never the same, just as we are never the same. This is existence. This is what existence is. This is being.

Okay, so as I've described, knowledge is something like the blob that ate New York City. The knowledge is that we are all one; that is the blob, and that is what we are. Yes, we are individuals, and the blob, the knowledge of us all, is there to care and protect each and every individual. Without the knowledge, we all die, and fairly quickly too. We are all one. The behaviours and actions of the past regarding residential schools, and the treatment of so many children, this satanic entity, this thing, is a living thing. It is alive. These children who have died are not locked in the past, they are one with us; they are in us, whether we acknowledge them or not. That is why we must embrace them or be no more. The evil, this satanic blob of darkness, exists, and it must find a place to live. It was created here in Canada; let us give it a place to be and enclose it in the knowledge that we are all one. Let us do so without hesitation.

But what does all that mean? What the hell does that look like? Does that mean the acknowledgement of a satanic entity that does not exist? We know that the satanic entity, as an anthropomorphic being, does not exist and has never existed but within the minds of the insane. It is the deeds and behaviour that exist. We simply accept these deeds. We take accountability for them, and we manifest the oneness of mankind every time we face the memory of these evil actions.

There is both the change in attitude through understanding and the change in behaviour when the universe offers us an opportunity. We do not deny being Canadian or the true hosers that we are; we add to what it means to be Canadian.

Nothing makes all of this clearer than the fact that no other race other than the white race carries with it the fundamental belief in original sin. The belief, absurd though it sounds, is that we are all born condemned to everlasting damnation and an eternity of torment simply because we were born. No other race, no other culture, even in the ancient recesses of history, has this fundamental belief in original sin or eternal damnation simply by being born. So, this idea of embracing the evil of our history and the horrors of children at residential schools is nowhere near as absurd as the fundamental belief of all Western Christianity that got us into this mess in the first place.

Please just think about it. We are all told that there is this fundamentally evil and repugnant entity, or place, and we are in it. That this world, this existence is an existence of evil, of condemnation and that is because we were born, because we are alive, that our natural state is is that of being condemned, of being in hell, that we are the damned and the minions of Satan as a natural state of being. And only if we are accepted into some dogma, or pay someone money, can we escape this fate and be "saved". I did not make this up; this is the way it is according to our cultural heritage. It's just that no one wants to talk about it.

Perhaps we Canadian men can understand why Native people think we are so screwed up and so stupid. It is not that we are not spiritual or lack spiritual sensitivity; we're actually good people who have been damaged. We may have had healthy, nurturing upbringings and be fortunate in many ways. We have been indoctrinated with a staunch belief in our own superiority, enforced by a backdrop of ever-present satanic fear. Small wonder we deny ourselves of our spiritual capacity.

Now, to deal with reality with maturity and in a healthy way, we know that this satanic ideal professed by the lunatics of religion does not actually exist, except for within the minds of the unsuspecting. I am talking about information. And information exists. Truth exists. This information, this truth, has no where to go and it has to go somewhere. We embrace this truth, the truth as told to us by the dead lying within our beloved country, and take accountability for it. We accept it and then overcome it by recognizing that we are all one. The dead children are not calling to Native people, or to churches, or governments; they are calling to us to embrace and comfort them with our love. That we are much more of them than they are of us. We are one.

Chapter 24

The stones sing
As anomalies
On a computer screen
Vibrating with screams and whimpers
In a dark and cold basement

Now, when that transformation occurs in your mind and your soul, there comes a time when you must plan for action. Before you do anything, after you have prayed and talked with the dead, read the 95 recommendations of the Truth and Reconciliation Commission. You don't have to agree with it; just read it. It's in the appendix. At least know what is being asked. Most, if not all, of the recommendations are actions that are supposed to be taken by our government, so it's pretty obvious that they won't get done. Remember, this is not a political issue; it's a spiritual issue. The healing is for us as those accepting accountability, not blame, for the injustice that has occurred. Please remember that.

Let's say you've completed step one and are ready to do something positive And if you jump ahead and don't do step one and you fall flat on your face, or create more problems than you're trying to solve, go back and do step one.

What are the problems on a reserve? What are the problems for off-reserve Native people? Apart from clean drinking water, they are kind of the same: education, housing and employment.

So, as a white guy with little or no money, and no political grunt, thank God, what can you do which will in turn give you the healing you need to be empowered to be able to make a difference?

First off, if you're making some sort of inroad to accompaniment, be aware that Native people are really pissed off and suspicious. And for good reason. Canadians are filled with feelings of superiority. So, you may find yourself in a room with the suspicious and those feeling superior. It takes getting used to. No one said love was easy. You cannot apologize. It's not your fault and it doesn't do any good. Let your actions speak louder than words. As a matter of fact, if you don't say anything, and even more importantly, if you don't offer any suggestions, you'll impress the hell out of them. Particularly as a white man. Believe me, white men, never shut up. I know; I'm a white man myself.

So what can be done is a hell of a lot more important than what can be said. And what is being said, through social media lately, Spring, 2024, is that we have to do something regarding clean drinking water and an admonition to anyone who tries to pan Canadian history or how nice we are. The admonition is to tell people that if you want to know Canadian history, start with the residential school system. Start with the thousands of children and women who have just disappeared or been lost to the fentanyl crisis. Becoming Canadian involves loving the winter and knowing the essence of the Truth and Reconciliation movement. Embrace the darkness.

This still doesn't get to what we should or could do. To be honest, I don't know. I wait for the dead to talk to me as we all do. And I wait for an opportunity. But it seems, we have all been robbed of our voice. And we are deprived of the opportunity to consult with each other. The world is antagonistic and the few have tremendous power over the many. And each and every day, we become more and more disempowered and more dissociated from the truth. What must we do to free ourselves? We are pretty powerless working as individuals.

Then again, there is knowledge. Let us not forget about knowledge. The ultimate power is to know wherein lies the source of knowledge. The source of knowledge lies with the individual who appears to be completely disempowered. This is going to get a bit out there as though we are not fairly out there now. This idea is about the mission. The most important knowledge is knowledge or alignment with our mission, whatever that is. We may not know what our mission is, and that may not be important. What is important is that we are aligned with our mission. So let's say that everything is knowledge. It's all information. And knowledge is a form of information that is organized to a level of being knowledge. Our mission is just information, organized into the knowledge that is our mission. We could call that our purpose, but white men don't need purpose – but a mission? Hey we're on it.

So, looking at a rock, which we are oft want to do, we see that the rock is just information. It contains history from long ago. As a matter of fact, we can deconstruct the rock into the information contained in the rock and the physical material of the rock. In our Western epistemology, we deconstruct everything and then make the mistake of confusing information, which is contained in the whole, with the material in which the information is contained. Knowledge is a different and separate thing. It is an entity in and of itself.

The knowledge of Euclidean geometry and the knowledge of ancient medicines are applications of the same source which has manifested itself in two different ways. There are rules to geometry and there are rules to medicine. Although they are different rules, they both follow the same principles. And they are the principles of integrity. So life itself is the manifestation of knowledge, which has integrity. If we have no integrity, we cease to exist. We cease to be. We die.

So there is a difference between knowledge that has integrity, or maybe information that is arranged with integrity, and just information. The information that is arranged with integrity is knowledge. The information that is disjoint and lacks integrity is just random information. It is not a living thing. Within a leaf, there is a phenomenal amount of knowledge. It is not so much as the integrity of the information, but the integrity of the arrangement of the information which, agreed, is also information but of a higher level. The integrity may also be a form, or thing, in and of itself and may be the building blocks of knowledge and consciousness.

By integrity, I mean something that lasts, something that doesn't collapse or decay and disintegrate. So many have built structures believing they will last forever only to have them fall. How about a mountain that has survived for millions of years? It has integrity, but it does not have knowledge and consciousness in the same way as a human being, or as a bear in the woods. So, I think I've laid out a model that there is order and chaos. There is integrity and corruption. There is knowledge and goodness versus ignorance and evil.

There is always the creation of ignorance upon the birth of knowledge. That is the result of information theory. Information is the arrangement of stuff in some sort of higher order. But as order increases there has to be the creation of more disorder in order that entropy increases. It is not that goodness begets evil, it is that knowledge will create more confusion somewhere. The confusion could be in the form of heat, or in the form of things being more decentralized. Please hear me out. We have so much evil in our history and we embrace it by acknowledging it, and by refusing to deny it. We can do all the goodness we like and use our history as a sink of chaos.

Our history is this box that has an infinite capacity for evil. We can do all the goodness we like and not worry about the consequence. We just stick the consequence into the sink of evil we carry around with us. Another way of putting it that may be easier to grasp but is really the same thing – we ask: Are we all going to heaven our hell? Easy. We're all going to hell. Well, now that we have that silly and meaningless question out of the road, we can carry on and do all the good we like. We are never going to receive salvation so we can be good people simply for the sake that it is a lot of fun. We as Canadians can reject the idea of doing the right thing because it's the right thing to do. We just do the right thing because we're Canadians. It's what we are. It's what we do.

Why? Because of our history, and the merciless torturing of tens of thousands of children to death, and the devastation of hundreds of thousands of human lives; that's why. Does that make it easier to understand? We don't do good for the sake of redemption. There is no redemption. We're all going to hell. There is no forgiveness. That's why we do that which is right. That's our identity. That's what being a Canadian is. So the most important thing in all of this is that we are not asked to take the blame. Guilt is not going to get us anywhere. Guilt will kill this whole thing.

Do not wear sackcloth and ashes and for God's sake, don't apologize. Jesus. What we are asked to do, or rather even without being asked, is to take accountability. We have to. Native people in Canada have suffered enough. We're going to have to attack the Indian Act. It's our legislation, not the legislation of Native people. They don't own it, we do. Now, there are things not to do and there are things we can do and should do. We can do these things as individuals or in groups. I'll explain.

What not to do:

1. Natives don't pay taxes.
   Uh, Natives are not citizens. Why the hell should they pay taxes? We're on their land, or the land that they gave us. They've paid enough in taxes already. If Natives get wealthy enough to have to pay taxes, we're done. We can declare a national holiday and dance in the streets.

2. Natives don't pay for a university education.
   Not true. They pay tuition and fees just like everybody else.

3. Natives are drunk all the time.
   At last count, 75 percent of Native people were following the path of sobriety. A vast majority don't drink at all.

   Natives, as a percentage of the Native population, have the same number of alcoholics and homeless as Canadians as a percentage of the Canadian population. Stop listening to rumours and check your numbers. Find the cause of a problem and then fix it, rather than making things worse by being a racist prick and celebrating the downfall and hardship of others.

   When was the last time you had a drink? When was the last day or time you went through a day without having a drink, including beer?

Okay, enough of that shit. Now, for what you can do, We have to get rid of the Indian Act. I'll get to that in a minute.

Your actions can be divided into two groups, what you can do by yourself and what you can do with others.

What you can do by yourself:

1. Be aware. There is a ton of racism in Canada and you can't do much about it. Keep yourself safe, but be aware. Be knowledgeable.

2. Read the recommendations of the Truth and Reconciliation Report. Know your history, know what happened and what life was like before Confederation before 1867 Avoid politics like the plague.

3. Visit Powwows. Even though they are not traditional, it's a great place to experience some of the dances and pageantry. Drop by a Native Friendship Centre. It's okay to ask questions there. It's what the place is for. Keep your mouth shut. You don't know anything. If you're there to learn, it's okay to ask questions. If you're being told just listen, you don't have to say anything. Even if you do say anything, it would be crap.

4. Find peace and just listen. There will come a time for you to speak, but it will be to other Canadians. We don't have anything to say to Native people. Remember, we are listening to the dead and are responding to their call. That's enough.

5. Mostly Native people teach by getting you to figure it out rather than telling you. It's expected that, at least, you know how to behave. Be polite.

Enough of that. Now, let's see what we can do as a group of people united. Even though we may all feel alone and are a country in name only, this is a delusion. Free yourself from it. Work in small groups, and build your communities. You'll find out very quickly that you are not alone regarding our relationship with Native people. The goal is to change the Indian Act; it is not to become the great white saviour. Even as a group of people, regardless of how much money and power that group has, it won't be able to get Native people clean drinking water, access to education, or access to decent housing, but it can change the Indian Act.

So, what kinds of groups are we looking at? Well, there are service groups like Lions, Elk, Moose, Rotary, Toastmasters, Masons and a rather large number of others. These groups have corresponding female organizations. Join one of them and ask around. How are we going to change the Indian Act?

If you get opposition, quit, and join another group. Then there are Church groups. Not all Christians are a bunch of racist pigs. A lot of Christians are nice. Ask around: Are we going to change the Indian Act? If you get nothing but opposition and racism, quit. Join another group. Keep away from political groups. They're a waste of time. Talk to ordinary people. The idea of working in groups is that you are working with a group rather than a collection of individuals, (even though that's what they are). We have lost the ability to consult.

The reason working within a group is so important is that we can talk with each other in a non-threatening environment. Even by going slow, it'll go remarkably quickly. I'm betting that everyone is on board; they just don't know what to do. If you say: hey, I got an idea, let's change the Indian Act, everyone can consider that goal.

If anyone asks can we do that? You can answer: Well, if we can't, then we're not a country. Let's change the Indian Act. Let's change the constitution. And that now brings us to the crux of the problem. How do we change the constitution? We cheat. You see, the most important thing for a government, or authority, is to maintain authority.

That authority is used to keep the populace, and even more importantly, the individual, encased in a cocoon of ignorance and powerlessness. This is done by creating enormous unapproachable organizations through which you must go, whose approval you need, to change authority. And believe me, we are going to change authority big time.

The stones and rocks have taught me that all of this is an illusion. The only authority that exists is your own personal and individual integrity. We just have to put that into practice. Many people, maybe everybody, think we have to go through the Supreme Court of Canada. And those guys are scumbags.

Remember what I wrote about accountability? If you want to bypass accountability, create a fake organization and be accountable to it, rather than an authority with teeth. For example, judges, in

Canada are accountable to an organization known as the Canadian Justice Council, which consists of the Supreme Court judges and chief justices of all the other courts, including chief justices of provincial courts. This is a sham. The head of the Canada Justice Council is the Chief Justice of the Supreme Court and that guy cannot be trusted. Because who is that guy accountable to? Himself. The same as all the other members. They are all accountable to themselves. There's no consequence and it is all contrary to our constitution.

The Chief Justice of the Supreme Court, as the chairman of the Canada Justice Council, is not pulling the strings. He does what he is told to do. The entire legal system of Canada, is rife with corruption. And for us, that is a good thing. You cannot establish such a huge organization of vapidity, incompetence and corruption, and keep it going with threats and pretension without everybody, knowing about it. This is because not everyone is a complete sleazebag. There are some people who have a sense of moral rectitude, and some of these people are judges. But the more entrenched the person is in authority, the further they are from moral rectitude. So look to the bottom of the organization, not the top. Consider the alternatives.

In 1991 we had a referendum concerning our constitution. It was the first time we got to change the thing for over 100 years. The referendum rejected all the proposed changes from the federal government and, of course, the will of the people was ignored and many of the proposed changes were applied anyway.

So the will of the people means nothing to our government, but that should surprise no one. One of the things that remained regarded a little item known as a constitutional question. During this referendum hubbub, the people of Canada very strongly insisted that constitutional questions remain, very firmly, under the jurisdiction of the lowest courts of the land: the provincial courts. Ordinarily, provincial court judges, the men and women who staunchly guard over the maintenance of traffic tickets, have jurisdiction over constitutional questions, not some dickhead in Ottawa. Furthermore under our constitution, our judges, all of them, are not accountable to some corrupt and lame bureaucratic institution created by the twits of confusion.

Judges are accountable to the bar. They are accountable only to the bar and to nothing else. That's in our constitution. It's the bar associations in each province that have the ability to fire judges simply by striking them from the bar. It is feasible and possible for the bar association of the appropriate province to strike the Chief Justice of the Supreme Court of Canada from the bar. And he is then no longer a judge; he is off the bench.

In making a decision over a constitutional question, it has to be presented to the nearest court. That's a provincial Court. This is how prostitution was decriminalized in Canada. Some hooker questioned the authority of the federal government and the constitutionality of criminalizing the sex trade. And she won; bless her heart.

If the jurisdiction of the sex, trade can be overturned by an individual Canadian, then changing the Indian Act can be done as well. And by individual Canadians, hundreds and thousands, even millions of them. All at once or one at a time. And if anyone on the Canada Justice Council tries to armstrong any of our judges, we move to strike them from the bar, question the constitutionality of the CJC and then annihilated it according to our constitution. Judges call their cases according to their own conscience and their personal relationship to the bar. The bar, by the way, is a piece of wood.

To digress: in Europe, not Scandinavia, in ancient times before the Romans, when a respected person, a storyteller, elder, healer, whatever, died they dug a hole, buried the body and planted a tree on top of the body. The tree grew, sustained and was nurtured by the decaying body of the respected one. The tree became the headstone, or grave marker, and the dead person's body lived again in the tree. The molecules of the decaying body were then absorbed and became molecules of the tree. Eventually the tree dies and the wood from the tree was used for sacred objects, like the bar, and contained the blood, etc., of the ancestor. The judge in Canada is therefore accountable to the dead.

However, in Canada, this is a tradition handed down from British and French law, and in Canada we do not remember the dead as our ancestors; we remember the dead as young and very brave, young men and women, Native and non-Native, who paid the ultimate sacrifice overseas so that we today may possibly have some access to justice.

The bar represents those who died so that we may possibly have access to justice, and those who died because they had no possibility of having access to justice.

Chapter 25

The Canadian Constitution is both written and unwritten. The written part is descended from the BNA Act into the bureaucratic gong show of today. And the unwritten part lies in the hearts of Canadians and with the dead. It does not matter what those who believe they have authority think; it only matters what we as individual Canadians think. If we maintain our personal and individual integrity we are all powerful. If we abandon our integrity then we are powerless. And those who believe they have authority will do all they can to annihilate our integrity. Money is not the issue. This is a spiritual battle. The issue is the integrity of the individual Canadian regardless of whether we work in groups or we work alone. Therefore, obviously, a movement to change the Indian Act must be apolitical.

The original document regarding our relationship with Native People lies within the Hudson Bay Charter, in which the royal cousin Prince Rupert and the Company of Adventurers could conduct business in the area of land which drained into the Hudson's Bay. Any land they got they had to buy from Native people. It was the granting of a monopoly over trade and to fish. There is acknowledgement of the rights of the inhabitant Native peoples and the Company of Adventurers obtained a monopoly to trade with them. In 1670 the crown recognized Hudson's Bay Company as the law in the territories mentioned and that they may have land and rule over it as a plantation. Right after Canada formed in 1867, the government of Canada bought the charter and now possess it.

It is an English document designed for trade and does acknowledge trading with Native people rather than enslaving them as per the

Doctrine of Discovery from 1493 by Pope Alexander VI. The Doctrine of Discovery applies to the United States as a result of some dickhead in their Supreme Court, but there is a strong legal argument that this doctrine does not apply in Canada, And legal arguments are what we are into.

If we are to change our constitution, keeping our eyes on the prize, the object of the game is to change the Indian Act into what it needs to be changed into. Skating and puck handling are all great, but don't forget to put the puck in the net. The Doctrine of Discovery was issued by the pope a year after the discovery of North America by Europeans. Native people discovered it long before.

If you're paying attention, Native people discovered North America considerably earlier; however, the Doctrine of Discovery removes the acknowledgement of the humanity of Native people and that humanity continues to be removed even if Native people become Christians. It's pretty ugly stuff. It endorsed the slave trade.

Cutting to the quick here, Henry VIIII deposed the pope as the legally defined head of the church and placed the Monarch of England in his place. So that would mean that the doctrine would have no legal bearing on the Monarch of England. This overrides its dictates. The Hudson's Bay charter comes close. In the early 1700s, England defeats Catholic France in North America with significant help from Native people. Then the Monarch of England, George III, completely abrogates the Doctrine of Discovery in 1763 with a Royal Proclamation. And that proclamation is worthy of study, since under our constitution the purpose of the Indian Act is to uphold and fulfill the objectives of that Royal Proclamation. That's where we should start. Think of it as a gift from our ancestors. The details of why both the Doctrine of Discovery and the Hudson's Bay Charter are not applicable anymore can be filled in later.

The Hudson's Bay Charter was bought by the Canadian government right after Confederation, and the pope no longer has legal jurisdiction in Canada. What we need to show is that the Indian Act does not fulfill its mandate to uphold the directives of the Royal Proclamation.

Right off the bat, King George III, after winning the Seven Years War, the first global conflict in history, acknowledges that Native people in North America have property rights. That's huge. Forget legal arguments based on human rights; property rights supersede human rights all day long. And for good reason. In our way of life, for those of European descent, property rights form the foundation of our legal system.

And by the Royal Proclamation, Native people have property rights. Actually, to be more correct, Native People always had property rights and by Royal Proclamation these rights are acknowledged and protected by law. And these rights are enshrined in our constitution. The nobility claims all the property of, say, Canada, or the area of North America, by right of God. Then the people are granted rights to buy and sell property under certain conditions.

Those conditions are, collectively, property rights. There was no such thing as human rights until some time in the 1970s. With the acknowledgment of property rights, Native people can buy and sell land, which has been done by treaties. Legally, there has to be recognition of "the other" for our laws and legal system to work.

In all this, the Royal Proclamation acknowledged that Native people have their own sovereignty, including their own military, legal system and courts as well as a mess of other stuff. That gives recognition of Native people's rights, and the crown must negotiate on a level playing field. So, in changing the Indian Act, the first thing we as white people Canadians have to do is get rid of anything that removes property rights for Native people.

It may be that certain lands were granted to Canadians by Native people and for a fair price at the time. However, and this is an important issue, if an unfair advantage was taken by the crown of Native people, because of disease, wars pestilence or famine, then the courts must favour the disadvantaged party. We have to also remember that any contract, and a treaty is a contract, that goes into contention or disagreement, then favour is given to the party that did not write the contract. Yes, you read that, right. If there was an agreement to share the land and the agreement was written up by the crown, then disagreements in that agreement accrue to Native people.

Please also remember that we are not fighting over land, we are fighting over the maintenance, or re-establishment, of the recognition of property rights for Native people.

And, of course, the reason we are getting the legal enforcement of property rights for Native people is so that we can get them clean drinking water. You see, you can't sign away your fundamental rights as a human being; and property rights and access to clean drinking water are fundamental rights. It is not so much that we as Canadians will get our country back by getting Native people clean drinking water through property rights; it is through overcoming opposition to getting people access to clean drinking water. And there are people among us who feel that Native people deserve what they get and all of this is their own fault. But who cares? They don't have clean drinking water.

I have no idea how that could have been the fault of Native people. They don't have clean drinking water. Jesus. To get them clean drinking water we have to legally establish property rights. And to do that, we have to deal with a lot of corrupt lawyers, judges, bureaucrats and political leaders, as well as a general collection of assholes who inhabit any society. Remember please, that a country consists of a citizenry that holds its government to account for the government's actions, past present and future. A colony cannot do that. We are a colony until we hold our government to account. To do that we get Native people clean drinking water.

We enforce property rights for Native people. We become a country.

Now, to follow along this line for a little while, when you get to the source and supply of clean drinking water, check for mercury, check the water. You are drinking that too. The relationship is important. If we mobilize the entire country and cause havoc in the courts on a national basis, we should have some idea of an end goal.

Sure. We get clean drinking water for everybody. We tear down and rebuild our national approach to education, and that subject deserves an entire book just on its own. We basically create a new way of life for ourselves and for Native people. Let's say we do that. What does our relationship become not only with Native people but also to the world? What becomes our relationship to each other? To the land? To this Canada? It's an alliance, and that alliance requires responsibilities and effort on our part to fulfil our obligations under that alliance. The stones are telling us to wake up, to cast aside the lethargy and somnolence of death. Wake up.

They say:
We are here for you.
Wake up.
Have a stretch from your slumber
Look around everywhere.
There is love, and you are part and parcel of that love everywhere.
There is love.
Work quietly.
Be at peace.
Get the job done.

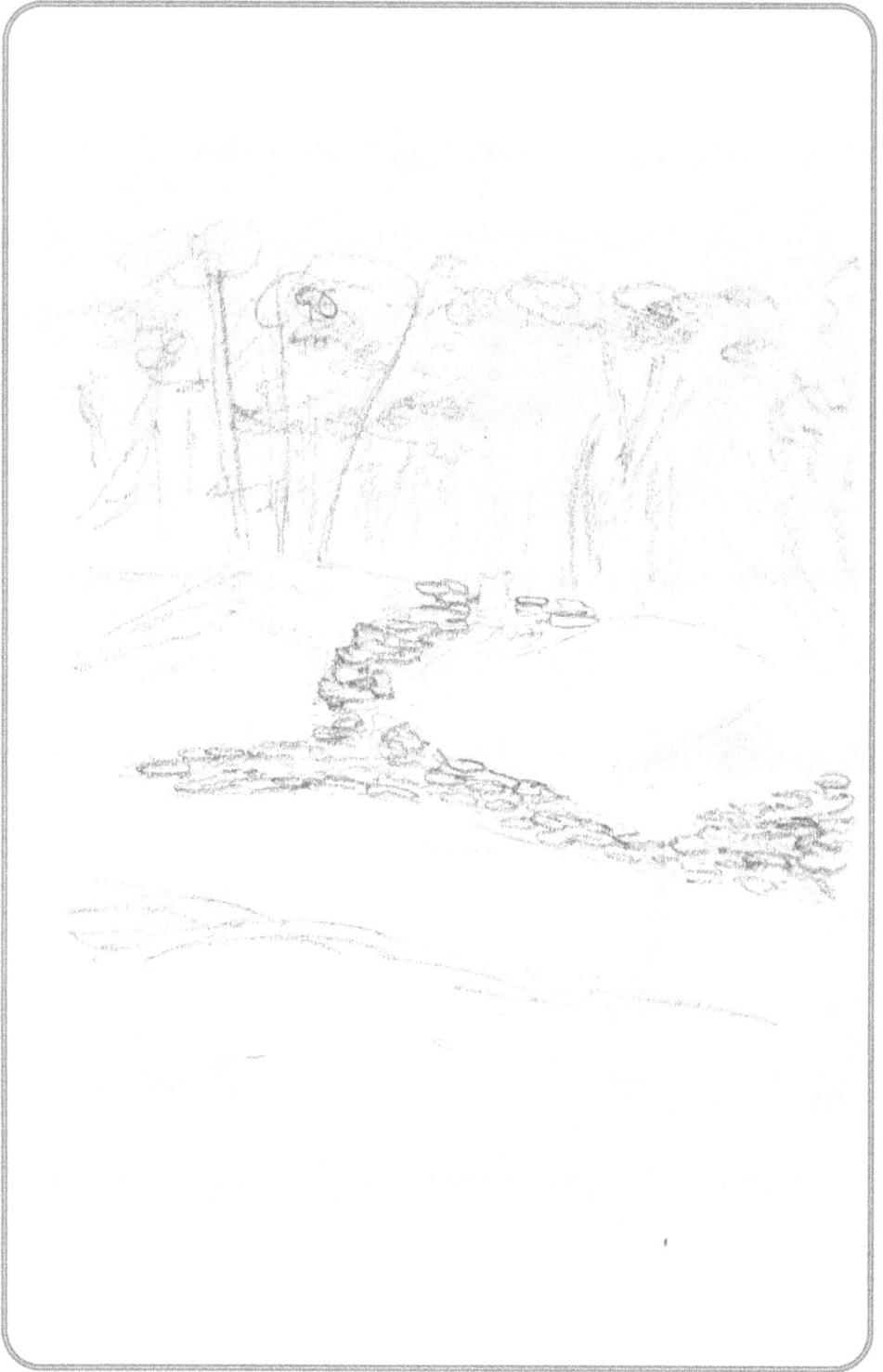

Chapter 26

Education

Learning, knowledge and so on determine who and what we are. It is the very foundation of our identity and our society. Education, according to Native people in Canada, is the new buffalo. It is the source of our economy. And education was everything at the time of signing the treaties.

Furthermore, in this day and age, education is a flash point. No other facet of our society, of who we are as Canadians, is more important than education. And education in Canada is a disaster. If anything shows our lack of being a country and the fact that we lack self-determination, it's our education system.

Our teachers are treated like shit.

Everyone thinks they are experts in education. That is because we have all had the experience of being taught and we all think we can do a better job than the teacher until we find ourselves at the front of a classroom of 30 to 35 kids who all hate you and don't want to be there. If you're not prepared and don't know what you are doing they will tear you apart. Education in this day and age is a disaster, but it wasn't always like this. There was a time when teachers were respected and acknowledged for their craft, but those times are no more. We are living in a world that is a product of a dumbing 'em down education system that has been in place since the 1970s. And this is 2024 as I write. That's 54 years – about three or four generations. Dumbing 'em down, is now an established pedagogy throughout the world.

I've been a teacher of mathematics and science for more than 35 years and have taught in all types of schools. Mostly I taught in marginal schools with wonderful children. Education usually is thought of as teaching some subject area to students. However, having been a teacher, education is much more about learning than it is about teaching. How we teach, how we transfer knowledge, is what is meant by a pedagogy. However, how we learn is mostly left up in the air. Without care and skill and applying means to learn, education becomes unproductive. I am writing about education because it offers a path for healing for Native people and Canadians. The real door for healing lies with truth. The acknowledgement of what is there has to be of mutual benefit in an alliance. The greatest gift for each side is the gift of knowledge. If we are to change the Indian Act, we must change it into something better or get rid of it. We can go through and try to correct a vast number of mistakes, or we can start with defining the basic principle of our relationship. Our basic principle is to defend ourselves against a common enemy. Our basic principle is also to build a country, a home that is much better than what we have now, and that will take time.

It will take generations of handing down knowledge of successes and failures. That involves education. It involves learning. So is it possible to make education or learning the basis of the relationship between Canadians and Native people? What would that look like? Well, first off, and most importantly, Native people refuse to be enslaved. That is important when it comes to education and to relationship. There are other differences between us but I'd say that's the biggest one. We as Canadians embrace our own enslavement. That's why we are still a colony and why we colonize others.

Institutionalized compulsory education began in the late 1800s as a result of the Industrial Revolution. The purpose of education was to train an agricultural population to become an industrialized population. It proved incredibly successful. The purpose of education is to produce semi-skilled factory workers. The First World War proved just how successful the education system of Europe had become. And countries strive for industrialization, for economic and military growth, and stability. The system of education is geared strictly for that purpose. Many disagree with the purpose of education which I have stated. It may be that you don't want the purpose of education to be to produce semi-skilled factory workers and I would fully agree with you. However, that does not contradict the reality of what education actually is in our society. Education and industrialization is a form of enslavement. It's just that the slaves are paid, given some hope of improving their lot, and are dehumanized through abject materialism. Canadians have been trained to live and think a certain way and to never try to imagine that any other way of life is possible. And, of course, the entire system is collapsing as it should, and as it is inevitable to do so. Does that mean we should all start living like Natives? Not really.

People can live however they like. Right now we live the way we do because we have to. Native people live the way they do because they have to. It's just that our houses are a lot nicer and we have clean drinking water. The recent pandemic demonstrated in spades just how dysfunctional we are. I live in Calgary and many here are in the oil industry. During the pandemic just about everyone was working from home. And no one wanted to go back to fighting traffic for an hour and a half every day to spend their working hours on a floor filled with cubicles with 600 others. Furthermore, not only could these people work from home and spend more time with their wife and kids, they could be working and living at the lake.

And Native people are mostly rural while living on reserve. Native people are packed onto reserves because the federal government insists on building the houses in which Native people must live because of the Indian Act and there aren't enough houses. On top of that, Natives don't own their houses; they have to rent them back from the federal government.

Surely, just from a housing perspective, we can all find a better way to live. That's what is meant by property rights. This clarifies something that Canadians are missing: The fact that we can compare our way of life, and it is a very privileged and fortunate way of life, to that of Native people. This blinds us to our disempowerment. Now that the pandemic is over, there is a massive push by management to get people to return to commuting to work. However, the entire system of work is changing. I am hoping that you will see that we can gain control over these changes by doing what is right as far as the Indian Act is concerned.

It is more than just a numbers game; it concerns our way of life and what it is going to look like to be a Canadian. This is the power of knowledge. An idea can completely change a nation. Can we consider knowledge as a form of property or capital? Can the way of life of both Canadians and various Native people be considered property and recognized by our constitution? I'm getting lost here. Obviously, when two people coexist, they exchange knowledge. They exchange all sorts of things: language, customs, religion. The two become different people. And that has occurred over the last 150 years.

But the way this interaction occurred was driven by the Indian Act. It did that through paternalizing Native people. The federal leaders believed being Native was a bad thing and being white and Anglo-Saxon Protestant was a good thing. Quebecers were tolerated and their language guaranteed, but they were still considered the "other" as far as being Canadian was concerned. Always the "other". And yet, none of us really fit in. We don't even know what a Canadian is other than some touques, maple syrup and hockey. We are presented as stupid, naive and illiterate and still we don't fit in.

I wonder if this is the key: how do we all fit in? How can we feel we are accepted in our home? I think Native people all fit in and feel they are home even though most social interactions are strained to say the least. This is a trick I learned from Māori people. We need to be welcomed on. We need to be allowed to be Canadians. We need to be certified. (I'm going backwards here). Usually we figure out what we are doing first, and then follow with some sort of ceremony to instigate what is to be done or what has to be done. Maybe we should start with the ceremony. Perhaps the ceremony will open the door for us to find this new constitution we all seek. There never was a Canada except in our imaginations. We're living a dream of emptiness and reality is everywhere around us. We seek significance in an ocean of unimaginable wealth. We seek love. There can be no love without a dichotomy. It takes two to tango. It takes French and English, East and West, North and South, Native and non-Native, child and adult, man and woman. The world is looking for meaning while love is lost to all.

Chapter 27

Wednesday July 10, 2024

It is evening, after returning from visiting Vimy Ridge, Passchendale, and Yprés, after walking through many graveyards and putting down tobacco, after saying thanks and asking for help and guidance. I'm really tired now, although I have a ton of ideas running through me. I've been investigating the crisis in physics and the need to change the Indian Act. And now I can see they are not just related but are manifestations of the same root cause. The fundamental cause is capitalism combined with the need for propaganda to sustain it.

We can look at this from a historical perspective and we can also look at using this knowledge to establish an everlasting world peace and justice for all. I've been deeply affected by the First World War and Canada's place in it. It marks a major shift in the affairs of mankind. Before the war, there was a solid chance, a very good chance of establishing an everlasting world peace.

- Architectural brutalism bears
- The art of the bunker child and lets loose
- Propaganda to continue the Spectre of War.
- To maintain and preserve capitalism we must
- Define terms of capitalism and
- Show the fallacy in its propaganda.
- Capitalism promotes incompetence.
- Capitalism is self-destructive.
- Define in terms of human labour how
- Capitalism is based on a system of wage labour and

- Propaganda.
- Capitalism requires propaganda in order to survive.
- You shall know the truth
- And it shall set you free.

By capitalism, I mean an economic system, or social order, based on wage labour. People are paid for their work rather than being forced to work through force of arms, or working for their own sake, or for the sake of others, or for the community through free choice.

The Museum of Flanders Fields in downtown Yprés, Belgium, is quite remarkable. So is the Museum of Passchendaele. While there I learned of the situation in Europe prior to the First World War and what led up to the conflict. There are some events that all occurred at the same time and the same place that led to the ability to have such a devastating conflict. Following the Napoleonic war in 1812, there was the re-establishment of the archaic state by Alexander I of Russia with the support of England. The archaic state had matured into a system of oligarchs, (monarchs), who governed the people with various elected representative governments. And the primary economic system was still based on agriculture with industrialism coming up fast. People had fought with swords on horseback, with muskets and and bayonets and cannon. Infantry charging with bayonets, along with cavalry and fixed cannon. They were all mostly farmers and wayward souls. There was also, philosophically, the establishment of the Enlightenment where reason took precedent over superstition. However, as I have written, superstition was fighting back but in the background. It would have its day.

Added onto all this, the entire planet had been colonized. Most of it very brutally so. And it had been colonized by Europe. The Napoleonic war was fought over Europe: Who would dominate and rule Europe? Now, in the aftermath of war, natural resources were pouring into Europe from all over the globe. Tons of it. Everything you could think of as a raw resource poured into Europe. There was a lot of money to be made. More money than had existed ever before in the entire history of the planet. More money than one could possible imagine. Industry was the new economic system almost overnight. There were a few rebellions/revolutions in the 1840s and labour became an organized economic force: a huge organized economic force based on the capital of Europe, of all these incredibly wealthy oli-garchs and their capitalist banks and financial systems. Labour was exploited to the hilt since it had no defence and the entire population of Europe was organized by the oligarchs as one massive body of humanity, trained through compulsory education, to do the bidding of the state.

In order to keep all this going, the state needed propaganda to convince labour to be happy in its lot. And the printing press became much more in use with pamphlets and so on, because the people could read. They couldn't read before the advent of free compulsory universal education. And education was geared towards converting humanity from an agricultural way of life into an industrial way of life. The people in Germany ridiculed the propaganda but the British ate it up like candy. Let us step back and take another look at the overall situation in Europe in the 1800s. There was created the ability to have a state over all of Europe. But not a political state: a state of mind. And everyone was committed to that state of mind. And so it was. Europe begat the global modern state. It was not a political body, but it contained all the political states. It was not an economy, but it incorporated all of the economies. It was not a particular philosophy or belief system; it embraced and utilized all of the philosophies and belief systems. Everything was utilized to promote and nourish this new Global Modern State. The new global modern state was all powerful, could do no wrong, could solve all your problems and was always right and committed to doing what was best for humanity. It was the birth of a new age.

But it had no soul.

Looking back from the vantage point of over a hundred years of history, we could have had it all. We could have establish a world peace and justice for all. We could have eliminated illiteracy, poverty, sickness, child mortality, and injustice throughout the world. We could have created an everlasting world peace and justice for all. We could have created a golden age of humanity. It would have been easy. The desire and motive was there as a result of the Enlightenment. There were lots of movements for world unity and active forces to eliminate slavery. Knowledge and rationality were supposed to be paramount. But no. The global modern state decided instead to be engaged in an inhuman and insane chess game over the resources of the world. There was no reason for the First World War. There were excuses, incredibly paltry excuses, but no real reason for the merciless slaughter of millions of people. Nothing was gained but for another war and eventual discovery of nuclear weapons. Men, by the hundreds of thousands, drowned in the mud at Passchendaele. They were canon fodder. The minions of the state were fighting using the tactics and methodologies of the Napoleonic war throwing cavalry charges and men with bayonets into barbed wire and machine guns. And the dead bodies piled higher and higher in no man's land. And the state could do no wrong. It was frozen and could not change how it was doing things. It was all for the glory of war. The glory of war with poison gas, with eyes burned out and melted, with shit and piss in an ocean of slaughter.

And in the middle of this horrid scene which created the incredible literature of J. R. Tolkien and the Lord of the Rings, there were the Canadians. And there was one Canadian in particular. A chubby friendly chap by the name of Arthur Currie. He had trained in the artillery on Vancouver Island before the war. He was an officer, he fought in the second battle of Yprés fighting off gas attacks and was considered by the British command as cowardly since he didn't want all his men to die in battle. Currie despised the British, the war and the incompetence of the state. After the second battle of Yprés he worked with Canadian parliament and the Canadians demanded that they would fight under their own command or else, you can fight the rest of this stupid war without the Canadians. And British command had to agree.

I really hope you see why this is so damned important. The Canadians would only fight under their own command. I am trying to establish peace and justice, but I have to resort to the annuls of war to find a way to establish such a desire. Canadians fight under their own command. This flies in the face of the principles of a global modern state.

Currie pulled all the Canadians off of the front line, away from the Yprés salient, went inland and started training the entire 80,000 of the newly-formed Canadian Corps how to fight with mobile artillery and as a cohesive unit. There was no glory, just the sober and unfeeling training of working together to get a job done. Every Canadian soldier knew their mission, where they had to be and when. They practised for six months on a mock-up of Vimy Ridge. They knew what they were doing. And that was the antithesis of the global state that demands unthinking automatons who sacrifice themselves for the cause.

Let me explain, please, the outlay at the time. The trenches of both sides of the war were about 30 feet or so apart and stretched in pretty well a straight line from English Channel to the Alps, like two parallel lines. Except for the city of Yprés in Belgium and the area of northern France. There was a bulge in this line protruding into German occupied territory all round the city of Yprés. This is called a salient. The reason it becomes a concentration of military conflict is that if the enemy, the Germans, can penetrate the base of this bulge, the salient, they can surround the allied forces and kill them. At the southern base of this salient, south and west of Yprés, was a ridge known as Vimy Ridge. The British and the French had been defending the ridge for three and a half years. An unimaginable number of men from both sides of the trenches died and their bodies abandoned in the dirt at Vimy Ridge. Bombardment, bayonet charges, underground tunnels and explosions, nothing had moved the parallel line of trenches one iota. The Canadians were given the job of taking the ridge. They relieved the allied forces and took over. They annihilated the Germans, routing them, and completely erased Germans off the ridge, down into the flats, and off the map in that area in four days with remarkably few losses in comparison. The Canadians had invented modern warfare.

Soon afterwards, they took Passchendaele, at the front of the salient, in seven days.

France gave Canada Vimy Ridge. If you go there today, you are on Canadian soil. You are in Canada.

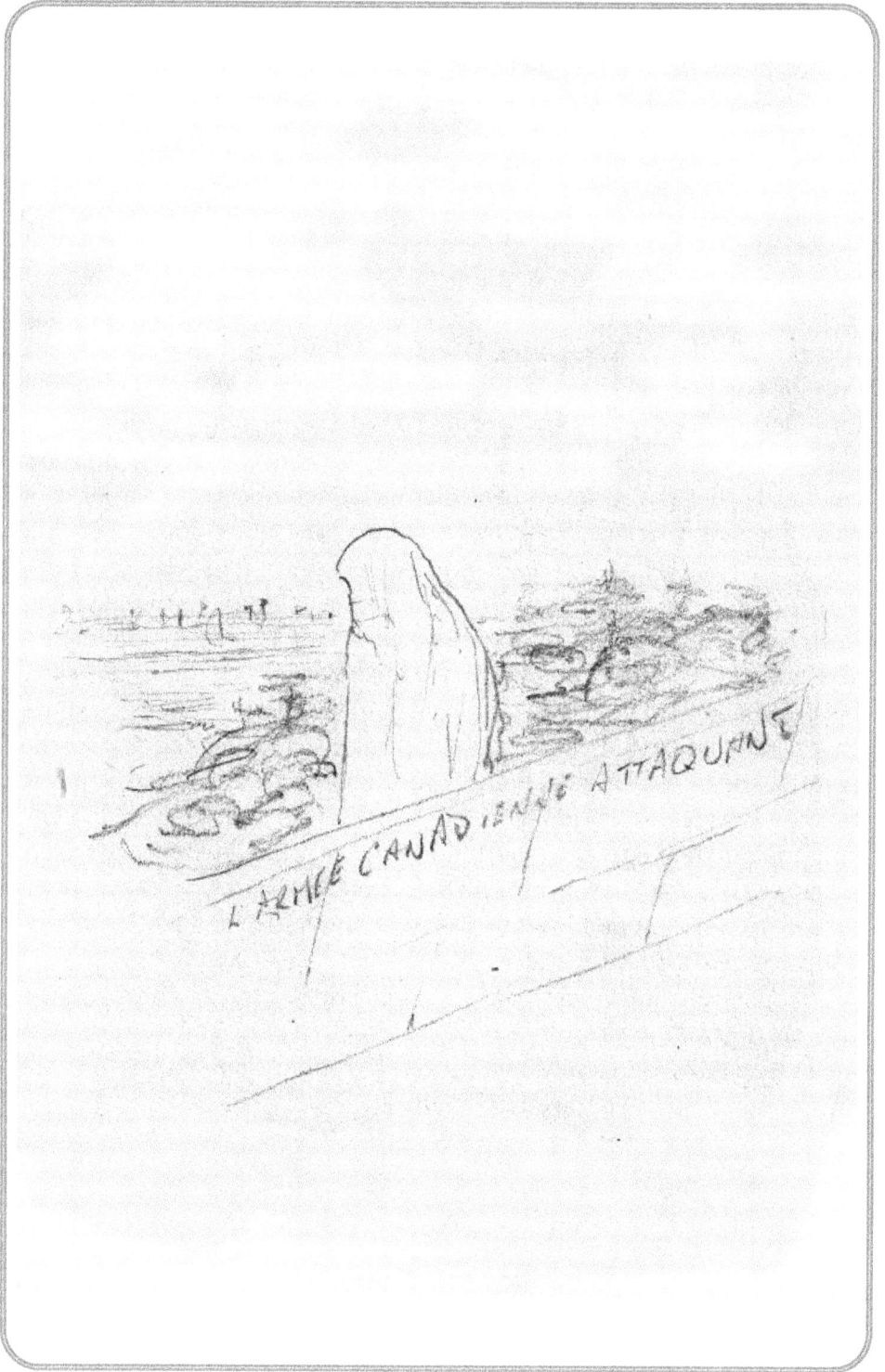

L ARMÉE CANADIENNE ATTAQUANT

Chapter 28

I shall now return to discussing the modern global state. It may be that wage labour provides some redistribution of wealth from the wealthy to the rest of society. But eventually the general public is trapped into an enslavement of working for a living until everyone, including management, is engaged in a form of slavery. Everybody ends up working for the man. Native people saw right through this charade and wanted no part of it when push came to shove. However, and this is a big however, It was the Hudson's Bay Company that begat mercantile capitalism which lead to industrialism.

You see, if the populace is enslaved through force of arms and then are offered to be paid for their work, they'll jump right on board and believe they are finally free. But Native people were never enslaved. Conquerors tried to enslave them at first, but it didn't work. Native people would rather die than be enslaved. Furthermore, before the advent of the modern global state after the Napoleaonic wars, Native people in Canada were our allies. That is of a paramount importance if we are going to change the Indian Act. We cannot change the Indian Act in order to impose a life based on wage labour. That won't work. There are a ton of alternatives to capitalism, or an economic system based on wage labour. There are economic systems that have been stable for tens of thousands of years and they don't use money. And I'm not talking about a barter system either. Such systems include the potlatch and give-away practices. They are amazingly efficient and allow everyone to live life to their full potential.

Please don't get me wrong. We're in an ongoing new age. We are not going back to a way of life that does not use all the advantages of modern technology. It's Canada. It gets cold in the winter. We all need to survive. But there are alternatives to forced wage labour and we don't have to freeze and starve in the dark. So what is it in the Indian Act that stops us from ensuring Natives have access to clean drinking water? The Indian Act does not include Metis or Inuit people. It came into effect 12th of April 1876 and here are some points:

- Definition of a reserve: section 2 (1)
- Definition of a band: section 2 (2)
- Powers of Band Council: section 2 (3)
- Section 3: Administration – Minister of indigenous Services is superintendent general of Indian Affairs
- Section 4: Applications of the Act
- Section 115 and 116: Canadian government completely controls education, housing and healthcare of Native people. They can abduct children from their parents.
- And it goes on

It's pretty obvious that the Indian Act assumes the surrendering of property rights through the signing of treaties, which may be illegal. The crown takes over all surrendered lands of Native people. Let's see if a treaty actually accomplishes this. In other words, check the treaty. Education, housing and health care . . . Do we even have to stop and think about this? And in our own country? By the way, they also don't have clean drinking water and no way to get it. And this is Canada, which is a country that blames others for violations of human rights. Something is very wrong here. The memories of walking through Vimy Ridge and Passchendaele are still fresh within my mind. Men, who drowned in mud and babies burned in school ovens joined forces to scream in darkness where no one will hear them. No one cares. Where no one knows they even existed. This is a reflection of us. This is the legacy of Canada. Look at the world today. We see propaganda that hounds us constantly that we are powerless and nothing can be done.

The plight of Native people in Canada is tolerated for a short while with some soul-searching and shame. Then the diversions begin and overtake the main thrust of the press impregnating our minds with the consistent germ of irrelevance: that we are irrelevant, that we are born, we consume stuff, we die. Therefore, organize and work together. Organize and awaken those who are already organized. Join the flow. Rejoin humanity. Work together. Coordinate a legal attack against our court system starting from the bottom.

Be humble.
Be strong.
Have courage.

Appendix

Appendix A

Truth and Reconciliation Recommendations

Truth and Reconciliation
Commission of Canada:
Calls to Action

This report is in the public domain. Anyone may, without charge or
request for permission, reproduce all or part of this report. 2015
Truth and Reconciliation Commission of Canada, 2012
1500–360 Main Street
Winnipeg, Manitoba
R3C 3Z3
Telephone: (204) 984-5885
Toll Free: 1-888-872-5554 (1-888-TRC-5554)
Fax: (204) 984-5915
E-mail: info@trc.ca
Website: www.trc.ca

A.1   Calls to Action

In order to redress the legacy of residential schools and advance
the process of Canadian reconciliation, the Truth and Reconciliation
Commission makes the following calls to action.

A.2 Legacy

A.2.1 Child welfare

1. We call upon the federal, provincial, territorial, and Aboriginal governments to commit to reducing the number of Aboriginal children in care by:
   (a) Monitoring and assessing neglect investigations.
   (b) Providing adequate resources to enable Aboriginal communities and child-welfare organizations to keep Aboriginal families together where it is safe to do so, and to keep children in culturally appropriate environments, regardless of where they reside.
   (c) Ensuring that social workers and others who conduct child-welfare investigations are properly educated and trained about the history and impacts of residential schools.
   (d) Ensuring that social workers and others who conduct child-welfare investigations are properly educated and trained about the potential for Aboriginal communities and families to provide more appropriate solutions to family healing.
   (e) Requiring that all child-welfare decision makers consider the impact of the residential school experience on children and their caregivers.
2. We call upon the federal government, in collaboration with the provinces and territories, to prepare and publish annual reports on the number of Aboriginal children (First Nations, Inuit, and Métis) who are in care, compared with non-Aboriginal children, as well as the reasons for apprehension, the total spending on preventive and care services by child-welfare agencies, and the effectiveness of various interventions.
3. We call upon all levels of government to fully implement Jordan's Principle.
4. We call upon the federal government to enact Aboriginal child-welfare legislation that establishes national standards for Aboriginal child apprehension and custody cases and includes principles that:

(a) Affirm the right of Aboriginal governments to establish and maintain their own child-welfare agencies.

(b) Require all child-welfare agencies and courts to take the residential school legacy into account in their decision making.

(c) Establish, as an important priority, a requirement that placements of Aboriginal children into temporary and permanent care be culturally appropriate.

5. We call upon the federal, provincial, territorial, and Aboriginal governments to develop culturally appropriate parenting programs for Aboriginal families. Education

6. We call upon the Government of Canada to repeal section* 43 of the Criminal Code of Canada.

7. We call upon the federal government to develop with Aboriginal groups a joint strategy to eliminate educational and employment gaps between Aboriginal and non-Aboriginal Canadians.

8. We call upon the federal government to eliminate the discrepancy in federal education funding for First Nations children being educated on reserves and those First Nations children being educated off reserves.

9. We call upon the federal government to prepare and publish annual reports comparing funding for the education of First Nations children on and off reserves, as well as educational and income attainments of Aboriginal peoples in Canada compared with non-Aboriginal people.

10. We call on the federal government to draft new Aboriginal education legislation with the full participation and informed consent of Aboriginal peoples. The new legislation would include a commitment to sufficient funding and would incorporate the following principles:

(a) Providing sufficient funding to close identified educational achievement gaps within one generation.

(b) Improving education attainment levels and success rates.

(c) Developing culturally appropriate curricula.

(d) Protecting the right to Aboriginal languages, including the teaching of Aboriginal languages as credit courses.

(e) Enabling parental and community responsibility, control, and accountability, similar to what parents enjoy in public school systems.

(f) Enabling parents to fully participate in the education of their children.

(g) Respecting and honouring Treaty relationships.

11. We call upon the federal government to provide adequate funding to end the backlog of First Nations students seeking a post-secondary education.

12. We call upon the federal, provincial, territorial, and Aboriginal governments to develop culturally appropriate early childhood education programs for Aboriginal families.

A.2.2 Language and culture

13. We call upon the federal government to acknowledge that Aboriginal rights include Aboriginal language rights.

14. We call upon the federal government to enact an Aboriginal Languages Act that incorporates the following principles:

(a) Aboriginal languages are a fundamental and valued element of Canadian culture and society, and there is an urgency to preserve them.

(b) Aboriginal language rights are reinforced by the Treaties.

(c) The federal government has a responsibility to provide sufficient funds for Aboriginal-language revitalization and preservation.

(d) The preservation, revitalization, and strengthening of Aboriginal languages and cultures are best managed by Aboriginal people and communities.

(e) Funding for Aboriginal language initiatives must reflect the diversity of Aboriginal languages.

15. We call upon the federal government to appoint, in consultation with Aboriginal groups, an Aboriginal Languages Commissioner. The commissioner should help promote Aboriginal languages and report on the adequacy of federal funding of Aboriginal-languages initiatives.

16. We call upon post-secondary institutions to create university and college degree and diploma programs in Aboriginal lan-

guages.

17. We call upon all levels of government to enable residential school Survivors and their families to reclaim names changed by the residential school system by waiving administrative costs for a period of five years for the name-change process and the revision of official identity documents, such as birth certificates, passports, driver's licenses, health cards, status cards, and social insurance numbers.

A.2.3   Health

18. We call upon the federal, provincial, territorial, and Aboriginal governments to acknowledge that the current state of Aboriginal health in Canada is a direct result of previous Canadian government policies, including residential schools, and to recognize and implement the health-care rights of Aboriginal people as identified in international law, constitutional law, and under the Treaties.

19. We call upon the federal government, in consultation with Aboriginal peoples, to establish measurable goals to identify and close the gaps in health outcomes between Aboriginal and non-Aboriginal communities, and to publish annual progress reports and assess longterm trends. Such efforts would focus on indicators such as: infant mortality, maternal health, suicide, mental health, addictions, life expectancy, birth rates, infant and child health issues, chronic diseases, illness and injury incidence, and the availability of appropriate health services.

20. In order to address the jurisdictional disputes concerning Aboriginal people who do not reside on reserves, we call upon the federal government to recognize, respect, and address the distinct health needs of the Métis, Inuit, and off-reserve Aboriginal peoples.

21. We call upon the federal government to provide sustainable funding for existing and new Aboriginal healing centres to address the physical, mental, emotional, and spiritual harms caused by residential schools, and to ensure that the funding of healing centres in Nunavut and the Northwest Territories is a

priority.

22. We call upon those who can effect change within the Canadian health-care system to recognize the value of Aboriginal healing practices and use them in the treatment of Aboriginal patients in collaboration with Aboriginal healers and Elders where requested by Aboriginal patients.

23. We call upon all levels of government to:
    (a) Increase the number of Aboriginal professionals working in the health-care field.
    (b) Ensure the retention of Aboriginal health-care providers in Aboriginal communities.
    (c) Provide cultural competency training for all healthcare professionals.

24. We call upon medical and nursing schools in Canada to require all students to take a course dealing with Aboriginal health issues, including the history and legacy of residential schools, the United Nations Declaration on the Rights of Indigenous Peoples, Treaties and Aboriginal rights, and Indigenous teachings and practices. This will require skills-based training in intercultural competency, conflict resolution, human rights, and anti-racism.

A.2.4   Justice

25. We call upon the federal government to establish a written policy that reaffirms the independence of the Royal Canadian Mounted Police to investigate crimes in which the government has its own interest as a potential or real party in civil litigation.

26. We call upon the federal, provincial, and territorial governments to review and amend their respective statutes of limitations to ensure that they conform to the principle that governments and other entities cannot rely on limitation defences to defend legal actions of historical abuse brought by Aboriginal people.

27. We call upon the Federation of Law Societies of Canada to ensure that lawyers receive appropriate cultural competency training, which includes the history and legacy of residential schools, the United Nations Declaration on the Rights of In-

digenous Peoples, Treaties and Aboriginal rights, Indigenous law, and Aboriginal- Crown relations. This will require skills-based training in intercultural competency, conflict resolution, human rights, and anti-racism.

28. We call upon law schools in Canada to require all law students to take a course in Aboriginal people and the law, which includes the history and legacy of residential schools, the United Nations Declaration on the Rights of Indigenous Peoples, Treaties and Aboriginal rights, Indigenous law, and Aboriginal–Crown relations. This will require skills-based training in intercultural competency, conflict resolution, human rights, and antiracism.

29. We call upon the parties and, in particular, the federal government, to work collaboratively with plaintiffs not included in the Indian Residential Schools Settlement Agreement to have disputed legal issues determined expeditiously on an agreed set of facts.

30. We call upon federal, provincial, and territorial governments to commit to eliminating the overrepresentation of Aboriginal people in custody over the next decade, and to issue detailed annual reports that monitor and evaluate progress in doing so.

31. We call upon the federal, provincial, and territorial governments to provide sufficient and stable funding to implement and evaluate community sanctions that will provide realistic alternatives to imprisonment for Aboriginal offenders and respond to the underlying causes of offending.

32. We call upon the federal government to amend the Criminal Code to allow trial judges, upon giving reasons, to depart from mandatory minimum sentences and restrictions on the use of conditional sentences.

33. We call upon the federal, provincial, and territorial governments to recognize as a high priority the need to address and prevent Fetal Alcohol Spectrum Disorder (FASD), and to develop, in collaboration with Aboriginal people, FASD preventive programs that can be delivered in a culturally appropriate manner.

34. We call upon the governments of Canada, the provinces, and territories to undertake reforms to the criminal justice system to better address the needs of offenders with Fetal Alcohol Spec-

trum Disorder (FASD), including:

(a) Providing increased community resources and powers for courts to ensure that FASD is properly diagnosed, and that appropriate community supports are in place for those with FASD.

(b) Enacting statutory exemptions from mandatory minimum sentences of imprisonment for offenders affected by FASD.

(c) Providing community, correctional, and parole resources to maximize the ability of people with FASD to live in the community.

(d) Adopting appropriate evaluation mechanisms to measure the effectiveness of such programs and ensure community safety.

35. We call upon the federal government to eliminate barriers to the creation of additional Aboriginal healing lodges within the federal correctional system.

36. We call upon the federal, provincial, and territorial governments to work with Aboriginal communities to provide culturally relevant services to inmates on issues such as substance abuse, family and domestic violence, and overcoming the experience of having been sexually abused.

37. We call upon the federal government to provide more supports for Aboriginal programming in halfway houses and parole services.

38. We call upon the federal, provincial, territorial, and Aboriginal governments to commit to eliminating the overrepresentation of Aboriginal youth in custody over the next decade.

39. We call upon the federal government to develop a national plan to collect and publish data on the criminal victimization of Aboriginal people, including data related to homicide and family violence victimization.

40. We call on all levels of government, in collaboration with Aboriginal people, to create adequately funded and accessible Aboriginal-specific victim programs and services with appropriate evaluation mechanisms.

41. We call upon the federal government, in consultation with Aboriginal organizations, to appoint a public inquiry into the causes

of, and remedies for, the disproportionate victimization of Aboriginal women and girls. The inquiry's mandate would include:
   (a) Investigation into missing and murdered Aboriginal women and girls.
   (b) Links to the intergenerational legacy of residential schools.
42. We call upon the federal, provincial, and territorial governments to commit to the recognition and implementation of Aboriginal justice systems in a manner consistent with the Treaty and Aboriginal rights of Aboriginal peoples, the Constitution Act, 1982, and the United Nations Declaration on the Rights of Indigenous Peoples, endorsed by Canada in November 2012.

A.3   Reconciliation

A.3.1   Canadian Governments and the United Nations Declaration on the Rights of Indigenous People

43. We call upon federal, provincial, territorial, and municipal governments to fully adopt and implement the United Nations Declaration on the Rights of Indigenous Peoples as the framework for reconciliation.
44. We call upon the Government of Canada to develop a national action plan, strategies, and other concrete measures to achieve the goals of the United Nations Declaration on the Rights of Indigenous Peoples.

A.3.2   Royal Proclamation and Covenant of Reconciliation

45. We call upon the Government of Canada, on behalf of all Canadians, to jointly develop with Aboriginal peoples a Royal Proclamation of Reconciliation to be issued by the Crown. The proclamation would build on the Royal Proclamation of 1763 and the Treaty of Niagara of 1764, and reaffirm the nation-to-nation relationship between Aboriginal peoples and the Crown. The proclamation would include, but not be limited to, the following

commitments:

(a) Repudiate concepts used to justify European sovereignty over Indigenous lands and peoples such as the Doctrine of Discovery and terra nullius.

(b) Adopt and implement the United Nations Declaration on the Rights of Indigenous Peoples as the framework for reconciliation.

(c) Renew or establish Treaty relationships based on principles of mutual recognition, mutual respect, and shared responsibility for maintaining those relationships into the future.

(d) Reconcile Aboriginal and Crown constitutional and legal orders to ensure that Aboriginal peoples are full partners in Confederation, including the recognition and integration of Indigenous laws and legal traditions in negotiation and implementation processes involving Treaties, land claims, and other constructive agreements.

46. We call upon the parties to the Indian Residential Schools Settlement Agreement to develop and sign a Covenant of Reconciliation that would identify principles for working collaboratively to advance reconciliation in Canadian society, and that would include, but not be limited to:

(a) Reaffirmation of the parties' commitment to reconciliation.

(b) Repudiation of concepts used to justify European sovereignty over Indigenous lands and peoples, such as the Doctrine of Discovery and terra nullius, and the reformation of laws, governance structures, and policies within their respective institutions that continue to rely on such concepts.

(c) Full adoption and implementation of the United Nations Declaration on the Rights of Indigenous Peoples as the framework for reconciliation.

(d) Support for the renewal or establishment of Treaty relationships based on principles of mutual recognition, mutual respect, and shared responsibility for maintaining those relationships into the future.

(e) Enabling those excluded from the Settlement Agreement to sign onto the Covenant of Reconciliation.

(f) Enabling additional parties to sign onto the Covenant of Reconciliation.

47. We call upon federal, provincial, territorial, and municipal governments to repudiate concepts used to justify European sovereignty over Indigenous peoples and lands, such as the Doctrine of Discovery and terra nullius, and to reform those laws, government policies, and litigation strategies that continue to rely on such concepts.

A.3.3   Settlement Agreement Parties and the United Nations Declaration on the Rights of Indigenous Peoples

48. We call upon the church parties to the Settlement Agreement, and all other faith groups and interfaith social justice groups in Canada who have not already done so, to formally adopt and comply with the principles, norms, and standards of the United Nations Declaration on the Rights of Indigenous Peoples as a framework for reconciliation. This would include, but not be limited to, the following commitments:
    (a) Ensuring that their institutions, policies, programs, and practices comply with the United Nations Declaration on the Rights of Indigenous Peoples.
    (b) Respecting Indigenous peoples' right to selfdetermination in spiritual matters, including the right to practise, develop, and teach their own spiritual and religious traditions, customs, and ceremonies, consistent with Article 12:1 of the United Nations Declaration on the Rights of Indigenous Peoples.
    (c) Engaging in ongoing public dialogue and actions to support the United Nations Declaration on the Rights of Indigenous Peoples.
    (d) Issuing a statement no later than March 31, 2016, from all religious denominations and faith groups, as to how they will implement the United Nations Declaration on the Rights of Indigenous Peoples.
49. We call upon all religious denominations and faith groups who

have not already done so to repudiate concepts used to justify European sovereignty over Indigenous lands and peoples, such as the Doctrine of Discovery and terra nullius.

A.3.4   Equity for Aboriginal People in the Legal System

50. In keeping with the United Nations Declaration on the Rights of Indigenous Peoples, we call upon the federal government, in collaboration with Aboriginal organizations, to fund the establishment of Indigenous law institutes for the development, use, and understanding of Indigenous laws and access to justice in accordance with the unique cultures of Aboriginal peoples in Canada.
51. We call upon the Government of Canada, as an obligation of its fiduciary responsibility, to develop a policy of transparency by publishing legal opinions it develops and upon which it acts or intends to act, in regard to the scope and extent of Aboriginal and Treaty rights.
52. We call upon the Government of Canada, provincial and territorial governments, and the courts to adopt the following legal principles:
    (a) Aboriginal title claims are accepted once the Aboriginal claimant has established occupation over a particular territory at a particular point in time.
    (b) Once Aboriginal title has been established, the burden of proving any limitation on any rights arising from the existence of that title shifts to the party asserting such a limitation.

A.3.5   National Council for Reconciliation

53. We call upon the Parliament of Canada, in consultation and collaboration with Aboriginal peoples, to enact legislation to establish a National Council for Reconciliation. The legislation would establish the council as an independent, national, oversight body with membership jointly appointed by the Gov-

ernment of Canada and national Aboriginal organizations, and consisting of Aboriginal and non-Aboriginal members. Its mandate would include, but not be limited to, the following:

(a) Monitor, evaluate, and report annually to Parliament and the people of Canada on the Government of Canada's post-apology progress on reconciliation to ensure that government accountability for reconciling the relationship between Aboriginal peoples and the Crown is maintained in the coming years.

(b) Monitor, evaluate, and report to Parliament and the people of Canada on reconciliation progress across all levels and sectors of Canadian society, including the implementation of the Truth and Reconciliation Commission of Canada's Calls to Action.

(c) Develop and implement a multi-year National Action Plan for Reconciliation, which includes research and policy development, public education programs, and resources.

(d) Promote public dialogue, public/private partnerships, and public initiatives for reconciliation.

54. We call upon the Government of Canada to provide multi-year funding for the National Council for Reconciliation to ensure that it has the financial, human, and technical resources required to conduct its work, including the endowment of a National Reconciliation Trust to advance the cause of reconciliation.

55. We call upon all levels of government to provide annual reports or any current data requested by the National Council for Reconciliation so that it can report on the progress towards reconciliation. The reports or data would include, but not be limited to:

(a) The number of Aboriginal children—including Métis and Inuit children—in care, compared with nonAboriginal children, the reasons for apprehension, and the total spending on preventive and care services by child-welfare agencies.

(b) Comparative funding for the education of First Nations children on and off reserves.

(c) The educational and income attainments of Aboriginal

peoples in Canada compared with non-Aboriginal people.

    (d) Progress on closing the gaps between Aboriginal and non-Aboriginal communities in a number of health indicators such as: infant mortality, maternal health, suicide, mental health, addictions, life expectancy, birth rates, infant and child health issues, chronic diseases, illness and injury incidence, and the availability of appropriate health services.

    (e) Progress on eliminating the overrepresentation of Aboriginal children in youth custody over the next decade.

    (f) Progress on reducing the rate of criminal victimization of Aboriginal people, including data related to homicide and family violence victimization and other crimes.

    (g) Progress on reducing the overrepresentation of Aboriginal people in the justice and correctional systems.

56. We call upon the prime minister of Canada to formally respond to the report of the National Council for Reconciliation by issuing an annual "State of Aboriginal Peoples" report, which would outline the government's plans for advancing the cause of reconciliation.

Professional Development and Training for Public Servants

57. We call upon federal, provincial, territorial, and municipal governments to provide education to public servants on the history of Aboriginal peoples, including the history and legacy of residential schools, the United Nations Declaration on the Rights of Indigenous Peoples, Treaties and Aboriginal rights, Indigenous law, and Aboriginal–Crown relations. This will require skills-based training in intercultural competency, conflict resolution, human rights, and anti-racism.

A.3.6   Church Apologies and Reconciliation

58. We call upon the Pope to issue an apology to Survivors, their families, and communities for the Roman Catholic Church's role in the spiritual, cultural, emotional, physical, and sexual abuse

of First Nations, Inuit, and Métis children in Catholic-run residential schools. We call for that apology to be similar to the 2010 apology issued to Irish victims of abuse and to occur within one year of the issuing of this Report and to be delivered by the Pope in Canada.

59. We call upon church parties to the Settlement Agreement to develop ongoing education strategies to ensure that their respective congregations learn about their church's role in colonization, the history and legacy of residential schools, and why apologies to former residential school students, their families, and communities were necessary.

60. We call upon leaders of the church parties to the Settlement Agreement and all other faiths, in collaboration with Indigenous spiritual leaders, Survivors, schools of theology, seminaries, and other religious training centres, to develop and teach curriculum for all student clergy, and all clergy and staff who work in Aboriginal communities, on the need to respect Indigenous spirituality in its own right, the history and legacy of residential schools and the roles of the church parties in that system, the history and legacy of religious conflict in Aboriginal families and communities, and the responsibility that churches have to mitigate such conflicts and prevent spiritual violence.

61. We call upon church parties to the Settlement Agreement, in collaboration with Survivors and representatives of Aboriginal organizations, to establish permanent funding to Aboriginal people for:

(a) Community-controlled healing and reconciliation projects.

(b) Community-controlled culture- and languagerevitalization projects.

(c) Community-controlled education and relationshipbuilding projects.

(d) Regional dialogues for Indigenous spiritual leaders and youth to discuss Indigenous spirituality, selfdetermination, and reconciliation.

A.3.7 Education for reconciliation

62. We call upon the federal, provincial, and territorial governments, in consultation and collaboration with Survivors, Aboriginal peoples, and educators, to:
    (a) Make age-appropriate curriculum on residential schools, Treaties, and Aboriginal peoples' historical and contemporary contributions to Canada a mandatory education requirement for Kindergarten to Grade Twelve students.
    (b) Provide the necessary funding to post-secondary institutions to educate teachers on how to integrate Indigenous knowledge and teaching methods into classrooms.
    (c) Provide the necessary funding to Aboriginal schools to utilize Indigenous knowledge and teaching methods in classrooms.
    (d) Establish senior-level positions in government at the assistant deputy minister level or higher dedicated to Aboriginal content in education.

63. We call upon the Council of Ministers of Education, Canada to maintain an annual commitment to Aboriginal education issues, including:
    (a) Developing and implementing Kindergarten to Grade Twelve curriculum and learning resources on Aboriginal peoples in Canadian history, and the history and legacy of residential schools.
    (b) Sharing information and best practices on teaching curriculum related to residential schools and Aboriginal history.
    (c) Building student capacity for intercultural understanding, empathy, and mutual respect.
    (d) Identifying teacher-training needs relating to the above.

64. We call upon all levels of government that provide public funds to denominational schools to require such schools to provide an education on comparative religious studies, which must include a segment on Aboriginal spiritual beliefs and practices developed in collaboration with Aboriginal Elders.

65. We call upon the federal government, through the Social Sciences and Humanities Research Council, and in collaboration

with Aboriginal peoples, post-secondary institutions and educators, and the National Centre for Truth and Reconciliation and its partner institutions, to establish a national research program with multi-year funding to advance understanding of reconciliation. Youth Programs

66. We call upon the federal government to establish multiyear funding for community-based youth organizations to deliver programs on reconciliation, and establish a national network to share information and best practices.

A.3.8 Museums and Archives

67. We call upon the federal government to provide funding to the Canadian Museums Association to undertake, in collaboration with Aboriginal peoples, a national review of museum policies and best practices to determine the level of compliance with the United Nations Declaration on the Rights of Indigenous Peoples and to make recommendations.

68. We call upon the federal government, in collaboration with Aboriginal peoples, and the Canadian Museums Association to mark the 150th anniversary of Canadian Confederation in 2017 by establishing a dedicated national funding program for commemoration projects on the theme of reconciliation.

69. We call upon Library and Archives Canada to:
    (a) Fully adopt and implement the United Nations Declaration on the Rights of Indigenous Peoples and the United Nations Joinet-Orentlicher Principles, as related to Aboriginal peoples' inalienable right to know the truth about what happened and why, with regard to human rights violations committed against them in the residential schools.
    (b) Ensure that its record holdings related to residential schools are accessible to the public.
    (c) Commit more resources to its public education materials and programming on residential schools.

70. We call upon the federal government to provide funding to the Canadian Association of Archivists to undertake, in collaboration with Aboriginal peoples, a national review of archival

policies and best practices to:

(a) Determine the level of compliance with the United Nations Declaration on the Rights of Indigenous Peoples and the United Nations Joinet-Orentlicher Principles, as related to Aboriginal peoples' inalienable right to know the truth about what happened and why, with regard to human rights violations committed against them in the residential schools.

(b) Produce a report with recommendations for full implementation of these international mechanisms as a reconciliation framework for Canadian archives. Missing Children and Burial Information

71. We call upon all chief coroners and provincial vital statistics agencies that have not provided to the Truth and Reconciliation Commission of Canada their records on the deaths of Aboriginal children in the care of residential school authorities to make these documents available to the National Centre for Truth and Reconciliation.

72. We call upon the federal government to allocate sufficient resources to the National Centre for Truth and Reconciliation to allow it to develop and maintain the National Residential School Student Death Register established by the Truth and Reconciliation Commission of Canada.

73. We call upon the federal government to work with churches, Aboriginal communities, and former residential school students to establish and maintain an online registry of residential school cemeteries, including, where possible, plot maps showing the location of deceased residential school children.

74. We call upon the federal government to work with the churches and Aboriginal community leaders to inform the families of children who died at residential schools of the child's burial location, and to respond to families' wishes for appropriate commemoration ceremonies and markers, and reburial in home communities where requested.

75. We call upon the federal government to work with provincial, territorial, and municipal governments, churches, Aboriginal communities, former residential school students, and current

landowners to develop and implement strategies and procedures for the ongoing identification, documentation, maintenance, commemoration, and protection of residential school cemeteries or other sites at which residential school children were buried. This is to include the provision of appropriate memorial ceremonies and commemorative markers to honour the deceased children.

76. We call upon the parties engaged in the work of documenting, maintaining, commemorating, and protecting residential school cemeteries to adopt strategies in accordance with the following principles:

   (a) The Aboriginal community most affected shall lead the development of such strategies.

   (b) Information shall be sought from residential school Survivors and other Knowledge Keepers in the development of such strategies.

   (c) Aboriginal protocols shall be respected before any potentially invasive technical inspection and investigation of a cemetery site.

A.3.9   National Centre for Truth and Reconciliation

77. We call upon provincial, territorial, municipal, and community archives to work collaboratively with the National Centre for Truth and Reconciliation to identify and collect copies of all records relevant to the history and legacy of the residential school system, and to provide these to the National Centre for Truth and Reconciliation.

78. We call upon the Government of Canada to commit to making a funding contribution of $10 million over seven years to the National Centre for Truth and Reconciliation, plus an additional amount to assist communities to research and produce histories of their own residential school experience and their involvement in truth, healing, and reconciliation. Commemoration

79. We call upon the federal government, in collaboration with Survivors, Aboriginal organizations, and the arts community, to develop a reconciliation framework for Canadian heritage and

commemoration. This would include, but not be limited to:

(a) Amending the Historic Sites and Monuments Act to include First Nations, Inuit, and Métis representation on the Historic Sites and Monuments Board of Canada and its Secretariat.

(b) Revising the policies, criteria, and practices of the National Program of Historical Commemoration to integrate Indigenous history, heritage values, and memory practices into Canada's national heritage and history.

(c) Developing and implementing a national heritage plan and strategy for commemorating residential school sites, the history and legacy of residential schools, and the contributions of Aboriginal peoples to Canada's history.

80. We call upon the federal government, in collaboration with Aboriginal peoples, to establish, as a statutory holiday, a National Day for Truth and Reconciliation to honour Survivors, their families, and communities, and ensure that public commemoration of the history and legacy of residential schools remains a vital component of the reconciliation process.

81. We call upon the federal government, in collaboration with Survivors and their organizations, and other parties to the Settlement Agreement, to commission and install a publicly accessible, highly visible, Residential Schools National Monument in the city of Ottawa to honour Survivors and all the children who were lost to their families and communities.

82. We call upon provincial and territorial governments, in collaboration with Survivors and their organizations, and other parties to the Settlement Agreement, to commission and install a publicly accessible, highly visible, Residential Schools Monument in each capital city to honour Survivors and all the children who were lost to their families and communities.

83. We call upon the Canada Council for the Arts to establish, as a funding priority, a strategy for Indigenous and non-Indigenous artists to undertake collaborative projects and produce works that contribute to the reconciliation process.

A.3.10 Media and Reconciliation

84. We call upon the federal government to restore and increase funding to the CBC/Radio-Canada, to enable Canada's national public broadcaster to support reconciliation, and be properly reflective of the diverse cultures, languages, and perspectives of Aboriginal peoples, including, but not limited to:
    (a) Increasing Aboriginal programming, including Aboriginal-language speakers.
    (b) Increasing equitable access for Aboriginal peoples to jobs, leadership positions, and professional development opportunities within the organization.
    (c) Continuing to provide dedicated news coverage and online public information resources on issues of concern to Aboriginal peoples and all Canadians, including the history and legacy of residential schools and the reconciliation process.
85. We call upon the Aboriginal Peoples Television Network, as an independent non-profit broadcaster with programming by, for, and about Aboriginal peoples, to support reconciliation, including but not limited to:
    (a) Continuing to provide leadership in programming and organizational culture that reflects the diverse cultures, languages, and perspectives of Aboriginal peoples.
    (b) Continuing to develop media initiatives that inform and educate the Canadian public, and connect Aboriginal and non-Aboriginal Canadians.
86. We call upon Canadian journalism programs and media schools to require education for all students on the history of Aboriginal peoples, including the history and legacy of residential schools, the United Nations Declaration on the Rights of Indigenous Peoples, Treaties and Aboriginal rights, Indigenous law, and Aboriginal– Crown relations.

A.3.11 Sports and Reconciliation

87. We call upon all levels of government, in collaboration with Aboriginal peoples, sports halls of fame, and other relevant or-

ganizations, to provide public education that tells the national story of Aboriginal athletes in history.

88. We call upon all levels of government to take action to ensure long-term Aboriginal athlete development and growth, and continued support for the North American Indigenous Games, including funding to host the games and for provincial and territorial team preparation and travel.

89. We call upon the federal government to amend the Physical Activity and Sport Act to support reconciliation by ensuring that policies to promote physical activity as a fundamental element of health and well-being, reduce barriers to sports participation, increase the pursuit of excellence in sport, and build capacity in the Canadian sport system, are inclusive of Aboriginal peoples.

90. We call upon the federal government to ensure that national sports policies, programs, and initiatives are inclusive of Aboriginal peoples, including, but not limited to, establishing:

   (a) In collaboration with provincial and territorial governments, stable funding for, and access to, community sports programs that reflect the diverse cultures and traditional sporting activities of Aboriginal peoples.

   (b) An elite athlete development program for Aboriginal athletes.

   (c) Programs for coaches, trainers, and sports officials that are culturally relevant for Aboriginal peoples.

   (d) Anti-racism awareness and training programs.

91. We call upon the officials and host countries of international sporting events such as the Olympics, Pan Am, and Commonwealth games to ensure that Indigenous peoples' territorial protocols are respected, and local Indigenous communities are engaged in all aspects of planning and participating in such events.

A.3.12 Business and Reconciliation

92. We call upon the corporate sector in Canada to adopt the United Nations Declaration on the Rights of Indigenous Peoples as a reconciliation framework and to apply its principles, norms, and standards to corporate policy and core operational activi-

ties involving Indigenous peoples and their lands and resources. This would include, but not be limited to, the following:

(a) Commit to meaningful consultation, building respectful relationships, and obtaining the free, prior, and informed consent of Indigenous peoples before proceeding with economic development projects.

(b) Ensure that Aboriginal peoples have equitable access to jobs, training, and education opportunities in the corporate sector, and that Aboriginal communities gain long-term sustainable benefits from economic development projects.

(c) Provide education for management and staff on the history of Aboriginal peoples, including the history and legacy of residential schools, the United Nations Declaration on the Rights of Indigenous Peoples, Treaties and Aboriginal rights, Indigenous law, and Aboriginal–Crown relations. This will require skills based training in intercultural competency, conflict resolution, human rights, and anti-racism.

A.3.13 Newcomers to Canada

93. We call upon the federal government, in collaboration with the national Aboriginal organizations, to revise the information kit for newcomers to Canada and its citizenship test to reflect a more inclusive history of the diverse Aboriginal peoples of Canada, including information about the Treaties and the history of residential schools.

94. We call upon the Government of Canada to replace the Oath of Citizenship with the following:
I swear (or affirm) that I will be faithful and bear true allegiance to Her Majesty Queen Elizabeth II, Queen of Canada, Her Heirs and Successors, and that I will faithfully observe the laws of Canada including Treaties with Indigenous Peoples, and fulfill my duties as a Canadian citizen.

Appendix B

The Hudson's Bay Charter

The Royal Charter for incorporating The Hudson's Bay Company, A.D. 1670.

Charles the Second By the grace of God King of England Scotland France and Ireland defender of the faith &c

To All to whome these presentes shall come greeting Whereas Our Deare and entirely Beloved cousin Prince Rupert Count Palatyne of the Rhyne Duke of Bavaria and Cumberland &c Christopher Duke of Albemarle William Earle of Craven Henry Lord Arlington Anthony Lord Ashley Sir John Robinson and Sir Robert Vyner Knightes and Baronettes Sir Peter Colliton Baronett Sir Edward Hungerford Knight of the Bath Sir Paul Neele Knight Sir John Griffith and Sir Phillipp Carteret Knightes James Hayes John Kirke Francis Millington William Prettyman John Fenn Esquires and John Portman Cittizen and Goldsmith of London have at theire owne great cost and charge undertaken an Expedicion for Hudsons Bay in the North west part of America for the discovery of a new Passage into the South Sea and for the finding some Trade for Furrs Mineralls and other considerable Commodityes and by such theire undertaking have already made such discoveryes as doe encourage them to proceed further in pursuance of theire said designe by meanes whereof there may probably arise very great advantage to us and our Kingdome

And whereas the said undertakers for theire further encouragement in the said designe have humbly besought us to Incorporate them and grant unto them and their successors the sole Trade and

Commerce of all those Seas Streightes Bayes Rivers Lakes Creekes and Soundes in whatsoever Latitude they shall bee that lye within the the entrance of the Streightes commonly called Hudsons Streightes together with all the Landes Countryes and Territoryes upon the Coastes and Confynes of the Seas Streightes Bayes Lakes Rivers Creekes and Soundes aforesaid which are not now actually possessed by any of our Subjectes or by the Subjectes of any other Christian Prince or State.

Now know yee that Wee being desirous to promote all Endeavours tending to the publique good of our people and to encourage the said undertaking have of our especiall grace certaine knowledge and meere mocion Given granted ratifyed and confirmed And by these Presentes for us our heires and Successors

Doe give grant ratifie and confirme unto our said Cousin Prince Rupert Christopher Duke of Albemarle William Earle of Craven Henry Lord Arlington Anthony Lord Ashley Sir John Robinson Sir Robert Vyner Sir Peter Colleton Sir Edward Hungerford Sir Paul Neile Sir John Griffith and Sir Phillipp Carterett James Hayes John Kirke Francis Millington William Prettyman John Fenn and John Portman That they and such others as shall bee admitted into the said Society as is hereafter expressed shall bee one Body Corporate and Politique in deed and in name by the name of the Governor and Company of Adventurers of England tradeing into Hudsons Bay and them by the name of the Governor and Company of Adventurers of England tradeing into Hudsons Bay one Body Corporate and Politique in deede and in name really and fully for ever for us our heirs and successors

doe make ordeyne constitute establish confirme and declare by these Presentes and that by the same name of Governor & Company of Adventurers of England Tradeing into Hudsons Bay they shall have perpetuall succession And that they and theire successors by the name of Governor and Company of Adventurers of England Tradeing into Hudsons Bay bee and at all tymes hereafter shall bee persons able and capable in Law to have purchase receive possesse enjoy and reteyne Landes Rentes priviledges libertyes Jurisdiccions Franchyses and hereditamentes of what kinde nature and quality soever they bee to them and theire Successors And alsoe to give grant demise alien assigne and dispose Landes Tenementes and hereditamentes and to doe and execute all and singuler other thinges by the same name that to them shall or may apperteyne to doe And that they and theire Successors by the name of the Governor and Company of Adventurers of England Tradeing into Hudsons Bay may pleade and bee impleaded answeare and bee answeared defend and bee defended in whatsoever Courtes and places before whatsoever Judges and Justices and other persons and Officers in all and singular Accions Pleas Suitts Quarrells causes and demandes whatsoever of whatsoever kinde nature or sort in such manner and forme as any other our Liege people of this our Realme of England being persons able and capable in Lawe may or can have purchase receive possesse enjoy reteyne give grant demise alien assigne dispose pleade defend and bee defended doe permit and execute And that the said Governor and Company of Adventurers of England Tradeing into Hudsons Bay and their successors may have a Common Seale to serve for all the causes and busnesses of them and theire Successors and that itt shall and may bee lawfull to the said Governor and Company and theire Successors the same Seall from tyme to tyme at theire will and pleasure to breake change and to make a new or alter as them shall seeme expedient

And further Wee will And by these presentes for us our Heires and successors Wee doe ordeyne that there shall bee from henceforth one of the same Company to bee elected and appointed in such forme as hereafter in these presentes is expressed which shall be called The Governor of the said Company And that the said Governor and Company shall or may elect seaven of theire number in such forme as hereafter in these presentes is expressed which shall bee called the Committee of the said Company which Committee of seaven or any three of them together with the Governor or Deputy Governor of the said Company for the tyme being shall have the direcion of the Voyages of and for the said Company and Provision of the Shipping and Merchandizes thereunto belonging and alsoe the sale of all merchandizes Goodes and other things returned in all or any the Voyages or Shippes of or for the said Company and the mannageing and handleing of all other business affaires and thinges belonging to the said Company And Wee will ordeyne and Grant by these presentes for us our heires and successors unto the said Governor and Company and theire successors that they the said Governor and Company and theire successors shall from henceforth for ever bee ruled ordered and governed according to such manner and forme as is hereafter in these presentes expressed and not otherwise And that they shall have hold reteyne and enjoy the Grantes Libertyes Priviledges Jurisdiccions and Immunityes only hereafter in these presentes granted and expressed and noe other

And for the better Wee have assigned nominated constituted and made And by these presentes for us our heires and successors Wee doe assigne nominate constitute and make our said Cousin Prince Rupert to bee the first and present Governor of the said Company and to continue in the said Office from the date of these presentes until the tenth of November then next following if hee the said Prince Rupert shall soe long live and soe until a new Governor bee chosen by the said Company in forme hereafter expressed

And alsoe Wee have assigned nominated and appointed And by these presentes for us our heirs and Successors Wee doe assigne nominate and constitute the said Sir John Robinson Sir Robert Vyner Sir Peter Colleton James Hayes John Kirke Francis Millington and John Portman to bee the seaven first and present Committees of the said Company from the date of these presentes until the said tenth Day of November then alsoe next following and soe until new Committees shall bee chosen in forme hereafter expressed And further Wee will and grant by these presentes for us our heires and Successors unto the said Governor and Company and theire successors that itt shall and may bee lawfull to and for the said Governor and Company for the tyme being or the greater part of them present at any publique Assembly commonly called the Court Generall to bee holden for the said Company the Governor of the said Company being alwayes one from tyme to tyme elect nominate and appoint one of the said Company to bee Deputy to the said Governor which Deputy shall take a corporall Oath before the Governor and three or more of the Committee of the said Company for the tyme being well truely and faithfully to execute his said Office of Deputy to the Governor of the said Company and after his Oath soe taken shall and may from tyme to tyme in the absence of the said Governor exercize and execute the Office of Governor of the said Company in such sort as the said Governor ought to doe

And further Wee will and grant and by these presentes for us our heires and Successors unto the said Governor and Company of Adventurers of England tradeing into Hudsons Bay and theire Successors That they or the greater part of them whereof the Governor for the Tyme being or his Deputy to bee one from tyme to tyme and at all tymes hereafter shall and may have authority and power yearely and every yeare betweene the first and last day of November to assemble and meete together in some convenient place to bee appointed from tyme to tyme by the Governor or in his absence by the Deputy of the said Governor for the tyme being And that they being soe assembled itt shall and may bee lawfull to and for the said Governor or Deputy of the said Governor and the said Company for the tyme being or the greater part of them which then shall happen to bee present whereof the Governor of the said Company or his Deputy for the tyme being to bee one to elect and nominate one of the said Company which shall bee Governor of the same Company for one whole yeare then next following which person being soe elected and nominated to bee Governor of the said Company as is aforesaid before hee bee admitted to the Execucion of the said Office shall take a Corporall Oath before the last Governor being his Predecessor or his Deputy and any three or more of the Committee of the said Company for the tyme being that hee shall from tyme to tyme well and truely execute the Office of Governor of the said Company in all thinges concerneing the same and that Ymediately after the same Oath soe taken hee shall and may execute and use the said Office of Governor of the said Company for one whole yeare from thence next following and in like sort Wee will and grant that as well every one of the above named to bee of the said Company or fellowshipp as all other hereafter to bee admitted or free of the said Company shall take a Corporall Oath before the Governor of the said Company or his Deputy for the tyme being to such effect as by the said Governor and Company or the greater part of them in any publick Court to bee held for the said Company shall bee in reasonable and legall manner sett down and devised before they shall bee allowed or admitted to Trade or traffique as a freeman of the said Company And further Wee will and grant by these presentes for us our heires and successors unto the said Governor and Company and theire successors that the said Governor or Deputy Governor and the rest of the said company and theire successors for the tyme being or the greater part of them whereof the Governor or the Deputy Governor from tyme to tyme to bee one shall and may from tyme to tyme and at all tymes hereafter have power and authority yearely and every yeare betweene the first and last day of November to assemble and meete together in some convenient place from tyme to tyme to bee appointed by the said Governor of the said Company or in his absence by his Deputy and that they being soe assembled itt shall and may bee lawfull to and for the said Governor or his Deputy and the Company for the tyme being or the greater part of them which then shall happen to bee present whereof the Governor of the said Company or his Deputy for the tyme being to bee one to elect and nominate seaven of the said Company which shall bee a Committee of the said Company for one whole yeare from thence next ensueing which persons being soe elected and nominated to bee a Committee of the said Company as aforesaid before they bee admitted to the execucion of theire Office shall take a Corporall Oath before the Governor or his Deputy and any three or more of the said Committee of the said Company being theire last Predecessors and that they and every of them shall well and faithfully performe theire said Office of Committees in all thinges concerneing the same And that imediately after the said Oath soe taken they shall and may execute and sue theire said Office of Committees of the said Company for one whole yeare from thence next following

And moreover Our will and pleasure is And by these presentes for us our heires and successors Wee doe grant unto the said Governor and Company and theire successors that when and as often as itt shall happen the Governor or Deputy Governor of the said Company for the tyme being at any tyme within one yeare after that hee shall bee nominated elected and sworne to the Office of the Governor of the said Company as is aforesaid to dye or to bee removed from the said Office which Governor or Deputy Governor not demeaneing himselfe well in his said Office

Wee will to bee removable at the Pleasure of the rest of the said Company or the greater part of them which shall bee present at theire publick assemblies commonly called theire Generall Courtes holden for the said Company that then and soe often itt shall and may bee lawfull to and for the Residue of the said Company for the tyme being or the greater part of them within convenient tyme after the death or removeing of any such Governor or Deputy Governor to assemble themselves in such convenient place as they shall think fitt for the eleccion of the Governor or Deputy Governor of the said Company and that the said Company or the greater part of them being then and there present shall and may then and there before theire departure from the said place elect and nominate one other of the said Company to bee Governor or Deputy Governor for the said Company in the place and stead of him that soe dyed or was removed which person being soe elected and nominated to the Office of Governor of Deputy Governor of the said Company shall have and exercize the said Office for and dureing the residue of the said yeare takeing first a Corporall Oath as is aforesaid for the due execucion thereof And this to bee done from tyme to tyme soe often as the case shall soe require The Royal Charter for incorporating The Hudson's Bay Company, A.D. 1670. 4 And also Our Will and Pleasure is and by these presentes for us our heires and successors

Wee doe grant unto the said Governor and Company that when and as often as itt shall happen any person or persons of the Committee of the said Company for the tyme being at any tyme within one yeare next after that they or any of them shall bee nominated elected and sworne to the Office of Committee of the said Company as is aforesaid to dye or to be removed from the said Office which Committees not demeaneing themselves well in theire said Office Wee will to be removeable at the pleasure of the said Governor and Company or the greater part of them whereof the Governor of the said Company for the tyme being or his Deputy to bee one that then and soe often itt shall and may bee lawfull to and for the said Governor and the rest of the Company for the tyme being or the greater part of them whereof the Governor for the tyme being or his Deputy to bee one within convenient tyme after the death or removeing of any of the said Committee to assemble themselves in such convenient place as is or shall bee usuall and accustomed for the eleccion of the Governor of the said Company or where else the Governor of the said Company for the tyme being or his Deputy shall appoint And that the said Governor and Company or the greater part of them whereof the Governor for the tyme being or his Deputy to bee one being then and there present shall and may then and there before theire Departure from the said place elect and nominate one or more of the said Company to bee of the Committee of the said Company in the place and stead of him or them that soe died or were or was soe removed which person or persons soe elected and nominated to the Office of Committee of the said Company shall have and exercize the said Office for and dureing the residue of the said yeare takeing first a Corporall Oath as is aforesaid for the due execucion thereof and this to bee done from tyme to tyme so often as the case shall require And to the end the said Governor and Company of Adventurers of England Tradeing into Hudsons Bay may bee encouraged to undertake and effectually to prosecute the said designe of our more especial grace certaine knowledge and meere Mocion

Wee have given granted and confirmed And by these presentes for us our heires and successors Doe give grant and confirme unto the said Governor and Company and theire successors the sole Trade and Commerce of all those Seas Streightes Bayes Rivers Lakes Creekes and Soundes in whatsoever Latitude they shall bee that lie within the entrance of the Streightes commonly called Hudsons Streightes together with all the Landes and Terriroryes upon the Countryes Coastes and confynes of the Seas Bayes Lakes Rivers Creekes and Soundes aforesaid that are not already actually possessed by or granted to any of our Subjectes or possessed by the Subjectes of any other Christian Prince or State with the Fishing of all Sortes of Fish Whales Sturgions and all other Royall Fishes in the Seas Bays Islets and Rivers within the premisses and the Fish therein taken together with the Royalty of the Sea upon the Coastes with the Lymittes aforesaid and all Mynes Royall as well discovered as not discovered of Gold Silver Gemms and pretious Stones to bee found or discovered within the Territoryes Lymittes and Places aforesaid And that the said Land bee from henceforth reckoned and reputed as one of our Plantacions or Colonyes in America called Ruperts Land And further We doe by these presentes for us our heires and successors make create and constitute the said Governor and Company for the tyme being and theire successors the true and absolute Lordes and Proprietors of the same

Territory lymittes and places aforesaid And of all other the premisses The Royal Charter for incorporating The Hudson's Bay Company, A.D. 1670. 5 Saving always the faith Allegiance and Soveraigne Dominion due to us our heires and successors for the same

To have hold possesse and enjoy the said Territory lymittes and places and all and singular other the premisses hereby granted as aforesaid with theire and every of theire Rightes Members Jurisdiccions Perogatives Royaltyes and Appurtenances whatsoever to them the said Governor and Company and theire Successors for ever To bee holden of us our heires and successors as of our Mannor of East Greenwich in our Country of Kent in free and common Soccage and not in Capite or by Knightes Service Yeilding and paying yearley to us our heirs and Successors for the same two Elkes and two Black beavers whensoever and as often as Wee our heirs and successors shall happen to enter into the said Countryes Territoryes and Regions hereby granted And further our will and pleasure is And by these presentes for us our heires and successors

Wee doe grant unto the said Governor and Company and to theire successors that itt shall and may be lawfull to and for the said Governor and Company and theire successors from tyme to tyme to assemble themselves for or about any the matters causes affaires or buisnesses of the said Trade in any place or places for the same convenient within our Dominions or elsewhere and there to hold Court for the said Company and the affaires thereof And that alsoe itt shall and may bee lawfull to and for them and the greater part of them being soe assembled and that shall then and there bee present in any such place or places whereof the Governor or his Deputy for the tyme being to bee one to make ordyne and constitute such and soe many reasonable Lawes Constitucions Orders and Ordinances as to them or the greater part of them being then and there present shall seeme necessary and convenient for the good Government of the said Company and of all Governors of Colonyes Fortes and Plantacions Factors Masters Mariners and other Officers employed or to bee employed in any of the Territories and Landes aforesaid and in any of theire Voyages and for the better advancement and contynuance of the said Trade or Traffick and Plantacions and the same Lawes Constitucions Orders and Ordinances soe made to putt in use and execute accordingly and at theire pleasure to revoake and alter the same or any of them as the occasion shall require And that the said Governor and Company soe often as they shall make ordeyne or establish any such Lawes Constitucions Orders and Ordinances in such forme as aforesaid shall and may lawfully impose ordeyne limitt and provide such paines penaltyes and punishmentes upon all Offenders contrary to such Lawes Constitucions Orders and Ordinances or any of them as to the said Governor and Company for the tyme being or the greater part of them then and there being present the said Governor or his Deputy being alwayes one shall seeme necessary requisite or convenient for the observacion of the same Lawes Constitucions Orders and Ordinances And the same Fynes and Amerciamentes shall and may by theire Officers and Servantes from tyme to tyme to bee appointed for that purpose levy take and have to the use of the said Governor and Company and theire successors without the impediment of us our heires or successors or of any the Officers or Ministers of us our heires or successors and without any accompt therefore to us our heires or successors to bee made All and singuler which Lawes Constitucions Orders and Ordinances soe as aforesaid to bee made Wee will to bee duely observed and kept under the paines and penaltyes therein to bee conteyned soe alwayes as the said Lawes Constitucions Orders and Ordinances Fynes and Amerciamentes bee reasonable and not contrary or repugnant but as neare as may bee agreeable to the Lawes Statutes or Customes of this our Realme

And furthermore of our ample and abundant grace certaine knowledge and meere mocion Wee have granted and by these presentes for us our heires and successors doe grant unto the said Governor and Company and theire Successors That they and theire Successors and theire Factors Servantes and Agentes for them and on theire behalfe and not otherwise shall for ever hereafter have use and enjoy not only the whole Entire and only Trade and Traffick and the whole entire and only liberty use and priviledge of tradeing and Trafficking to and from the Territory Lymittes and places aforesaid but alsoe the whole and entire Trade and Trafficke to and from all Havens Bayes Creekes Rivers Lakes and Seas into which they shall find entrance or passage by water or Land out of the Territoryes Lymittes or places aforesaid and to and with all the Natives and People Inhabitting or which shall inhabit within the Territoryes Lymittes and places aforesaid and to and with all other Nacions Inhabitting any the Coaste adjacent to the said Territoryes Lymittes and places which are not already possessed as aforesaid or whereof the sole liberty or priviledge of Trade and Trafficke is not granted to any other of our Subjectes And Wee of our further Royall favour And of our more especiall grace certaine knowledge and meere Mocion Have granted and by these presentes for us our heires and Successors doe grant to the said Governor and Company and to theire Successors That neither the said Territoryes Lymittes and places hereby Granted as aforesaid nor any part thereof nor the islandes Havens Portes Cittyes Townes or places thereof or therein conteyned shall bee visited frequented or haunted by any of the Subjectes of us our heires or successors contrary to the true meaneing of these presentes and by vertue of our Perogative Royall which wee will not have in that behalfe argued or brought into Question

Wee streightly Charge Command and prohibitt for us our heires and Successors all the subjectes of us our heires and Successors of what degree or Quality soever they bee that none of them directly or indirectly doe visit haunt frequent or Trade Trafficke or Adventure by way of Merchandize into or from any the said Territoryes Lymittes or Places hereby granted or any or either of them other then the said Governor and Company and such perticuler persons as now bee or hereafter shall bee of that Company theire Agentes Factors and Assignes unlesse itt bee by the Lycence and agreement of the said Governor and Company in writing first had and obteyned under theire Common Seale to bee granted upon paine that every such person or persons that shall Trade or Traffick into or from any the Countryes Territoryes or Lymittes aforesaid other then the said Governor and Company and theire Successors shall incurr our Indignacion and the forfeiture and the losse of the Goodes Merchandizes and other thinges whatsoever which soe shall bee brought into this Realme of England or any the Dominions of the same contrary to our said Prohibicion or the purport or true meaneing of these presentes for which the said Governor and Company shall finde take and seize in other places out of our Dominions where the said Company theire Agentes Factors or Ministers shall Trade Traffick inhabitt by vertue of these our Letters Patente As alsoe the Shipp and Shippes with the Furniture thereof wherein such goodes Merchandizes and other thinges shall bee brought or found the one halfe of all the said Forfeitures to bee to us our heires and successors and the other halfe thereof

Wee doe by these Presentes cleerely and wholly for us our heires and Successors Give and Grant unto the said Governor and Company and theire Successors The Royal Charter for incorporating The Hudson's Bay Company, A.D. 1670. 7 And further all and every the said Offenders for theire said contempt to suffer such other punishment as to us our heires or Successors for soe high a contempt shall seeme meete and convenient and not to bee in any wise delivered untill they and every of them shall become bound unto the said Governor for the tyme being in the summe of one thousand Poundes at the least at noe tyme then after to Trade or Traffick into any of the said places Seas Streightes Bayes Portes Havens or Territoryes aforesaid contrary to our Expresse Commandment in the behalfe herein sett downe and published And further of our more especiall grace

Wee have condiscended and granted And by these presentes for us our heires and Successors doe grant unto the said Governor and Company and theire successors That Wee our heires and Successors will not Grant liberty lycence or power to any person or persons whatsoever contrary to the tenour of these our Letters Patente to Trade trafficke or inhabit unto or upon any the Territoryes lymittes or places afore specifyed contrary to the true meaneing of these presentes without the consent of the said Governor and Company or the most part of them And of our more abundant grace and favour to the said Governor and Company Wee doe hereby declare our will and pleasure to bee that if it shall soe happen that any of the persons free or to bee free of the said Company of Adventurers of England Tradeing into Hudsons Bay who shall before goeing forth of any Shipp or Shipps appointed for A Voyage or otherwise promise or agree by Writeing under his or theire handes to adventure any summe or Sumes of money towardes the furnishing any provision or maintainance of any voyage or voyages sett forth or to bee sett forth or intended or meant to bee sett forth by the said Governor and Company or the more part of them present at any Publick Assembly commonly called theire Generall Court shall not within the Space of twenty Dayes next after Warneing given to him or them by the said Governor or Company or theire knowne Officer or Minister bring in and deliver to the Treasurer or Treasurers appointed for the Company such summes of money as shall have been expressed and sett downe in writeing by the said Person or Persons subscribed with the name of the said Adventurer or Adventurers that then and at all Tymes after itt shall and may bee lawfull to and for the said Governor and Company or the more part of them present

Whereof the said Governor or his Deputy to bee one at any of theire Generall Courtes or Generall Assemblyes to remove and disfranchise him or them and every such person and persons at their wills and pleasures and hee or they soe removed and disfranchised not to bee permitted to trade into the Countryes Territoryes Lymittes aforesaid or any part thereof nor to have any Adventure or Stock goeing or remaining with or amongst the said Company without the speciall lycence of the said Governor and Company or the more part of them present at any Generall Court first had and obteyned in that behalfe Any thing before in these presentes to the contrary thereof in any wise notwithstanding And Our Will and Pleasure is And hereby wee doe alsoe ordeyne that itt shall and may bee lawfull to and for the said Governor and Company or the greater part of them whereof the Governor for the tyme being or his Deputy to bee one to admitt into and to bee of the said Company all such Servantes or Factors of or for the said Company and all such others as to them or the most part of them present at any Court held for the said Company the Governor or his Deputy being one shall be thought fitt and agreeable with the Orders and Ordinances made and to bee made for the Government of the said Company And further Our will and pleasure is And by these presentes for us our heires and Successors

Wee doe grant unto the said Governor and Company and to theire Successors that itt shall and may bee lawfull in all Eleccions and By-Lawes to bee made by the Generall Court of the Adventurers of the said Company that every person shall have a number of votes according to his Stock that is to say for every hundred poundes by him subscribed or brought into the present Stock one vote and that any of these that have Subscribed lesse then one hundred poundes may joyne theire respective summes to make upp one hundred poundes and have one vote joyntly for the same and not otherwise And further of our expeciall grace certaine knowledge and meere mocion Wee doe for us our heires and successors grant to and with the said Governor and Company of Adventurers of England Tradeing into Hudsons Bay that all Landes Islandes Territoryes Plantacions Fortes Fortificacions Factoryes or Colonyes where the said Companyes Factoryes and Trade are or shall bee within any the Portes and places afore lymitted shall bee ymediately and from henceforth under the power and command of the said Governor and Company theire Successors and Assignes Saving the faith and Allegiance due to bee performed to us our heires and successors as aforesaid and that the said Governor and Company shall have liberty full Power and authority to appoint and establish Governors and all other Officers to governe them And that the Governor and his Councill of the severall and respective places where the said Company shall have Plantacions Fortes Factoryes Colonyes or Places of Trade within any the Countryes Landes or Territoryes hereby granted may have power to judge all persons belonging to the said Governor and Company or that shall live under them in all Causes whether Civil or Criminall according to the Lawes of this Kingdome and to execute Justice accordingly And in case any crime or misdemeanor shall bee committed in any of the said Companyes Plantacions Fortes Factoryes or Places of Trade within the Lymittes aforesaid where Judicature cannot bee executed for want of a Governor and Councill there then in such case itt shall and may bee lawfull for the chiefe Factor of that place and his Councill to transmitt the party together with the offence to such other Plantacion Factory or Fort where there shall bee a Governor and Councill where Justice may bee executed or into this Kingdome of England as shall bee thought most convenient there to receive such punishment as the nature of his offence shall deserve And Moreover Our will and pleasure is And by these presentes for us our heires and Successors

Wee doe give and grant unto the said Governor and Company and theire Successors free Liberty and Lycence in case they conceive it necessary to send either Shippes of War Men or Amunicion unto any theire Plantacions Fortes Factoryes or Places of Trade aforesaid for the security and defence of the same and to choose Commanders and Officers over them and to give them power and authority by

Commission under theire Common Seale or otherwise to continue or make peace or Warre with any Prince or People whatsoever that are not Christians in any places where the said Company shall have any Plantacions Fortes or Factoryes or adjacent thereunto as shall The Royal Charter for incorporating The Hudson's Bay Company, A.D. 1670. 9 bee most for the advantage and benefitt of the said Governor and Company and of theire Trade and alsoe to right and recompence themselves upon the Goodes Estates or people of those partes by whome the said Governor and Company shall sustyne any injury losse or dammage or upon any other People whatsoever that shall any way contrary to the intent of these presentes interrupt wrong or injure them in theire said Trade within the said places Territoryes and Lymittes granted by this Charter and that itt shall and may bee lawfull to and for the said Governor and Company and theire Successors from tyme to tyme and at all tymes from henceforth to Erect and build such Castles Fortifications Fortes Garrisons Colonyes Plantacions Townes or Villages in any partes or places within the Lymittes and Boundes granted before in these presentes unto the said Governor and Company as they in theire Discrecions shall thinke fitt and requisite and for the supply of such as shall bee needefull and convenient to keepe and bee in the same to send out of this Kingdome to the said Castles Fortes Fortifications Garrisons Colonyes Plantacions Townes or Villages all Kindes of Cloathing Provision of Victuales Ammunicion and Implementes necessary for such purpose paying the Dutyes and Customes for the same As alsoe to transport and carry over such number of Men being willing thereunto or not prohibited as they shall thinke fitt and alsoe to governe them in such legall and reasonable manner as the said Governor and Company shall thinke best and to inflict punishment for misdemeanors or impose such Fynes upon them for breach of theire Orders as in these Presentes are formerly expressed And further Our will and pleasure is And by these presentes for us our heires and Successors

Wee doe grant unto the said Governor and Company and to theire Successors full Power and lawfull authority to seize upon the Persons of all such English or any other of our Subjects which shall saile into Hudsons Bay or Inhabit in any of the Countryes Islandes or Territoryes hereby Granted to the said Governor and Company without theire leave and Licence in that Behalfe first had and obteyned or that shall contemne or disobey theire Orders and send them to England and that all and every Person and Persons being our Subjectes any wayes Imployed by the said Governor and Company within any the Partes places and Lymittes aforesaid shall bee lyable unto and suffer such punnishment for any Offences by them committed in the Partes aforesaid as the President and Councill for the said Governor and Company there shall thinke fitt and the meritt of the offence shall require as aforesaid. And in case any Person or Persons being convicted and Sentenced by the President and Councill of the said Governor and Company in the Countryes Landes or Lymittes aforesaid theire Factors or Agentes there for any Offence by them done shall appeale from the same That then and in such Case itt shall and may bee lawfull to and for the said President and Councill Factors or Agentes to seize upon him or them and to carry him or them home Prisoners into England to the said Governor and Company there to receive such condigne punnishment as his Cause shall require and the Law of this Nacion allow of and for the better discovery of abuses and injuryes to bee done unto the said Governor and Company or theire Successors by any Servant by them to bee imployed in the said Voyages and Plantacions itt shall and may be lawfull to and for the said Governor and Company and theire respective Presidentes Chiefe Agent or Governor in the partes aforesaid to examine upon Oath all Factors Masters Pursers Supra Cargoes Commanders of Castles Fortes Fortificacions Plantacions or Colonyes or other Persons touching or concerning any matter or thing in which by Law or usage an Oath may bee administered soe as the said Oath and the matter therein conteyned bee not repugnant but agreeable to the Lawes of this Realme And Wee doe hereby streightly charge and Command all and singuler our Admiralls Vice Admiralls Justices Mayors Sherriffs Constables Bayliffes and all and singuler other our Officers Ministers Liege Men and Subjects whatsoever to bee ayding favouring helping and assisting to the said Governor and Company and to theire Successors and to theire Deputyes Officers Factors Servantes Assignes and Ministers and every of them in executeing and enjoying the premisses as well on Land as on Sea from tyme to tyme when any of you shall thereunto bee required Any Statute Act Ordinance Proviso

Proclamacion or restraint heretofore had made sett forth ordeyned or provided or any other matter cause or thing whatsoever to the contrary in any wise notwithstanding

In witness whereof we have caused these our Letters to bee made Patentes Witness Ourself at Westminster the second day of May in the two and twentieth yeare of our Raigne By Writt of Privy Seale

Appendix C

The Royal Proclamation 1763

The Royal Proclamation
October 7, 1763
BY THE KING A PROCLAMATION GEORGE R.
Whereas We have taken into Our Royal Consideration the extensive
and valuable Acquisitions in America, secured to our Crown by the
late Definitive Treaty of Peace, concluded at Paris the 10th Day of
February last; and being desirous that all Our loving Subjects, as well
of our Kingdom as of our Colonies in America, may avail themselves
with all convenient Speed, of the great Benefits and Advantages which
must accrue therefrom to their Commerce, Manufactures, and Nav-
igation, We have thought fit, with the Advice of our Privy Council.
to issue this our Royal Proclamation, hereby to publish and declare
to all our loving Subjects, that we have, with the Advice of our Said
Privy Council, granted our Letters Patent, under our Great Seal of
Great Britain, to erect, within the Countries and Islands ceded and
confirmed to Us by the said Treaty, Four distinct and separate Governments, styled and called by the names of Quebec, East Florida,
West Florida and Grenada, and limited and bounded as follows, viz.

First–The Government of Quebec bounded on the Labrador Coast
by the River St. John, and from thence by a Line drawn from the
Head of that River through the Lake St. John, to the South end of
the Lake Nipissim; from whence the said Line, crossing the River St.
Lawrence, and the Lake Champlain, in 45. Degrees of North Latitude, passes along the High Lands which divide the Rivers that empty

themselves into the said River St. Lawrence from those which fall into the Sea; and also along the North Coast of the Baye des Chaleurs, and the Coast of the Gulph of St. Lawrence to Cape Rosieres, and from thence crossing the Mouth of the River St. Lawrence by the West End of the Island of Anticosti, terminates at the aforesaid River of St. John.

Secondly – The Government of East Florida bounded to the Westward by the Gulph of Mexico and the Apalachicola River; to the Northward by a Line drawn from that part of the said River where the Chatahouchee and Flint Rivers meet, to the source of St. Mary's River and by the course of the said River to the Atlantic Ocean; and to the Eastward and Southward by the Atlantic Ocean and the Gulph of Florida, including all Islands within Six Leagues of the Sea Coast.

Thirdly – The Government of West Florida bounded to the Southward by the Gulph of Mexico. including all Islands within Six Leagues of the Coast from the River Apalachicola to Lake Pontchartrain; to the Westward by the said Lake, the Lake Maurepas, and the River Mississippi; to the Northward by a Line drawn due East from that part of the River Mississippi which lies in 31 Degrees North Latitude. to the River Apalachicola or Chatahouchee; and to the Eastward by the said River.

Fourthly – The Government of Grenada, comprehending the Island of that name, together with the Grenadines, and the Islands of Dominico, St. Vincent's and Tobago. And to the end that the open and free Fishery of our Subjects may be extended to and carried on upon the Coast of Labrador, and the adjacent Islands We have thought fit with the advice of our said Privy Council to put all that Coast, from the River St. John's to Hudson's Streights, together with the Islands of Anticosti and Madelaine, and all other smaller Islands Iying upon the said Coast, under the care and Inspection of our Governor of Newfoundland.

We have also, with the advice of our Privy Council thought fit to annex the Islands of St. John's and Cape Breton, or Isle Royale, with the lesser Islands adjacent thereto, to our Government of Nova Scotia.

We have also, with the advice of our Privy Council aforesaid, annexed to our Province of Georgia all the Lands lying between the

Rivers Alatamaha and St. Mary's. And whereas it will greatly contribute to the speedy settling of our said new Governments, that our loving Subjects should be informed of our Paternal care, for the security of the Liberties and Properties of those who are and shall become Inhabitants thereof, We have thought fit to publish and declare, by this Our Proclamation, that We have, in the Letters Patent under our Great Seal of Great Britain, by which the said Governments are constituted given express Power and Direction to our Governors of our Said Colonies respectively, that so soon as the state and circumstances of the said Colonies will admit thereof, they shall, with the Advice and Consent of the Members of our Council, summon and call General Assemblies within the said Governments respectively, in such Manner and Form as is used and directed in those Colonies and Provinces in America which are under our immediate Government: And We have also given Power to the said Governors, with the consent of our Said Councils, and the Representatives of the People so to be summoned as aforesaid, to make, constitute, and ordain Laws. Statutes, and Ordinances for the Public Peace, Welfare, and good Government of our said Colonies, and of the People and Inhabitants thereof, as near as may be agreeable to the Laws of England, and under such Regulations and Restrictions as are used in other Colonies; and in the mean Time, and until such Assemblies can be called as aforesaid, all Persons Inhabiting in or resorting to our Said Colonies may confide in our Royal Protection for the Enjoyment of the Benefit of the Laws of our Realm of England; for which Purpose We have given Power under our Great Seal to the Governors of our said Colonies respectively to erect and constitute, with the Advice of our said Councils respectively, Courts of Judicature and public Justice within our Said Colonies for hearing and determining all Causes, as well Criminal as Civil, according to Law and Equity, and as near as may be agreeable to the Laws of England, with Liberty to all Persons who may think themselves aggrieved by the Sentences of such Courts, in all Civil Cases to appeal, under the usual Limitations and Restrictions, to Us in our Privy Council.

We have also thought fit, with the advice of our Privy Council as aforesaid, to give unto the Governors and Councils of our said Three new Colonies, upon the Continent full Power and Authority to settle and agree with the Inhabitants of our said new Colonies or with any other Persons who shall resort thereto, for such Lands. Tenements and Hereditaments, as are now or hereafter shall be in our Power to dispose of; and them to grant to any such Person or Persons upon such Terms, and under such moderate Quit Rents, Services and Acknowledgments, as have been appointed and settled in our other Colonies, and under such other Conditions as shall appear to us to be necessary and expedient for the Advantage of the Grantees, and the Improvement and settlement of our said Colonies.

And Whereas, We are desirous, upon all occasions, to testify our Royal Sense and Approbation of the Conduct and bravery of the Officers and Soldiers of our Armies, and to reward the same, We do hereby command and impower our Governors of our said Three new Colonies, and all other our Governors of our several Provinces on the Continent of North America, to grant without Fee or Reward, to such reduced Officers as have served in North America during the late War, and to such Private Soldiers as have been or shall be disbanded in America, and are actually residing there, and shall personally apply for the same, the following Quantities of Lands, subject, at the Expiration of Ten Years, to the same Quit-Rents as other Lands are subject to in the Province within which they are granted, as also subject to the same Conditions of Cultivation and Improvement; viz.

To every Person having the Rank of a Field Officer – 5,000 Acres.
To every Captain – 3,000 Acres.
To every Subaltern or Staff Officer – 2,000 Acres.
To every Non-Commission Office – 200 Acres . To every Private Man – 50 Acres.

We do likewise authorize and require the Governors and Commanders in Chief of all our said Colonies upon the Continent of North America to grant the like Quantities of Land, and upon the same conditions, to such reduced Officers of our Navy of like Rank as served on board our Ships of War in North America at the times of the Reduction of Louisbourg and Quebec in the late War, and who shall personally apply to our respective Governors for such Grants.

And whereas it is just and reasonable, and essential to our Interest, and the Security of our Colonies, that the several Nations or Tribes of Indians with whom We are connected, and who live under our Protection, should not be molested or disturbed in the Possession of such Parts of Our Dominions and Territories as, not having been ceded to or purchased by Us, are reserved to them. or any of them, as their Hunting Grounds.–We do therefore, with the Advice of our Privy Council, declare it to be our Royal Will and Pleasure that no Governor or Commander in Chief in any of our Colonies of Quebec, East Florida or West Florida, do presume, upon any Pretence whatever, to grant Warrants of Survey, or pass any Patents for Lands beyond the Bounds of their respective Governments as described in their Commissions: as also that no Governor or Commander in Chief in any of our other Colonies or Plantations in America do presume for the present, and until our further Pleasure be known, to grant Warrants of Survey, or pass Patents for any Lands beyond the Heads or Sources of any of the Rivers which fall into the Atlantic Ocean from the West and North West, or upon any Lands whatever, which, not having been ceded to or purchased by Us as aforesaid, are reserved to the said Indians, or any of them.

And We do further declare it to be Our Royal Will and Pleasure, for the present as aforesaid, to reserve under our Sovereignty, Protection, and Dominion, for the use of the said Indians, all the Lands and Territories not included within the Limits of Our said Three new Governments, or within the Limits of the Territory granted to the Hudson's Bay Company, as also all the Lands and Territories lying to the Westward of the Sources of the Rivers which fall into the Sea from the West and North West as aforesaid.

And We do hereby strictly forbid, on Pain of our Displeasure, all our loving Subjects from making any Purchases or Settlements whatever, or taking Possession of any of the Lands above reserved without our especial leave and Licence for that Purpose first obtained. And We do further strictly enjoin and require all Persons whatever who have either wilfully or inadvertently seated themselves upon any Lands within the Countries above described or upon any other Lands which, not having been ceded to or purchased by Us, are still reserved to the said Indians as aforesaid, forthwith to remove themselves from such Settlements.

And whereas great Frauds and Abuses have been committed in

purchasing Lands of the Indians, to the great Prejudice of our Interests and to the great Dissatisfaction of the said Indians: In order, therefore, to prevent such Irregularities for the future, and to the end that the Indians may be convinced of our Justice and determined Resolution to remove all reasonable Cause of Discontent, We do with the Advice of our Privy Council strictly enjoin and require that no private Person do presume to make any purchase from the said Indians of any Lands reserved to the said Indians, within those parts of our Colonies where, We have thought proper to allow Settlement: but that. if at any Time any of the Said Indians should be inclined to dispose of the said Lands, the same shall be Purchased only for Us, in our Name, at some public Meeting or Assembly of the said Indians, to be held for that Purpose by the Governor or Commander in Chief of our Colony respectively within which they shall lie: and in case they shall lie within the limits of any Proprietary Government they shall be purchased only for the Use and in the name of such Proprietaries, conformable to such Directions and Instructions as We or they shall think proper to give for that Purpose: And we do. by the Advice of our Privy Council, declare and enjoin, that the Trade with the said Indians shall be free and open to all our Subjects whatever provided that every Person who may incline to Trade with the said Indians do take out a Licence for carrying on such Trade from the Governor or Commander in Chief of any of our Colonies respectively where such Person shall reside and also give Security to observe such Regulations as We shall at any Time think fit by ourselves or by our Commissaries to be appointed for this Purpose, to direct and appoint for the Benefit of the said Trade:

And we do hereby authorize, enjoin, and require the Governors and Commanders in Chief of all our Colonies respectively, as well those under Our immediate Government as those under the Government and Direction of Proprietaries, to grant such Licences without Fee or Reward, taking especial Care to insert therein a Condition, that such Licence shall be void, and the Security forfeited in case the Person to whom the same is granted shall refuse or neglect to observe such Regulations as We shall think proper to prescribe as aforesaid.

And we do further expressly conjoin and require all Officers whatever, as well Military as those Employed in the Management and

Direction of Indian Affairs, within the Territories reserved as afore-said for the use of the said Indians, to seize and apprehend all Persons whatever. who standing charged with Treason, Misprisions of Trea-son, Murders, or other Felonies or Misdemeanors shall fly from Justice and take Refuge in the said Territory and to send them under a proper guard to the Colony where the Crime was committed of which they, stand accused in order to take their Trial for the same.

Given at our Court at St. James's the 7th Day of October 1763 in the Third Year of our Reign. GOD SAVE THE KING

Appendix D

The Indian Act

CONSOLIDATION

Indian Act

R.S.C., 1985, c. I-5

CODIFICATION

Loi sur les Indiens

L.R.C. (1985), ch. I-5

Current to August 18, 2024

Last amended on August 15, 2019

À jour au 18 août 2024

Dernière modification le 15 août 2019

Published by the Minister of Justice at the following address:
http://laws-lois.justice.gc.ca

Publié par le ministre de la Justice à l'adresse suivante :
http://lois-laws.justice.gc.ca

An Act respecting Indians

Short Title

Short title

1 This Act may be cited as the *Indian Act*.

R.S., c. I-6, s. 1.

Interpretation

Definitions

2 (1) In this Act,

band means a body of Indians

(a) for whose use and benefit in common, lands, the legal title to which is vested in Her Majesty, have been set apart before, on or after September 4, 1951,

(b) for whose use and benefit in common, moneys are held by Her Majesty, or

(c) declared by the Governor in Council to be a band for the purposes of this Act; (*bande*)

Band List means a list of persons that is maintained under section 8 by a band or in the Department; (*liste de bande*)

child includes a legally adopted child and a child adopted in accordance with Indian custom; (*enfant*)

common-law partner, in relation to an individual, means a person who is cohabiting with the individual in a conjugal relationship, having so cohabited for a period of at least one year; (*conjoint de fait*)

council of the band means

(a) in the case of a band to which section 74 applies, the council established pursuant to that section,

Loi concernant les Indiens

Titre abrégé

Titre abrégé

1 *Loi sur les Indiens*.

S.R., ch. I-6, art. 1.

Définitions

Définitions

2 (1) Les définitions qui suivent s'appliquent à la présente loi.

argent des Indiens Les sommes d'argent perçues, reçues ou détenues par Sa Majesté à l'usage et au profit des Indiens ou des bandes. (*Indian moneys*)

bande Groupe d'Indiens, selon le cas :

a) à l'usage et au profit communs desquels des terres appartenant à Sa Majesté ont été mises de côté avant ou après le 4 septembre 1951;

b) à l'usage et au profit communs desquels, Sa Majesté détient des sommes d'argent;

c) que le gouverneur en conseil a déclaré être une bande pour l'application de la présente loi. (*band*)

biens Tout bien meuble ou immeuble, y compris un droit sur des terres. (*estate*)

boisson alcoolisée Tout liquide — alcoolisé ou non —, mélange ou préparation ayant des propriétés enivrantes et susceptible de consommation humaine. (*intoxicant*)

conjoint de fait La personne qui vit avec la personne en cause dans une relation conjugale depuis au moins un an. (*common-law partner*)

conseil de la bande

Indian
Interpretation
Section 2

Indiens
Définitions
Article 2

(b) in the case of a band that is named in the schedule to the *First Nations Elections Act*, the council elected or in office in accordance with that Act,

(c) in the case of a band whose name has been removed from the schedule to the *First Nations Elections Act* in accordance with section 42 of that Act, the council elected or in office in accordance with the community election code referred to in that section, or

(d) in the case of any other band, the council chosen according to the custom of the band, or, if there is no council, the chief of the band chosen according to the custom of the band; (*conseil de la bande*)

Department means the Department of Indigenous Services; (*ministère*)

designated lands means a tract of land or any interest therein the legal title to which remains vested in Her Majesty and in which the band for whose use and benefit it was set apart as a reserve has, otherwise than absolutely, released or surrendered its rights or interests, whether before or after the coming into force of this definition; (*terres désignées*)

elector means a person who

(a) is registered on a Band List,

(b) is of the full age of eighteen years, and

(c) is not disqualified from voting at band elections; (*électeur*)

estate includes real and personal property and any interest in land; (*biens*)

Indian means a person who pursuant to this Act is registered as an Indian or is entitled to be registered as an Indian; (*Indien*)

Indian moneys means all moneys collected, received or held by Her Majesty for the use and benefit of Indians or bands; (*argent des Indiens*)

Indian Register means the register of persons that is maintained under section 5; (*registre des Indiens*)

intoxicant includes alcohol, alcoholic, spirituous, vinous, fermented malt or other intoxicating liquor or combination of liquors and mixed liquor a part of which is spirituous, vinous, fermented or otherwise intoxicating and all drinks, drinkable liquids, preparations or mixtures capable of human consumption that are intoxicating; (*boisson alcoolisée*)

a) Dans le cas d'une bande à laquelle s'applique l'article 74, le conseil constitué conformément à cet article;

b) s'agissant d'une bande dont le nom figure à l'annexe de la *Loi sur les élections au sein de premières nations*, le conseil élu ou en place conformément à cette loi;

c) s'agissant d'une bande dont le nom a été radié de l'annexe de la *Loi sur les élections au sein de premières nations* conformément à l'article 42 de cette loi, le conseil élu ou en place conformément au code électoral communautaire visé à cet article;

d) s'agissant de toute autre bande, le conseil choisi selon la coutume de celle-ci ou, en l'absence d'un conseil, le chef de la bande choisi selon la coutume de celle-ci. (*council of the band*)

électeur Personne qui remplit les conditions suivantes :

a) être inscrit sur une liste de bande;

b) avoir dix-huit ans;

c) ne pas avoir perdu son droit de vote aux élections de la bande. (*elector*)

enfant Sont compris parmi les enfants les enfants légalement adoptés, ainsi que les enfants adoptés selon la coutume indienne. (*child*)

Indien Personne qui, conformément à la présente loi, est inscrite à titre d'Indien ou a droit de l'être. (*Indian*)

Indien mentalement incapable Indien qui, conformément aux lois de la province où il réside, a été déclaré mentalement déficient ou incapable, pour l'application de toute loi de cette province régissant l'administration des biens de personnes mentalement déficientes ou incapables. (*mentally incompetent Indian*)

inscrit Inscrit comme Indien dans le registre des Indiens. (*registered*)

liste de bande Liste de personnes tenue en vertu de l'article 8 par une bande ou au ministère. (*Band List*)

membre d'une bande Personne dont le nom apparaît sur une liste de bande ou qui a droit à ce que son nom y figure. (*member of a band*)

ministère Le ministère des Services aux Autochtones. (*Department*)

member of a band means a person whose name appears on a Band List or who is entitled to have his name appear on a Band List; (*membre d'une bande*)

mentally incompetent Indian means an Indian who, pursuant to the laws of the province in which he resides, has been found to be mentally defective or incompetent for the purposes of any laws of that province providing for the administration of estates of mentally defective or incompetent persons; (*Indien mentalement incapable*)

Minister means the Minister of Indigenous Services; (*ministre*)

registered means registered as an Indian in the Indian Register; (*inscrit*)

Registrar means the officer in the Department who is in charge of the Indian Register and the Band Lists maintained in the Department; (*registraire*)

reserve

(a) means a tract of land, the legal title to which is vested in Her Majesty, that has been set apart by Her Majesty for the use and benefit of a band, and

(b) except in subsection 18(2), sections 20 to 25, 28, 37, 38, 42, 44, 46, 48 to 51 and 58 to 60 and the regulations made under any of those provisions, includes designated lands; (*réserve*)

superintendent includes a commissioner, regional supervisor, Indian superintendent, assistant Indian superintendent and any other person declared by the Minister to be a superintendent for the purposes of this Act, and with reference to a band or a reserve, means the superintendent for that band or reserve; (*surintendant*)

surrendered lands means a reserve or part of a reserve or any interest therein, the legal title to which remains vested in Her Majesty, that has been released or surrendered by the band for whose use and benefit it was set apart; (*terres cédées*)

survivor, in relation to a deceased individual, means their surviving spouse or common-law partner. (*survivant*)

Definition of *band*

(2) The expression **band**, with reference to a reserve or surrendered lands, means the band for whose use and benefit the reserve or the surrendered lands were set apart.

ministre Le ministre des Services aux Autochtones. (*Minister*)

registraire Le fonctionnaire du ministère responsable du registre des Indiens et des listes de bande tenus au ministère. (*Registrar*)

registre des Indiens Le registre de personnes tenu en vertu de l'article 5. (*Indian Register*)

réserve Parcelle de terrain dont Sa Majesté est propriétaire et qu'elle a mise de côté à l'usage et au profit d'une bande; y sont assimilées les terres désignées, sauf pour l'application du paragraphe 18(2), des articles 20 à 25, 28, 37, 38, 42, 44, 46, 48 à 51 et 58 à 60, ou des règlements pris sous leur régime. (*reserve*)

surintendant Sont assimilés à un surintendant un commissaire, un surveillant régional, un surintendant des Indiens, un surintendant adjoint des Indiens et toute autre personne que le ministre a déclarée un surintendant pour l'application de la présente loi; relativement à une bande ou une réserve, le surintendant de cette bande ou réserve. (*superintendent*)

survivant L'époux ou conjoint de fait survivant d'une personne décédée. (*survivor*)

terres cédées Réserve ou partie d'une réserve, ou tout droit sur celle-ci, propriété de Sa Majesté et que la bande à l'usage et au profit de laquelle il avait été mis de côté a abandonné ou cédé. (*surrendered lands*)

terres désignées Parcelle de terrain, ou tout droit sur celle-ci, propriété de Sa Majesté et relativement à laquelle la bande à l'usage et au profit de laquelle elle a été mise de côté à titre de réserve a cédé, avant ou après l'entrée en vigueur de la présente définition, ses droits autrement qu'à titre absolu. (*designated lands*)

Définition de *bande*

(2) En ce qui concerne une réserve ou des terres cédées, **bande** désigne la bande à l'usage et au profit de laquelle la réserve ou les terres cédées ont été mises de côté.

3

Indian
Interpretation
Sections 2-4

Indiens
Définitions
Articles 2-4

Exercise of powers conferred on band or council

(3) Unless the context otherwise requires or this Act otherwise provides,

(a) a power conferred on a band shall be deemed not to be exercised unless it is exercised pursuant to the consent of a majority of the electors of the band; and

(b) a power conferred on the council of a band shall be deemed not to be exercised unless it is exercised pursuant to the consent of a majority of the councillors of the band present at a meeting of the council duly convened.

R.S., 1985, c. I-5, s. 2; R.S., 1985, c. 32 (1st Supp.), s. 1, c. 17 (4th Supp.), s. 1; 2000, c. 12, s. 148; 2014, c. 5, s. 43, c. 38, s. 3; 2019, c. 29, s. 372; 2019, c. 29, s. 375.

Administration

Superintendent general

3 The Minister of Indigenous Services shall be the superintendent general of Indian affairs.

R.S., 1985, c. I-5, s. 3; 2019, c. 29, s. 357.

Application of Act

Application of Act

4 (1) A reference in this Act to an Indian does not include any person of the race of aborigines commonly referred to as Inuit.

Act may be declared inapplicable

(2) The Governor in Council may by proclamation declare that this Act or any portion thereof, except sections 5 to 14.3 or sections 37 to 41, shall not apply to

(a) any Indians or any group or band of Indians, or

(b) any reserve or any surrendered lands or any part thereof,

and may by proclamation revoke any such declaration.

Authority confirmed for certain cases

(2.1) For greater certainty, and without restricting the generality of subsection (2), the Governor in Council shall be deemed to have had the authority to make any declaration under subsection (2) that the Governor in Council has made in respect of section 11, 12 or 14, or any

Exercice des pouvoirs conférés à une bande ou un conseil

(3) Sauf indication contraire du contexte ou disposition expresse de la présente loi :

a) un pouvoir conféré à une bande est censé ne pas être exercé, à moins de l'être en vertu du consentement donné par une majorité des électeurs de la bande;

b) un pouvoir conféré au conseil d'une bande est censé ne pas être exercé à moins de l'être en vertu du consentement donné par une majorité des conseillers de la bande présents à une réunion du conseil dûment convoquée.

L.R. (1985), ch. I-5, art. 2; L.R. (1985), ch. 32 (1er suppl.), art. 1, ch. 17 (4e suppl.), art. 1; 2000, ch. 12, art. 148; 2014, ch. 5, art. 43, ch. 38, art. 3; 2019, ch. 29, art. 372; 2019, ch. 29, art. 375.

Administration

Surintendant général

3 Le ministre des Services aux Autochtones est le surintendant général des affaires indiennes.

L.R. (1985), ch. I-5, art. 3; 2019, ch. 29, art. 357.

Application de la loi

Application de la loi

4 (1) La mention d'un Indien, dans la présente loi, exclut une personne de la race d'aborigènes communément appelés Inuit.

Pouvoir de déclarer la loi inapplicable

(2) Le gouverneur en conseil peut, par proclamation, déclarer que la présente loi, ou toute partie de celle-ci, sauf les articles 5 à 14.3 et 37 à 41, ne s'applique pas :

a) à des Indiens ou à un groupe ou une bande d'Indiens;

b) à une réserve ou à des terres cédées, ou à une partie y afférente.

Il peut en outre, par proclamation, révoquer toute semblable déclaration.

Confirmation de la validité de certaines déclarations

(2.1) Sans que soit limitée la portée générale du paragraphe (2), il demeure entendu que le gouverneur en conseil est réputé avoir eu le pouvoir de faire, en vertu du paragraphe (2), toute déclaration qu'il a faite à l'égard des articles 11, 12 ou 14, ou d'une disposition de ceux-ci, dans leur version antérieure au 17 avril 1985.

Indian
Application of Act
Sections 4-5

Indiens
Application de la loi
Articles 4-5

provision thereof, as each section or provision read immediately prior to April 17, 1985.

Certain sections inapplicable to Indians living off reserves

(3) Sections 114 to 117 and, unless the Minister otherwise orders, sections 42 to 52 do not apply to or in respect of any Indian who does not ordinarily reside on a reserve or on lands belonging to Her Majesty in right of Canada or a province.

R.S., 1985, c. I-5, s. 4; R.S., 1985, c. 32 (1st Supp.), s. 2; 2014, c. 38, s. 4.

Provisions that apply to all band members

4.1 A reference to an Indian in any of the following provisions shall be deemed to include a reference to any person whose name is entered in a Band List and who is entitled to have it entered therein: the definitions *band*, *Indian moneys* and *mentally incompetent Indian* in section 2, subsections 4(2) and (3) and 18(2), sections 20 and 22 to 25, subsections 31(1) and (3) and 35(4), sections 51, 52, 52.2 and 52.3, subsections 58(3) and 61(1), sections 63 and 65, subsections 66(2) and 70(1) and (4), section 71, paragraphs 73(g) and (h), subsection 74(4), section 84, paragraph 87(1)(a), section 88, subsection 89(1) and paragraph 107(b).

R.S., 1985, c. 32 (1st Supp.), s. 3, c. 48 (4th Supp.), s. 1.

Definition and Registration of Indians

Indian Register

Indian Register

5 (1) There shall be maintained in the Department an Indian Register in which shall be recorded the name of every person who is entitled to be registered as an Indian under this Act.

Existing Indian Register

(2) The names in the Indian Register immediately prior to April 17, 1985 shall constitute the Indian Register on April 17, 1985.

Deletions and additions

(3) The Registrar may at any time add to or delete from the Indian Register the name of any person who, in accordance with this Act, is entitled or not entitled, as the case may be, to have his name included in the Indian Register.

Certains articles ne s'appliquent pas aux Indiens vivant hors des réserves

(3) Les articles 114 à 117 et, sauf si le ministre en ordonne autrement, les articles 42 à 52 ne s'appliquent à aucun Indien, ni à l'égard d'aucun Indien, ne résidant pas ordinairement dans une réserve ou sur des terres qui appartiennent à Sa Majesté du chef du Canada ou d'une province.

L.R. (1985), ch. I-5, art. 4; L.R. (1985), ch. 32 (1er suppl.), art. 2; 2014, ch. 38, art. 4.

Dispositions applicables à tous les membres d'une bande

4.1 La mention du terme « Indien » dans les définitions de *bande*, *argent des Indiens* ou *Indien mentalement incapable* à l'article 2 et la mention de ce terme aux paragraphes 4(2) et (3) et 18(2), aux articles 20 et 22 à 25, aux paragraphes 31(1) et (3) et 35(4), aux articles 51, 52, 52.2 et 52.3, aux paragraphes 58(3) et 61(1), aux articles 63 et 65, aux paragraphes 66(2) et 70(1) et (4), à l'article 71, aux alinéas 73g) et h), au paragraphe 74(4), à l'article 84, à l'alinéa 87(1)a), à l'article 88, au paragraphe 89(1) et à l'alinéa 107b) valent également mention de toute personne qui a droit à ce que son nom soit consigné dans une liste de bande et dont le nom y est consigné.

L.R. (1985), ch. 32 (1er suppl.), art. 3, ch. 48 (4e suppl.), art. 1.

Définition et enregistrement des indiens

Registre des Indiens

Tenue du registre

5 (1) Est tenu au ministère un registre des Indiens où est consigné le nom de chaque personne ayant le droit d'être inscrite comme Indien en vertu de la présente loi.

Registre existant

(2) Les noms figurant au registre des Indiens le 16 avril 1985 constituent le registre des Indiens au 17 avril 1985.

Additions et retranchements

(3) Le registraire peut ajouter au registre des Indiens, ou en retrancher, le nom de la personne qui, aux termes de la présente loi, a ou n'a pas droit, selon le cas, à l'inclusion de son nom dans ce registre.

Indian
Definition and Registration of Indians
Indian Register
Sections 5-6

Indiens
Définition et enregistrement des indiens
Registre des Indiens
Articles 5-6

Date of change

(4) The Indian Register shall indicate the date on which each name was added thereto or deleted therefrom.

Application for registration

(5) The name of a person who is entitled to be registered is not required to be recorded in the Indian Register unless an application for registration is made to the Registrar.

Unknown or unstated parentage

(6) If a parent, grandparent or other ancestor of a person in respect of whom an application is made is unknown — or is unstated on a birth certificate that, if the parent, grandparent or other ancestor were named on it, would help to establish the person's entitlement to be registered — the Registrar shall, without being required to establish the identity of that parent, grandparent or other ancestor, determine, after considering all of the relevant evidence, whether that parent, grandparent or other ancestor is, was or would have been entitled to be registered. In making the determination, the Registrar shall rely on any credible evidence that is presented by the applicant in support of the application or that the Registrar otherwise has knowledge of and shall draw from it every reasonable inference in favour of the person in respect of whom the application is made.

No presumption

(7) For greater certainty, if the identity of a parent, grandparent or other ancestor of an applicant is unknown or unstated on a birth certificate, there is no presumption that this parent, grandparent or other ancestor is not, was not or would not have been entitled to be registered.

R.S., 1985, c. I-5, s. 5; R.S., 1985, c. 32 (1st Supp.), s. 4; 2017, c. 25, s. 1.

Persons entitled to be registered

6 (1) Subject to section 7, a person is entitled to be registered if

(a) that person was registered or entitled to be registered immediately before April 17, 1985;

(a.1) the name of that person was omitted or deleted from the Indian Register, or from a band list before September 4, 1951, under subparagraph 12(1)(a)(iv), paragraph 12(1)(b) or subsection 12(2) or under subparagraph 12(1)(a)(iii) pursuant to an order made under subsection 109(2), as each provision read immediately before April 17, 1985, or under any former provision of this Act relating to the same subject matter as any of those provisions;

Date du changement

(4) Le registre des Indiens indique la date où chaque nom y a été ajouté ou en a été retranché.

Demande

(5) Il n'est pas requis que le nom d'une personne qui a le droit d'être inscrite soit consigné dans le registre des Indiens, à moins qu'une demande à cet effet soit présentée au registraire.

Ascendants inconnus ou non déclarés

(6) Si une demande est présentée à l'égard d'une personne dont le parent ou un autre de ses ascendants est inconnu — ou est non déclaré sur un certificat de naissance, lequel serait utile pour établir le droit à l'inscription de la personne si le nom du parent ou de l'ascendant y était inscrit —, le registraire, sans devoir établir l'identité du parent ou de l'ascendant, décide, après avoir considéré toute la preuve pertinente, si ce parent ou cet ascendant a le droit d'être inscrit, ou avait ou aurait eu ce droit. Pour arriver à la décision, le registraire se fonde sur tout élément de preuve crédible que lui fournit le demandeur à l'appui de sa demande, ou sur tout élément de preuve crédible dont il a connaissance par ailleurs, et en tire les conclusions raisonnables les plus favorables à la personne à l'égard de laquelle la demande est présentée.

Aucune présomption

(7) Il est entendu que, si l'identité d'un parent ou un autre des ascendants du demandeur est inconnue ou non déclarée sur un certificat de naissance, il n'y a aucune présomption que le parent ou l'autre ascendant n'a pas le droit d'être inscrit ou n'avait pas ou n'aurait pas eu ce droit.

L.R. (1985), ch. I-5, art. 5; L.R. (1985), ch. 32 (1er suppl.), art. 4; 2017, ch. 25, art. 1.

Personnes ayant droit à l'inscription

6 (1) Sous réserve de l'article 7, toute personne a le droit d'être inscrite dans les cas suivants :

a) elle était inscrite ou avait le droit de l'être le 16 avril 1985;

a.1) son nom a été omis ou retranché du registre des Indiens ou, avant le 4 septembre 1951, d'une liste de bande, en vertu du sous-alinéa 12(1)a)(iv), de l'alinéa 12(1)b) ou du paragraphe 12(2) ou en vertu du sous-alinéa 12(1)a)(iii) conformément à une ordonnance prise en vertu du paragraphe 109(2), dans leur version antérieure au 17 avril 1985, ou en vertu de toute disposition antérieure de la présente loi portant sur le même sujet que celui de l'une de ces dispositions;

Indian
Definition and Registration of Indians
Indian Register
Section 6

Indiens
Définition et enregistrement des indiens
Registre des Indiens
Article 6

(a.2) that person meets the following conditions:

(i) they were born female during the period beginning on September 4, 1951 and ending on April 16, 1985 and their parents were not married to each other at the time of the birth,

(ii) their father was at the time of that person's birth entitled to be registered or, if he was no longer living at that time, was at the time of death entitled to be registered, and

(iii) their mother was not at the time of that person's birth entitled to be registered;

(a.3) that person is a direct descendant of a person who is, was or would have been entitled to be registered under paragraph (a.1) or (a.2) and

(i) they were born before April 17, 1985, whether or not their parents were married to each other at the time of the birth, or

(ii) they were born after April 16, 1985 and their parents were married to each other at any time before April 17, 1985;

(b) that person is a member of a body of persons that has been declared by the Governor in Council on or after April 17, 1985 to be a band for the purposes of this Act;

(c) [Repealed, 2017, c. 25, s. 2.1]

(c.01) [Repealed, 2017, c. 25, s. 2.1]

(c.02) [Repealed, 2017, c. 25, s. 2.1]

(c.1) [Repealed, 2017, c. 25, s. 2.1]

(c.2) [Repealed, 2017, c. 25, s. 2.1]

(c.3) [Repealed, 2017, c. 25, s. 2.1]

(c.4) [Repealed, 2017, c. 25, s. 2.1]

(c.5) [Repealed, 2017, c. 25, s. 2.1]

(c.6) [Repealed, 2017, c. 25, s. 2.1]

(d) the name of that person was omitted or deleted from the Indian Register, or from a band list prior to September 4, 1951, under subparagraph 12(1)(a)(iii) pursuant to an order made under subsection 109(1), as each provision read immediately prior to April 17, 1985, or under any former provision of this Act relating to the same subject-matter as any of those provisions;

a.2) elle remplit les conditions suivantes :

(i) elle est une personne née de sexe féminin pendant la période commençant le 4 septembre 1951 et se terminant le 16 avril 1985, et ses parents n'étaient pas mariés l'un à l'autre au moment de sa naissance,

(ii) son père avait le droit d'être inscrit au moment de sa naissance ou, s'il était décédé à ce moment, avait ce droit à la date de son décès,

(iii) sa mère n'avait pas le droit d'être inscrite au moment de sa naissance;

a.3) elle est un descendant en ligne directe d'une personne qui a droit à l'inscription, ou qui avait ou aurait eu ce droit, en vertu de l'un des alinéas a.1) ou a.2) et elle est née soit avant le 17 avril 1985, que ses parents aient été ou non mariés l'un à l'autre au moment de sa naissance, soit après le 16 avril 1985 et ses parents se sont mariés à n'importe quel moment avant le 17 avril 1985;

b) elle est membre d'un groupe de personnes déclaré par le gouverneur en conseil après le 16 avril 1985 être une bande pour l'application de la présente loi;

c) [Abrogé, 2017, ch. 25, art. 2.1]

c.01) [Abrogé, 2017, ch. 25, art. 2.1]

c.02) [Abrogé, 2017, ch. 25, art. 2.1]

c.1) [Abrogé, 2017, ch. 25, art. 2.1]

c.2) [Abrogé, 2017, ch. 25, art. 2.1]

c.3) [Abrogé, 2017, ch. 25, art. 2.1]

c.4) [Abrogé, 2017, ch. 25, art. 2.1]

c.5) [Abrogé, 2017, ch. 25, art. 2.1]

c.6) [Abrogé, 2017, ch. 25, art. 2.1]

d) son nom a été omis ou retranché du registre des Indiens ou, avant le 4 septembre 1951, d'une liste de bande, en vertu du sous-alinéa 12(1)a)(iii) conformément à une ordonnance prise en vertu du paragraphe 109(1), dans leur version antérieure au 17 avril 1985, ou en vertu de toute disposition antérieure de la présente loi portant sur le même sujet que celui d'une de ces dispositions;

e) son nom a été omis ou retranché du registre des Indiens ou, avant le 4 septembre 1951, d'une liste de bande :

Indian
Definition and Registration of Indians
Indian Register
Section 6

Indiens
Définition et enregistrement des indiens
Registre des Indiens
Article 6

(e) the name of that person was omitted or deleted from the Indian Register, or from a band list prior to September 4, 1951,

(i) under section 13, as it read immediately prior to September 4, 1951, or under any former provision of this Act relating to the same subject-matter as that section, or

(ii) under section 111, as it read immediately prior to July 1, 1920, or under any former provision of this Act relating to the same subject-matter as that section; or

(f) both parents of that person are entitled to be registered under this section or, if the parents are no longer living, were so entitled at the time of death.

Persons entitled to be registered

(2) Subject to section 7, a person is entitled to be registered if one of their parents is entitled to be registered under subsection (1) or, if that parent is no longer living, was so entitled at the time of death.

Clarification

(2.1) A person who is entitled to be registered under both paragraph (1)(f) and any other paragraph of subsection (1) is considered to be entitled to be registered under that other paragraph only, and a person who is entitled to be registered under both subsection (2) and any paragraph of subsection (1) is considered to be entitled to be registered under that paragraph only.

Deeming provision

(3) For the purposes of paragraphs (1)(a.3) and (f) and subsection (2),

(a) a person who was no longer living immediately prior to April 17, 1985 but who was at the time of death entitled to be registered shall be deemed to be entitled to be registered under paragraph (1)(a);

(b) a person who is described in paragraph (1)(a.1), (d), (e) or (f) or subsection (2) and who was no longer living on April 17, 1985 is deemed to be entitled to be registered under that paragraph or subsection; and

(c) [Repealed, 2017, c. 25, s. 2.1]

(d) a person who is described in paragraph (1)(a.2) or (a.3) and who was no longer living on the day on which that paragraph came into force is deemed to be entitled to be registered under that paragraph.

R.S., 1985, c. I-5, s. 6; R.S., 1985, c. 32 (1st Supp.), s. 4, c. 43 (4th Supp.), s. 1; 2010, c. 18, s. 2; 2017, c. 25, s. 2; 2017, c. 25, s. 2.1.

(i) soit en vertu de l'article 13, dans sa version antérieure au 4 septembre 1951, ou en vertu de toute disposition antérieure de la présente loi portant sur le même sujet que celui de cet article,

(ii) soit en vertu de l'article 111, dans sa version antérieure au 1er juillet 1920, ou en vertu de toute disposition antérieure de la présente loi portant sur le même sujet que celui de cet article;

f) ses parents ont tous deux le droit d'être inscrits en vertu du présent article ou, s'ils sont décédés, avaient ce droit à la date de leur décès.

Personnes ayant droit à l'inscription

(2) Sous réserve de l'article 7, une personne a le droit d'être inscrite si l'un de ses parents a le droit d'être inscrit en vertu du paragraphe (1) ou, s'il est décédé, avait ce droit à la date de son décès.

Précision

(2.1) La personne qui a le droit d'être inscrite à la fois en vertu de l'alinéa (1)f) et d'un autre alinéa du paragraphe (1) est considérée avoir le droit d'être inscrite en vertu de cet autre alinéa seulement et celle qui a le droit d'être inscrite à la fois en vertu du paragraphe (2) et d'un alinéa du paragraphe (1) est considérée avoir le droit d'être inscrite en vertu de cet alinéa seulement.

Présomption

(3) Pour l'application des alinéas (1)a.3) et f) et du paragraphe (2) :

a) la personne qui est décédée avant le 17 avril 1985 mais qui avait le droit d'être inscrite à la date de son décès est réputée avoir le droit d'être inscrite en vertu de l'alinéa (1)a);

b) la personne qui est visée à l'un des alinéas (1)a.1), d), e) ou f) ou au paragraphe (2) et qui est décédée avant le 17 avril 1985 est réputée avoir le droit d'être inscrite en vertu de l'alinéa ou du paragraphe en cause;

c) [Abrogé, 2017, ch. 25, art. 2.1]

d) la personne qui est visée à l'un des alinéas (1)a.2) ou a.3) et qui est décédée avant la date d'entrée en vigueur de l'alinéa en cause est réputée avoir le droit d'être inscrite en vertu de celui-ci.

L.R. (1985), ch. I-5, art. 6; L.R. (1985), ch. 32 (1er suppl.), art. 4, ch. 43 (4e suppl.), art. 1; 2010, ch. 18, art. 2; 2017, ch. 25, art. 2; 2017, ch. 25, art. 2.1.

Indian
Definition and Registration of Indians
Indian Register
Sections 7-9

Indiens
Définition et enregistrement des indiens
Registre des Indiens
Articles 7-9

Persons not entitled to be registered

7 (1) The following persons are not entitled to be registered:

(a) a person who was registered under paragraph 11(1)(f), as it read immediately prior to April 17, 1985, or under any former provision of this Act relating to the same subject-matter as that paragraph, and whose name was subsequently omitted or deleted from the Indian Register under this Act; or

(b) a person who is the child of a person who was registered or entitled to be registered under paragraph 11(1)(f), as it read immediately prior to April 17, 1985, or under any former provision of this Act relating to the same subject-matter as that paragraph, and is also the child of a person who is not entitled to be registered.

Exception

(2) Paragraph (1)(a) does not apply in respect of a female person who was, at any time prior to being registered under paragraph 11(1)(f), entitled to be registered under any other provision of this Act.

Idem

(3) Paragraph (1)(b) does not apply in respect of the child of a female person who was, at any time prior to being registered under paragraph 11(1)(f), entitled to be registered under any other provision of this Act.

R.S., 1985, c. I-5, s. 7; R.S., 1985, c. 32 (1st Supp.), s. 4.

Band Lists

Band Lists

8 There shall be maintained in accordance with this Act for each band a Band List in which shall be entered the name of every person who is a member of that band.

R.S., 1985, c. I-5, s. 8; R.S., 1985, c. 32 (1st Supp.), s. 4.

Band Lists maintained in Department

9 (1) Until such time as a band assumes control of its Band List, the Band List of that band shall be maintained in the Department by the Registrar.

Existing Band Lists

(2) The names in a Band List of a band immediately prior to April 17, 1985 shall constitute the Band List of that band on April 17, 1985.

Deletions and additions

(3) The Registrar may at any time add to or delete from a Band List maintained in the Department the name of any

Personnes n'ayant pas droit à l'inscription

7 (1) Les personnes suivantes n'ont pas le droit d'être inscrites :

a) celles qui étaient inscrites en vertu de l'alinéa 11(1)f), dans sa version antérieure au 17 avril 1985, ou en vertu de toute disposition antérieure de la présente loi portant sur le même sujet que celui de cet alinéa, et dont le nom a ultérieurement été omis ou retranché du registre des Indiens en vertu de la présente loi;

b) celles qui sont les enfants d'une personne qui était inscrite ou avait le droit de l'être en vertu de l'alinéa 11(1)f), dans sa version antérieure au 17 avril 1985, ou en vertu de toute disposition antérieure de la présente loi portant sur le même sujet que celui de cet alinéa, et qui sont également les enfants d'une personne qui n'a pas le droit d'être inscrite.

Exception

(2) L'alinéa (1)a) ne s'applique pas à une personne de sexe féminin qui, avant qu'elle ne soit inscrite en vertu de l'alinéa 11(1)f), avait le droit d'être inscrite en vertu de toute autre disposition de la présente loi.

Idem

(3) L'alinéa (1)b) ne s'applique pas à l'enfant d'une personne de sexe féminin qui, avant qu'elle ne soit inscrite en vertu de l'alinéa 11(1)f), avait le droit d'être inscrite en vertu de toute autre disposition de la présente loi.

L.R. (1985), ch. I-5, art. 7; L.R. (1985), ch. 32 (1er suppl.), art. 4.

Listes de bande

Tenue

8 Est tenue conformément à la présente loi la liste de chaque bande où est consigné le nom de chaque personne qui en est membre.

L.R. (1985), ch. I-5, art. 8; L.R. (1985), ch. 32 (1er suppl.), art. 4.

Liste de bande tenue au ministère

9 (1) Jusqu'à ce que la bande assume la responsabilité de sa liste, celle-ci est tenue au ministère par le registraire.

Listes existantes

(2) Les noms figurant à la liste d'une bande le 16 avril 1985 constituent la liste de cette bande au 17 avril 1985.

Additions et retranchements

(3) Le registraire peut ajouter à une liste de bande tenue au ministère, ou en retrancher, le nom de la personne

Indian
Definition and Registration of Indians
Band Lists
Sections 9-10

Indiens
Définition et enregistrement des indiens
Listes de bande
Articles 9-10

person who, in accordance with this Act, is entitled or not entitled, as the case may be, to have his name included in that List.

Date of change

(4) A Band List maintained in the Department shall indicate the date on which each name was added thereto or deleted therefrom.

Application for entry

(5) The name of a person who is entitled to have his name entered in a Band List maintained in the Department is not required to be entered therein unless an application for entry therein is made to the Registrar.

R.S., 1985, c. I-5, s. 9; R.S., 1985, c. 32 (1st Supp.), s. 4.

Band control of membership

10 (1) A band may assume control of its own membership if it establishes membership rules for itself in writing in accordance with this section and if, after the band has given appropriate notice of its intention to assume control of its own membership, a majority of the electors of the band gives its consent to the band's control of its own membership.

Membership rules

(2) A band may, pursuant to the consent of a majority of the electors of the band,

(a) after it has given appropriate notice of its intention to do so, establish membership rules for itself; and

(b) provide for a mechanism for reviewing decisions on membership.

Exception relating to consent

(3) Where the council of a band makes a by-law under paragraph 81(1)(p.4) bringing this subsection into effect in respect of the band, the consents required under subsections (1) and (2) shall be given by a majority of the members of the band who are of the full age of eighteen years.

Acquired rights

(4) Membership rules established by a band under this section may not deprive any person who had the right to have his name entered in the Band List for that band, immediately prior to the time the rules were established, of the right to have his name so entered by reason only of a situation that existed or an action that was taken before the rules came into force.

---

qui, aux termes de la présente loi, a ou n'a pas droit, selon le cas, à l'inclusion de son nom dans cette liste.

Date du changement

(4) La liste de bande tenue au ministère indique la date où chaque nom y a été ajouté ou en a été retranché.

Demande

(5) Il n'est pas requis que le nom d'une personne qui a droit à ce que celui-ci soit consigné dans une liste de bande tenue au ministère y soit consigné, à moins qu'une demande à cet effet soit présentée au registraire.

L.R. (1985), ch. I-5, art. 9; L.R. (1985), ch. 32 (1er suppl.), art. 4.

Pouvoir de décision

10 (1) La bande peut décider de l'appartenance à ses effectifs si elle en fixe les règles par écrit conformément au présent article et si, après qu'elle a donné un avis convenable de son intention de décider de cette appartenance, elle y est autorisée par la majorité de ses électeurs.

Règles d'appartenance

(2) La bande peut, avec l'autorisation de la majorité de ses électeurs :

a) après avoir donné un avis convenable de son intention de ce faire, fixer les règles d'appartenance à ses effectifs;

b) prévoir une procédure de révision des décisions portant sur l'appartenance à ses effectifs.

Statut administratif sur l'autorisation requise

(3) Lorsque le conseil d'une bande prend, en vertu de l'alinéa 81(1)p.4), un règlement administratif mettant en vigueur le présent paragraphe à l'égard de la bande, l'autorisation requise en vertu des paragraphes (1) et (2) doit être donnée par la majorité des membres de la bande âgés d'au moins dix-huit ans.

Droits acquis

(4) Les règles d'appartenance fixées par une bande en vertu du présent article ne peuvent priver quiconque avait droit à ce que son nom soit consigné dans la liste de bande avant leur établissement du droit à ce que son nom y soit consigné en raison uniquement d'un fait ou d'une mesure antérieurs à leur prise d'effet.

Indian
Definition and Registration of Indians
Band Lists
Section 10

Indiens
Définition et enregistrement des indiens
Listes de bande
Article 10

Idem

(5) For greater certainty, subsection (4) applies in respect of a person who was entitled to have his name entered in the Band List under paragraph 11(1)(c) immediately before the band assumed control of the Band List if that person does not subsequently cease to be entitled to have his name entered in the Band List.

Notice to the Minister

(6) Where the conditions set out in subsection (1) have been met with respect to a band, the council of the band shall forthwith give notice to the Minister in writing that the band is assuming control of its own membership and shall provide the Minister with a copy of the membership rules for the band.

Notice to band and copy of Band List

(7) On receipt of a notice from the council of a band under subsection (6), the Minister shall, if the conditions set out in subsection (1) have been complied with, forthwith

(a) give notice to the band that it has control of its own membership; and

(b) direct the Registrar to provide the band with a copy of the Band List maintained in the Department.

Effective date of band's membership rules

(8) Where a band assumes control of its membership under this section, the membership rules established by the band shall have effect from the day on which notice is given to the Minister under subsection (6), and any additions to or deletions from the Band List of the band by the Registrar on or after that day are of no effect unless they are in accordance with the membership rules established by the band.

Band to maintain Band List

(9) A band shall maintain its own Band List from the date on which a copy of the Band List is received by the band under paragraph (7)(b), and, subject to section 13.2, the Department shall have no further responsibility with respect to that Band List from that date.

Deletions and additions

(10) A band may at any time add to or delete from a Band List maintained by it the name of any person who, in accordance with the membership rules of the band, is entitled or not entitled, as the case may be, to have his name included in that list.

Idem

(5) Il demeure entendu que le paragraphe (4) s'applique à la personne qui avait droit à ce que son nom soit consigné dans la liste de bande en vertu de l'alinéa 11(1)c) avant que celle-ci n'assume la responsabilité de la tenue de sa liste si elle ne cesse pas ultérieurement d'avoir droit à ce que son nom y soit consigné.

Avis au ministre

(6) Une fois remplies les conditions du paragraphe (1), le conseil de la bande, sans délai, avise par écrit le ministre du fait que celle-ci décide désormais de l'appartenance à ses effectifs et lui transmet le texte des règles d'appartenance.

Transmission de la liste

(7) Sur réception de l'avis du conseil de bande prévu au paragraphe (6), le ministre, sans délai, s'il constate que les conditions prévues au paragraphe (1) sont remplies :

a) avise la bande qu'elle décide désormais de l'appartenance à ses effectifs;

b) ordonne au registraire de transmettre à la bande une copie de la liste de bande tenue au ministère.

Date d'entrée en vigueur des règles d'appartenance

(8) Lorsque la bande décide de l'appartenance à ses effectifs en vertu du présent article, les règles d'appartenance fixées par celle-ci entrent en vigueur à compter de la date où l'avis au ministre a été donné en vertu du paragraphe (6); les additions ou retranchements effectués par le registraire à l'égard de la liste de la bande après cette date ne sont valides que s'ils sont effectués conformément à ces règles.

Transfert de responsabilité

(9) À compter de la réception de l'avis prévu à l'alinéa (7)b), la bande est responsable de la tenue de sa liste. Sous réserve de l'article 13.2, le ministère, à compter de cette date, est dégagé de toute responsabilité à l'égard de cette liste.

Additions et retranchements

(10) La bande peut ajouter à la liste de bande tenue par elle, ou en retrancher, le nom de la personne qui, aux termes des règles d'appartenance de la bande, a ou n'a pas droit, selon le cas, à l'inclusion de son nom dans la liste.

Indian
Definition and Registration of Indians
Band Lists
Sections 10-11

Indiens
Définition et enregistrement des indiens
Listes de bande
Articles 10-11

Date of change

(11) A Band List maintained by a band shall indicate the date on which each name was added thereto or deleted therefrom.

R.S., 1985, c. I-5, s. 10; R.S., 1985, c. 32 (1st Supp.), s. 4.

Membership rules for Departmental Band List

11 (1) Commencing on April 17, 1985, a person is entitled to have his name entered in a Band List maintained in the Department for a band if

(a) the name of that person was entered in the Band List for that band, or that person was entitled to have it entered in the Band List for that band, immediately prior to April 17, 1985;

(b) that person is entitled to be registered under paragraph 6(1)(b) as a member of that band;

(c) that person is entitled to be registered under paragraph 6(1)(a.1) and ceased to be a member of that band by reason of the circumstances set out in that paragraph; or

(d) that person was born on or after April 17, 1985 and is entitled to be registered under paragraph 6(1)(f) and both parents of that person are entitled to have their names entered in the Band List or, if no longer living, were at the time of death entitled to have their names entered in the Band List.

Additional membership rules for Departmental Band List

(2) Commencing on the day that is two years after the day that an Act entitled *An Act to amend the Indian Act*, introduced in the House of Commons on February 28, 1985, is assented to, or on such earlier day as may be agreed to under section 13.1, where a band does not have control of its Band List under this Act, a person is entitled to have his name entered in a Band List maintained in the Department for the band

(a) if that person is entitled to be registered under paragraph 6(1)(d) or (e) and ceased to be a member of that band by reason of the circumstances set out in that paragraph; or

(b) if that person is entitled to be registered under paragraph 6(1)(f) or subsection 6(2) and a parent referred to in that provision is entitled to have his name entered in the Band List or, if no longer living, was at the time of death entitled to have his name entered in the Band List.

Date du changement

(11) La liste de bande tenue par celle-ci indique la date où chaque nom y a été ajouté ou en a été retranché.

L.R. (1985), ch. I-5, art. 10; L.R. (1985), ch. 32 (1er suppl.), art. 4.

Règles d'appartenance pour une liste tenue au ministère

11 (1) À compter du 17 avril 1985, une personne a droit à ce que son nom soit consigné dans une liste de bande tenue pour cette dernière au ministère si elle remplit une des conditions suivantes :

a) son nom a été consigné dans cette liste, ou elle avait droit à ce qu'il le soit le 16 avril 1985;

b) elle a le droit d'être inscrite en vertu de l'alinéa 6(1)b) comme membre de cette bande;

c) elle a le droit d'être inscrite en vertu de l'alinéa 6(1)a.1) et a cessé d'être un membre de cette bande en raison des circonstances prévues à cet alinéa;

d) elle est née après le 16 avril 1985 et a le droit d'être inscrite en vertu de l'alinéa 6(1)f) et ses parents ont tous deux droit à ce que leur nom soit consigné dans la liste de bande ou, s'ils sont décédés, avaient ce droit à la date de leur décès.

Règles d'appartenance supplémentaires pour les listes tenues au ministère

(2) À compter du jour qui suit de deux ans la date de sanction de la loi intitulée *Loi modifiant la Loi sur les Indiens*, déposée à la Chambre des communes le 28 février 1985, ou de la date antérieure choisie en vertu de l'article 13.1, lorsque la bande n'a pas la responsabilité de la tenue de sa liste prévue à la présente loi, une personne a droit à ce que son nom soit consigné dans la liste de bande tenue au ministère pour cette dernière dans l'un ou l'autre des cas suivants :

a) elle a le droit d'être inscrite en vertu des alinéas 6(1)d) ou e) et elle a cessé d'être un membre de la bande en raison des circonstances prévues à l'un de ces alinéas;

b) elle a le droit d'être inscrite en vertu de l'alinéa 6(1)f) ou du paragraphe 6(2) et un de ses parents visés à l'une de ces dispositions a droit à ce que son nom soit consigné dans la liste de bande ou, s'il est décédé, avait ce droit à la date de son décès.

Indian
Definition and Registration of Indians
Band Lists
Section 11

Indiens
Définition et enregistrement des indiens
Listes de bande
Article 11

Deeming provision

(3) For the purposes of paragraph (1)(d) and subsection (2),

(a) a person whose name was omitted or deleted from the Indian Register or a Band List in the circumstances set out in paragraph 6(1)(a.1), (d) or (e) and who was no longer living on the first day on which the person would otherwise be entitled to have the person's name entered in the Band List of the band of which the person ceased to be a member is deemed to be entitled to have the person's name so entered;

(a.1) a person who would have been entitled to be registered under paragraph 6(1)(a.2) or (a.3), had they been living on the day on which that paragraph came into force, and who would otherwise have been entitled, on that day, to have their name entered in a Band List, is deemed to be entitled to have their name so entered; and

(b) a person described in paragraph (2)(b) shall be deemed to be entitled to have the person's name entered in the Band List in which the parent referred to in that paragraph is or was, or is deemed by this section to be, entitled to have the parent's name entered.

Additional membership rules — paragraphs 6(1)(c.01) to (c.6)

(3.1) A person is entitled to have their name entered in a Band List that is maintained in the Department for a band if

(a) they are entitled to be registered under paragraph 6(1)(a.2) and their father is entitled to have his name entered in the Band List or, if their father is no longer living, was so entitled at the time of death; or

(b) they are entitled to be registered under paragraph 6(1)(a.3) and one of their parents, grandparents or other ancestors

(i) ceased to be entitled to be a member of that band by reason of the circumstances set out in paragraph 6(1)(a.1), or

(ii) was not entitled to be a member of that band immediately before April 17, 1985.

(c) [Repealed, 2017, c. 25, s. 3.1]

(d) [Repealed, 2017, c. 25, s. 3.1]

(e) [Repealed, 2017, c. 25, s. 3.1]

(f) [Repealed, 2017, c. 25, s. 3.1]

Présomption

(3) Pour l'application de l'alinéa (1)d) et du paragraphe (2) :

a) la personne dont le nom a été omis ou retranché du registre des Indiens ou d'une liste de bande dans les circonstances prévues à l'un des alinéas 6(1)a.1), d) ou e) et qui est décédée avant le premier jour où elle a acquis le droit à ce que son nom soit consigné dans la liste de la bande dont elle a cessé d'être membre est réputée avoir droit à ce que son nom y soit consigné;

a.1) la personne qui, n'eût été son décès, aurait eu le droit d'être inscrite en vertu des alinéas 6(1)a.2) ou a.3) à la date d'entrée en vigueur de l'alinéa en cause et qui aurait eu, à cette date, le droit à ce que son nom soit consigné dans la liste de bande est réputée avoir droit à ce que son nom y soit consigné;

b) la personne visée à l'alinéa (2)b) est réputée avoir droit à ce que son nom soit consigné dans la même liste de bande que celle dans laquelle le parent visé au même paragraphe a ou avait, ou est réputé avoir, en vertu du présent article, droit à ce que son nom y soit consigné.

Règles d'appartenance supplémentaires — alinéas 6(1)c.01) à c.6)

(3.1) Toute personne a droit à ce que son nom soit consigné dans une liste de bande tenue pour celle-ci au ministère dans l'un ou l'autre des cas suivants :

a) elle a le droit d'être inscrite en vertu de l'alinéa 6(1)a.2) et son père a droit à ce que son nom soit consigné dans la liste de bande ou, s'il est décédé, avait ce droit à la date de son décès;

b) elle a le droit d'être inscrite en vertu de l'alinéa 6(1)a.3) et l'un de ses parents ou un autre de ses ascendants, selon le cas :

(i) a cessé d'avoir le droit d'être membre de la bande en raison des circonstances prévues à l'alinéa 6(1)a.1),

(ii) n'avait pas droit d'être membre de la bande le 16 avril 1985.

c) [Abrogé, 2017, ch. 25, art. 3.1]

d) [Abrogé, 2017, ch. 25, art. 3.1]

e) [Abrogé, 2017, ch. 25, art. 3.1]

f) [Abrogé, 2017, ch. 25, art. 3.1]

Indian
Definition and Registration of Indians
Band Lists
Sections 11-13.1

Indiens
Définition et enregistrement des indiens
Listes de bande
Articles 11-13.1

(g) [Repealed, 2017, c. 25, s. 3.1]

(h) [Repealed, 2017, c. 25, s. 3.1]

(i) [Repealed, 2017, c. 25, s. 3.1]

g) [Abrogé, 2017, ch. 25, art. 3.1]

h) [Abrogé, 2017, ch. 25, art. 3.1]

i) [Abrogé, 2017, ch. 25, art. 3.1]

Where band amalgamates or is divided

(4) Where a band amalgamates with another band or is divided so as to constitute new bands, any person who would otherwise have been entitled to have his name entered in the Band List of that band under this section is entitled to have his name entered in the Band List of the amalgamated band or the new band to which that person has the closest family ties, as the case may be.

R.S., 1985, c. I-5, s. 11; R.S., 1985, c. 32 (1st Supp.), s. 4, c. 43 (4th Supp.), s. 2; 2010, c. 18, s. 3; 2017, c. 25, s. 3; 2017, c. 25, s. 3.1.

Fusion ou division de bandes

(4) Lorsqu'une bande fusionne avec une autre ou qu'elle est divisée pour former de nouvelles bandes, toute personne qui aurait par ailleurs eu droit à ce que son nom soit consigné dans la liste de la bande en vertu du présent article a droit à ce que son nom soit consigné dans la liste de la bande issue de la fusion ou de celle de la nouvelle bande à l'égard de laquelle ses liens familiaux sont les plus étroits.

L.R. (1985), ch. I-5, art. 11; L.R. (1985), ch. 32 (1er suppl.), art. 4, ch. 43 (4e suppl.), art. 2; 2010, ch. 18, art. 3; 2017, ch. 25, art. 3; 2017, ch. 25, art. 3.1.

Entitlement with consent of band

12 Commencing on the day that is two years after the day that an Act entitled *An Act to amend the Indian Act*, introduced in the House of Commons on February 28, 1985, is assented to, or on such earlier day as may be agreed to under section 13.1, any person who

(a) is entitled to be registered under section 6, but is not entitled to have his name entered in the Band List maintained in the Department under section 11, or

(b) is a member of another band,

is entitled to have his name entered in the Band List maintained in the Department for a band if the council of the admitting band consents.

R.S., 1985, c. I-5, s. 12; R.S., 1985, c. 32 (1st Supp.), s. 4.

Inscription sujette au consentement du conseil

12 À compter du jour qui suit de deux ans la date de sanction de la loi intitulée *Loi modifiant la Loi sur les Indiens*, déposée à la Chambre des communes le 28 février 1985, ou de la date antérieure choisie en vertu de l'article 13.1, la personne qui :

a) soit a le droit d'être inscrite en vertu de l'article 6 sans avoir droit à ce que son nom soit consigné dans une liste de bande tenue au ministère en vertu de l'article 11;

b) soit est membre d'une autre bande,

a droit à ce que son nom soit consigné dans la liste d'une bande tenue au ministère pour cette dernière si le conseil de la bande qui l'admet en son sein y consent.

L.R. (1985), ch. I-5, art. 12; L.R. (1985), ch. 32 (1er suppl.), art. 4.

Limitation to one Band List

13 Notwithstanding sections 11 and 12, no person is entitled to have his name entered at the same time in more than one Band List maintained in the Department.

R.S., 1985, c. I-5, s. 13; R.S., 1985, c. 32 (1st Supp.), s. 4.

Nom consigné dans une seule liste

13 Par dérogation aux articles 11 et 12, nul n'a droit à ce que son nom soit consigné en même temps dans plus d'une liste de bande tenue au ministère.

L.R. (1985), ch. I-5, art. 13; L.R. (1985), ch. 32 (1er suppl.), art. 4.

Decision to leave Band List control with Department

13.1 (1) A band may, at any time prior to the day that is two years after the day that an Act entitled *An Act to amend the Indian Act*, introduced in the House of Commons on February 28, 1985, is assented to, decide to leave the control of its Band List with the Department if a majority of the electors of the band gives its consent to that decision.

Première décision

13.1 (1) Une bande peut, avant le jour qui suit de deux ans la date de sanction de la loi intitulée *Loi modifiant la Loi sur les Indiens*, déposée à la Chambre des communes le 28 février 1985, décider de laisser la responsabilité de la tenue de sa liste au ministère à condition d'y être autorisée par la majorité de ses électeurs.

Notice to the Minister

(2) Where a band decides to leave the control of its Band List with the Department under subsection (1), the

Avis au ministre

(2) Si la bande décide de laisser la responsabilité de la tenue de sa liste au ministère en vertu du paragraphe (1), le

Indian
Definition and Registration of Indians
Band Lists
Sections 13.1-14

Indiens
Définition et enregistrement des indiens
Listes de bande
Articles 13.1-14

council of the band shall forthwith give notice to the Minister in writing to that effect.

Subsequent band control of membership

(3) Notwithstanding a decision under subsection (1), a band may, at any time after that decision is taken, assume control of its Band List under section 10.

R.S., 1985, c. 32 (1st Supp.), s. 4.

Return of control to Department

13.2 (1) A band may, at any time after assuming control of its Band List under section 10, decide to return control of the Band List to the Department if a majority of the electors of the band gives its consent to that decision.

Notice to the Minister and copy of membership rules

(2) Where a band decides to return control of its Band List to the Department under subsection (1), the council of the band shall forthwith give notice to the Minister in writing to that effect and shall provide the Minister with a copy of the Band List and a copy of all the membership rules that were established by the band under subsection 10(2) while the band maintained its own Band List.

Transfer of responsibility to Department

(3) Where a notice is given under subsection (2) in respect of a Band List, the maintenance of that Band List shall be the responsibility of the Department from the date on which the notice is received and from that time the Band List shall be maintained in accordance with the membership rules set out in section 11.

R.S., 1985, c. 32 (1st Supp.), s. 4.

Entitlement retained

13.3 A person is entitled to have his name entered in a Band List maintained in the Department pursuant to section 13.2 if that person was entitled to have his name entered, and his name was entered, in the Band List immediately before a copy of it was provided to the Minister under subsection 13.2(2), whether or not that person is also entitled to have his name entered in the Band List under section 11.

R.S., 1985, c. 32 (1st Supp.), s. 4.

Notice of Band Lists

Copy of Band List provided to band council

14 (1) Within one month after the day an Act entitled *An Act to amend the Indian Act*, introduced in the House of Commons on February 28, 1985, is assented to, the Registrar shall provide the council of each band with a

conseil de la bande, sans délai, avise par écrit le ministre de la décision.

Seconde décision

(3) Malgré la décision visée au paragraphe (1), la bande peut, à tout moment par la suite, assumer la responsabilité de la tenue de sa liste en vertu de l'article 10.

L.R. (1985), ch. 32 (1er suppl.), art. 4.

Transfert de responsabilités au ministère

13.2 (1) La bande peut, à tout moment après avoir assumé la responsabilité de la tenue de sa liste en vertu de l'article 10, décider d'en remettre la responsabilité au ministère à condition d'y être autorisée par la majorité de ses électeurs.

Avis au ministre et texte des règles

(2) Lorsque la bande décide de remettre la responsabilité de la tenue de sa liste au ministère en vertu du paragraphe (1), le conseil de la bande, sans délai, avise par écrit le ministre de la décision et lui transmet une copie de la liste et le texte des règles d'appartenance fixées par la bande conformément au paragraphe 10(2) pendant qu'elle assumait la responsabilité de la tenue de sa liste.

Transfert de responsabilités au ministère

(3) Lorsque est donné l'avis prévu au paragraphe (2) à l'égard d'une liste de bande, la tenue de cette dernière devient la responsabilité du ministère à compter de la date de réception de l'avis. Elle est tenue, à compter de cette date, conformément aux règles d'appartenance prévues à l'article 11.

L.R. (1985), ch. 32 (1er suppl.), art. 4.

Maintien du droit d'être consigné dans la liste

13.3 Une personne a droit à ce que son nom soit consigné dans une liste de bande tenue par le ministère en vertu de l'article 13.2 si elle avait droit à ce que son nom soit consigné dans cette liste, et qu'il y a effectivement été consigné, avant qu'une copie en soit transmise au ministre en vertu du paragraphe 13.2(2), que cette personne ait ou non droit à ce que son nom soit consigné dans cette liste en vertu de l'article 11.

L.R. (1985), ch. 32 (1er suppl.), art. 4.

Affichage des listes de bande

Copie de la liste de bande transmise au conseil de bande

14 (1) Au plus tard un mois après la date de sanction de la loi intitulée *Loi modifiant la Loi sur les Indiens*, déposée à la Chambre des communes le 28 février 1985, le registraire transmet au conseil de chaque bande une copie

Indian
Definition and Registration of Indians
Notice of Band Lists
Sections 14-14.2

Indiens
Définition et enregistrement des indiens
Affichage des listes de bande
Articles 14-14.2

copy of the Band List for the band as it stood immediately prior to that day.

List of additions and deletions

(2) Where a Band List is maintained by the Department, the Registrar shall, at least once every two months after a copy of the Band List is provided to the council of a band under subsection (1), provide the council of the band with a list of the additions to or deletions from the Band List not included in a list previously provided under this subsection.

Lists to be posted

(3) The council of each band shall, forthwith on receiving a copy of the Band List under subsection (1), or a list of additions to and deletions from its Band List under subsection (2), post the copy or the list, as the case may be, in a conspicuous place on the reserve of the band.

R.S., 1985, c. I-5, s. 14; R.S., 1985, c. 32 (1st Supp.), s. 4.

Inquiries

Inquiries relating to Indian Register or Band Lists

14.1 The Registrar shall, on inquiry from any person who believes that he or any person he represents is entitled to have his name included in the Indian Register or a Band List maintained in the Department, indicate to the person making the inquiry whether or not that name is included therein.

R.S., 1985, c. 32 (1st Supp.), s. 4.

Protests

Protests

14.2 (1) A protest may be made in respect of the inclusion or addition of the name of a person in, or the omission or deletion of the name of a person from, the Indian Register, or a Band List maintained in the Department, within three years after the inclusion or addition, or omission or deletion, as the case may be, by notice in writing to the Registrar, containing a brief statement of the grounds therefor.

Protest in respect of Band List

(2) A protest may be made under this section in respect of the Band List of a band by the council of the band, any member of the band or the person in respect of whose name the protest is made or that person's representative.

de la liste de la bande dans son état antérieur à cette date.

Listes des additions et des retranchements

(2) Si la liste de bande est tenue au ministère, le registraire, au moins une fois tous les deux mois après la transmission prévue au paragraphe (1) d'une copie de la liste au conseil de la bande, transmet à ce dernier une liste des additions à la liste et des retranchements de celle-ci non compris dans une liste antérieure transmise en vertu du présent paragraphe.

Affichage de la liste

(3) Le conseil de chaque bande, dès qu'il reçoit copie de la liste de bande prévue au paragraphe (1) ou la liste des additions et des retranchements prévue au paragraphe (2), affiche la copie ou la liste, selon le cas, en un lieu bien en évidence sur la réserve de la bande.

L.R. (1985), ch. I-5, art. 14; L.R. (1985), ch. 32 (1er suppl.), art. 4.

Demandes

Demandes relatives au registre des Indiens ou aux listes de bande

14.1 Le registraire, à la demande de toute personne qui croit qu'elle-même ou que la personne qu'elle représente a droit à l'inclusion de son nom dans le registre des Indiens ou une liste de bande tenue au ministère, indique sans délai à l'auteur de la demande si ce nom y est inclus ou non.

L.R. (1985), ch. 32 (1er suppl.), art. 4.

Protestations

Protestations

14.2 (1) Une protestation peut être formulée, par avis écrit au registraire renfermant un bref exposé des motifs invoqués, contre l'inclusion ou l'addition du nom d'une personne dans le registre des Indiens ou une liste de bande tenue au ministère ou contre l'omission ou le retranchement de son nom de ce registre ou d'une telle liste dans les trois ans suivant soit l'inclusion ou l'addition, soit l'omission ou le retranchement.

Protestation relative à la liste de bande

(2) Une protestation peut être formulée en vertu du présent article à l'égard d'une liste de bande par le conseil de cette bande, un membre de celle-ci ou la personne dont le nom fait l'objet de la protestation ou son représentant.

Indian
Definition and Registration of Indians
Protests
Sections 14.2-14.3

Indiens
Définition et enregistrement des indiens
Protestations
Articles 14.2-14.3

Protest in respect of Indian Register

(3) A protest may be made under this section in respect of the Indian Register by the person in respect of whose name the protest is made or that person's representative.

Onus of proof

(4) The onus of establishing the grounds of a protest under this section lies on the person making the protest.

Registrar to cause investigation

(5) Where a protest is made to the Registrar under this section, the Registrar shall cause an investigation to be made into the matter and render a decision.

Evidence

(6) For the purposes of this section, the Registrar may receive such evidence on oath, on affidavit or in any other manner, whether or not admissible in a court of law, as the Registrar, in his discretion, sees fit or deems just.

Decision final

(7) Subject to section 14.3, the decision of the Registrar under subsection (5) is final and conclusive.

R.S., 1985, c. 32 (1st Supp.), s. 4.

Appeal

14.3 (1) Within six months after the Registrar renders a decision on a protest under section 14.2,

(a) in the case of a protest in respect of the Band List of a band, the council of the band, the person by whom the protest was made, or the person in respect of whose name the protest was made or that person's representative, or

(b) in the case of a protest in respect of the Indian Register, the person in respect of whose name the protest was made or that person's representative,

may, by notice in writing, appeal the decision to a court referred to in subsection (5).

Copy of notice of appeal to the Registrar

(2) Where an appeal is taken under this section, the person who takes the appeal shall forthwith provide the Registrar with a copy of the notice of appeal.

Material to be filed with the court by Registrar

(3) On receipt of a copy of a notice of appeal under subsection (2), the Registrar shall forthwith file with the court a copy of the decision being appealed together with all documentary evidence considered in arriving at that

Protestation relative au registre des Indiens

(3) Une protestation peut être formulée en vertu du présent article à l'égard du registre des Indiens par la personne dont le nom fait l'objet de la protestation ou son représentant.

Charge de la preuve

(4) La personne qui formule la protestation prévue au présent article a la charge d'en prouver le bien-fondé.

Le registraire fait tenir une enquête

(5) Lorsqu'une protestation lui est adressée en vertu du présent article, le registraire fait tenir une enquête sur la question et rend une décision.

Preuve

(6) Pour l'application du présent article, le registraire peut recevoir toute preuve présentée sous serment, par affidavit ou autrement, si celui-ci, à son appréciation, l'estime indiquée ou équitable, que cette preuve soit ou non admissible devant les tribunaux.

Décision finale

(7) Sous réserve de l'article 14.3, la décision du registraire visée au paragraphe (5) est définitive et sans appel.

L.R. (1985), ch. 32 (1er suppl.), art. 4.

Appel

14.3 (1) Dans les six mois suivant la date de la décision du registraire sur une protestation prévue à l'article 14.2, peuvent, par avis écrit, en interjeter appel devant le tribunal visé au paragraphe (5) :

a) s'il s'agit d'une protestation formulée à l'égard d'une liste de bande, le conseil de la bande, la personne qui a formulé la protestation ou la personne dont le nom fait l'objet de la protestation ou son représentant;

b) s'il s'agit d'une protestation formulée à l'égard du registre des Indiens, la personne dont le nom a fait l'objet de la protestation ou son représentant.

Copie de l'avis d'appel au registraire

(2) Lorsqu'il est interjeté appel en vertu du présent article, l'appelant transmet sans délai au registraire une copie de l'avis d'appel.

Documents à déposer par le registraire

(3) Sur réception de la copie de l'avis d'appel prévu au paragraphe (2), le registraire dépose sans délai au tribunal une copie de la décision en appel, toute la preuve documentaire prise en compte pour la décision, ainsi que

Indian
Definition and Registration of Indians
Protests
Sections 14.3-15

Indiens
Définition et enregistrement des indiens
Protestations
Articles 14.3-15

decision and any recording or transcript of any oral proceedings related thereto that were held before the Registrar.

Decision

(4) The court may, after hearing an appeal under this section,

(a) affirm, vary or reverse the decision of the Registrar; or

(b) refer the subject-matter of the appeal back to the Registrar for reconsideration or further investigation.

Court

(5) An appeal may be heard under this section

(a) in the Province of Quebec, before the Superior Court for the district in which the band is situated or in which the person who made the protest resides, or for such other district as the Minister may designate;

(a.1) in the Province of Ontario, before the Superior Court of Justice;

(b) in the Province of New Brunswick, Manitoba, Saskatchewan or Alberta, before the Court of Queen's Bench;

(c) in the Province of Newfoundland and Labrador, before the Trial Division of the Supreme Court;

(c.1) [Repealed, 1992, c. 51, s. 54]

(d) in the Province of Nova Scotia, British Columbia or Prince Edward Island, in Yukon or in the Northwest Territories, before the Supreme Court; or

(e) in Nunavut, before the Nunavut Court of Justice.

R.S., 1985, c. 32 (1st Supp.), s. 4, c. 27 (2nd Supp.), s. 10; 1990, c. 16, s. 14, c. 17, s. 25; 1992, c. 51, s. 54; 1998, c. 30, s. 14; 1999, c. 3, s. 69; 2002, c. 7, s. 183; 2015, c. 3, s. 118.

Payments in Respect of Persons Ceasing To Be Band Members

15 (1) to (4) [Repealed, R.S., 1985, c. 32 (1st Supp.), s. 5]

Commutation of payments under former Act

(5) Where, prior to September 4, 1951, any woman became entitled, under section 14 of the *Indian Act*, chapter 98 of the Revised Statutes of Canada, 1927, or any prior

Décision

(4) Le tribunal peut, à l'issue de l'audition de l'appel prévu au présent article :

a) soit confirmer, modifier ou renverser la décision du registraire;

b) soit renvoyer la question en appel au registraire pour réexamen ou nouvelle enquête.

Tribunal

(5) L'appel prévu au présent article peut être entendu :

a) dans la province de Québec, par la Cour supérieure du district où la bande est située ou dans lequel réside la personne qui a formulé la protestation, ou de tel autre district désigné par le ministre;

a.1) dans la province d'Ontario, par la Cour supérieure de justice;

b) dans la province du Nouveau-Brunswick, du Manitoba, de la Saskatchewan ou d'Alberta, par la Cour du Banc de la Reine;

c) dans la province de Terre-Neuve-et-Labrador, par la Section de première instance de la Cour suprême;

c.1) [Abrogé, 1992, ch. 51, art. 54]

d) dans les provinces de la Nouvelle-Écosse, de la Colombie-Britannique et de l'Île-du-Prince-Édouard, au Yukon et dans les Territoires du Nord-Ouest, par la Cour suprême;

e) au Nunavut, par la Cour de justice.

L.R. (1985), ch. 32 (1er suppl.), art. 4, ch. 27 (2e suppl.), art. 10; 1990, ch. 16, art. 14, ch. 17, art. 25; 1992, ch. 51, art. 54; 1998, ch. 30, art. 14; 1999, ch. 3, art. 69; 2002, ch. 7, art. 183; 2015, ch. 3, art. 118.

Paiements aux personnes qui cessent d'être membres d'une bande

15 (1) à (4) [Abrogés, L.R. (1985), ch. 32 (1er suppl.), art. 5]

Commutation de paiements prévus par une loi antérieure

(5) Lorsque, avant le 4 septembre 1951, une femme est devenue admissible, selon l'article 14 de la *Loi des Indiens*, chapitre 98 des Statuts revisés du Canada de 1927,

Indian
Definition and Registration of Indians
Payments in Respect of Persons Ceasing To Be Band Members
Sections 15-17

Indiens
Définition et enregistrement des indiens
Paiements aux personnes qui cessent d'être membres d'une bande
Articles 15-17

provisions to the like effect, to share in the distribution of annuities, interest moneys or rents, the Minister may, in lieu thereof, pay to that woman out of the moneys of the band an amount equal to ten times the average annual amounts of the payments made to her during the ten years last preceding or, if they were paid for less than ten years, during the years they were paid.

R.S., 1985, c. I-5, s. 15; R.S., 1985, c. 32 (1st Supp.), s. 5.

16 (1) [Repealed, R.S., 1985, c. 32 (1st Supp.), s. 6]

Transferred member's interest

(2) A person who ceases to be a member of one band by reason of becoming a member of another band is not entitled to any interest in the lands or moneys held by Her Majesty on behalf of the former band, but is entitled to the same interest in common in lands and moneys held by Her Majesty on behalf of the latter band as other members of that band.

(3) [Repealed, R.S., 1985, c. 32 (1st Supp.), s. 6]

R.S., 1985, c. I-5, s. 16; R.S., 1985, c. 32 (1st Supp.), s. 6.

New Bands

Minister may constitute new bands

17 (1) The Minister may, whenever he considers it desirable,

(a) amalgamate bands that, by a vote of a majority of their electors, request to be amalgamated; and

(b) constitute new bands and establish Band Lists with respect thereto from existing Band Lists, or from the Indian Register, if requested to do so by persons proposing to form the new bands.

Division of reserves and funds

(2) Where pursuant to subsection (1) a new band has been established from an existing band or any part thereof, such portion of the reserve lands and funds of the existing band as the Minister determines shall be held for the use and benefit of the new band.

No protest

(3) No protest may be made under section 14.2 in respect of the deletion from or the addition to a Band List consequent on the exercise by the Minister of any of the Minister's powers under subsection (1).

R.S., 1985, c. I-5, s. 17; R.S., 1985, c. 32 (1st Supp.), s. 7.

ou selon quelque disposition antérieure ayant le même effet, à participer à la distribution d'annuités, intérêts ou rentes, le ministre peut, en remplacement de ceux-ci, payer à cette femme, sur l'argent de la bande, un montant égal à dix fois les montants annuels moyens de ces paiements qui lui ont été versés au cours des dix années précédentes ou, s'ils l'ont été pendant moins de dix ans, au cours des années pendant lesquelles ils ont été faits.

L.R. (1985), ch. I-5, art. 15; L.R. (1985), ch. 32 (1er suppl.), art. 5.

16 (1) [Abrogé, L.R. (1985), ch. 32 (1er suppl.), art. 6]

Le droit d'un membre transféré

(2) Une personne qui cesse de faire partie d'une bande du fait qu'elle est devenue membre d'une autre bande n'a aucun droit sur les terres ou sommes d'argent détenues par Sa Majesté au nom de la bande dont elle faisait partie, mais elle jouit des mêmes droits en commun, sur les terres et les sommes d'argent détenues par Sa Majesté au nom de l'autre bande, que les membres de cette dernière.

(3) [Abrogé, L.R. (1985), ch. 32 (1er suppl.), art. 6]

L.R. (1985), ch. I-5, art. 16; L.R. (1985), ch. 32 (1er suppl.), art. 6.

Nouvelles bandes

Constitution de nouvelles bandes par le ministre

17 (1) Le ministre peut, lorsqu'il l'estime à propos :

a) fusionner les bandes qui, par un vote majoritaire de leurs électeurs, demandent la fusion;

b) constituer de nouvelles bandes et établir à leur égard des listes de bande à partir des listes de bande existantes, ou du registre des Indiens, s'il lui en est fait la demande par des personnes proposant la constitution de nouvelles bandes.

Division des réserves et des fonds

(2) Si, conformément au paragraphe (1), une nouvelle bande a été constituée à même une bande existante ou une partie de cette dernière, la fraction des terres de réserve et des fonds de la bande existante que le ministre détermine est détenue à l'usage et au profit de la nouvelle bande.

Aucune protestation

(3) Aucune protestation ne peut être formulée en vertu de l'article 14.2 à l'égard d'un retranchement d'une liste de bande ou d'une addition à celle-ci qui découle de l'exercice par le ministre de l'un de ses pouvoirs prévus au paragraphe (1).

L.R. (1985), ch. I-5, art. 17; L.R. (1985), ch. 32 (1er suppl.), art. 7.

Indian
Reserves
Sections 18-19

Indiens
Réserves
Articles 18-19

Reserves

Reserves to be held for use and benefit of Indians

18 (1) Subject to this Act, reserves are held by Her Majesty for the use and benefit of the respective bands for which they were set apart, and subject to this Act and to the terms of any treaty or surrender, the Governor in Council may determine whether any purpose for which lands in a reserve are used or are to be used is for the use and benefit of the band.

Use of reserves for schools, etc.

(2) The Minister may authorize the use of lands in a reserve for the purpose of Indian schools, the administration of Indian affairs, Indian burial grounds, Indian health projects or, with the consent of the council of the band, for any other purpose for the general welfare of the band, and may take any lands in a reserve required for those purposes, but where an individual Indian, immediately prior to the taking, was entitled to the possession of those lands, compensation for that use shall be paid to the Indian, in such amount as may be agreed between the Indian and the Minister, or, failing agreement, as may be determined in such manner as the Minister may direct.

R.S., c. I-6, s. 18.

Children of band members

18.1 A member of a band who resides on the reserve of the band may reside there with his dependent children or any children of whom the member has custody.

R.S., 1985, c. 32 (1st Supp.), s. 8.

Surveys and subdivisions

19 The Minister may

(a) authorize surveys of reserves and the preparation of plans and reports with respect thereto;

(b) divide the whole or any portion of a reserve into lots or other subdivisions; and

(c) determine the location and direct the construction of roads in a reserve.

R.S., c. I-6, s. 19.

Réserves

Les réserves sont détenues à l'usage et au profit des Indiens

18 (1) Sous réserve des autres dispositions de la présente loi, Sa Majesté détient des réserves à l'usage et au profit des bandes respectives pour lesquelles elles furent mises de côté; sous réserve des autres dispositions de la présente loi et des stipulations de tout traité ou cession, le gouverneur en conseil peut décider si tout objet, pour lequel des terres dans une réserve sont ou doivent être utilisées, se trouve à l'usage et au profit de la bande.

Emploi de réserves aux fins des écoles, etc.

(2) Le ministre peut autoriser l'utilisation de terres dans une réserve aux fins des écoles indiennes, de l'administration d'affaires indiennes, de cimetières indiens, de projets relatifs à la santé des Indiens, ou, avec le consentement du conseil de la bande, pour tout autre objet concernant le bien-être général de la bande, et il peut prendre toutes terres dans une réserve, nécessaires à ces fins, mais lorsque, immédiatement avant cette prise, un Indien particulier avait droit à la possession de ces terres, il doit être versé à cet Indien, pour un semblable usage, une indemnité d'un montant dont peuvent convenir l'Indien et le ministre, ou, à défaut d'accord, qui peut être fixé de la manière que détermine ce dernier.

S.R., ch. I-6, art. 18.

Enfants des membres d'une bande

18.1 Le membre d'une bande qui réside sur la réserve de cette dernière peut y résider avec ses enfants à charge ou tout enfant dont il a la garde.

L.R. (1985), ch. 32 (1er suppl.), art. 8.

Levés et subdivisions

19 Le ministre peut :

a) autoriser des levés de réserves et la préparation de plans et de rapports à cet égard;

b) séparer la totalité ou une partie d'une réserve en lots ou autres subdivisions;

c) décider de l'emplacement des routes dans une réserve et en prescrire la construction.

S.R., ch. I-6, art. 19.

Indian
Possession of Lands in Reserves
Section 20

Indiens
Possession de terres dans des réserves
Article 20

Possession of Lands in Reserves

Possession de terres dans des réserves

Possession of lands in a reserve

20 (1) No Indian is lawfully in possession of land in a reserve unless, with the approval of the Minister, possession of the land has been allotted to him by the council of the band.

Certificate of Possession

(2) The Minister may issue to an Indian who is lawfully in possession of land in a reserve a certificate, to be called a Certificate of Possession, as evidence of his right to possession of the land described therein.

Location tickets issued under previous legislation

(3) For the purposes of this Act, any person who, on September 4, 1951, held a valid and subsisting Location Ticket issued under *The Indian Act, 1880*, or any statute relating to the same subject-matter, shall be deemed to be lawfully in possession of the land to which the location ticket relates and to hold a Certificate of Possession with respect thereto.

Temporary possession

(4) Where possession of land in a reserve has been allotted to an Indian by the council of the band, the Minister may, in his discretion, withhold his approval and may authorize the Indian to occupy the land temporarily and may prescribe the conditions as to use and settlement that are to be fulfilled by the Indian before the Minister approves of the allotment.

Certificate of Occupation

(5) Where the Minister withholds approval pursuant to subsection (4), he shall issue a Certificate of Occupation to the Indian, and the Certificate entitles the Indian, or those claiming possession by devise or descent, to occupy the land in respect of which it is issued for a period of two years from the date thereof.

Extension and approval

(6) The Minister may extend the term of a Certificate of Occupation for a further period not exceeding two years, and may, at the expiration of any period during which a Certificate of Occupation is in force

(a) approve the allotment by the council of the band and issue a Certificate of Possession if in his opinion the conditions as to use and settlement have been fulfilled; or

Possession de terres dans une réserve

20 (1) Un Indien n'est légalement en possession d'une terre dans une réserve que si, avec l'approbation du ministre, possession de la terre lui a été accordée par le conseil de la bande.

Certificat de possession

(2) Le ministre peut délivrer à un Indien légalement en possession d'une terre dans une réserve un certificat, appelé certificat de possession, attestant son droit de posséder la terre y décrite.

Billets de location délivrés en vertu de lois antérieures

(3) Pour l'application de la présente loi, toute personne qui, le 4 septembre 1951, détenait un billet de location valide délivré sous le régime de l'*Acte relatif aux Sauvages, 1880*, ou de toute loi sur le même sujet, est réputée légalement en possession de la terre visée par le billet de location et est censée détenir un certificat de possession à cet égard.

Possession temporaire

(4) Lorsque le conseil de la bande a attribué à un Indien la possession d'une terre dans une réserve, le ministre peut, à sa discrétion, différer son approbation et autoriser l'Indien à occuper la terre temporairement, de même que prescrire les conditions, concernant l'usage et l'établissement, que doit remplir l'Indien avant que le ministre approuve l'attribution.

Certificat d'occupation

(5) Lorsque le ministre diffère son approbation conformément au paragraphe (4), il délivre un certificat d'occupation à l'Indien, et le certificat autorise l'Indien, ou ceux qui réclament possession par legs ou par transmission sous forme d'héritage, à occuper la terre concernant laquelle il est délivré, pendant une période de deux ans, à compter de sa date.

Prorogation et approbation

(6) Le ministre peut proroger la durée d'un certificat d'occupation pour une nouvelle période n'excédant pas deux ans et peut, à l'expiration de toute période durant laquelle un certificat d'occupation est en vigueur :

a) soit approuver l'attribution faite par le conseil de la bande et délivrer un certificat de possession si, d'après lui, on a satisfait aux conditions concernant l'usage et l'établissement;

Indian
Possession of Lands in Reserves
Sections 20-25

Indiens
Possession de terres dans des réserves
Articles 20-25

(b) refuse approval of the allotment by the council of the band and declare the land in respect of which the Certificate of Occupation was issued to be available for re-allotment by the council of the band.

R.S., c. I-6, s. 20.

Register

21 There shall be kept in the Department a register, to be known as the Reserve Land Register, in which shall be entered particulars relating to Certificates of Possession and Certificates of Occupation and other transactions respecting lands in a reserve.

R.S., c. I-6, s. 21.

Improvements on lands

22 Where an Indian who is in possession of lands at the time they are included in a reserve made permanent improvements thereon before that time, he shall be deemed to be in lawful possession of those lands at the time they are included.

R.S., c. I-6, s. 22.

Compensation for improvements

23 An Indian who is lawfully removed from lands in a reserve on which he has made permanent improvements may, if the Minister so directs, be paid compensation in respect thereof in an amount to be determined by the Minister, either from the person who goes into possession or from the funds of the band, at the discretion of the Minister.

R.S., c. I-6, s. 23.

Transfer of possession

24 An Indian who is lawfully in possession of lands in a reserve may transfer to the band or another member of the band the right to possession of the land, but no transfer or agreement for the transfer of the right to possession of lands in a reserve is effective until it is approved by the Minister.

R.S., c. I-6, s. 24.

Indian ceasing to reside on reserve

25 (1) An Indian who ceases to be entitled to reside on a reserve may, within six months or such further period as the Minister may direct, transfer to the band or another member of the band the right to possession of any lands in the reserve of which he was lawfully in possession.

When right of possession reverts

(2) Where an Indian does not dispose of his right of possession in accordance with subsection (1), the right to possession of the land reverts to the band, subject to the

b) soit refuser d'approuver l'attribution faite par le conseil de la bande et déclarer que la terre, à l'égard de laquelle le certificat d'occupation a été délivré, peut être attribuée de nouveau par le conseil de la bande.

S.R., ch. I-6, art. 20.

Registre

21 Il doit être tenu au ministère un registre, connu sous le nom de Registre des terres de réserve, où sont inscrits les détails concernant les certificats de possession et certificats d'occupation et les autres opérations relatives aux terres situées dans une réserve.

S.R., ch. I-6, art. 21.

Améliorations apportées aux terres

22 Un Indien qui a fait des améliorations à des terres en sa possession avant leur inclusion dans une réserve, est considéré comme étant en possession légale de ces terres au moment de leur inclusion.

S.R., ch. I-6, art. 22.

Indemnité à l'égard des améliorations

23 Un Indien qui est légalement retiré de terres situées dans une réserve et sur lesquelles il a fait des améliorations permanentes peut, si le ministre l'ordonne, recevoir à cet égard une indemnité d'un montant que le ministre détermine, soit de la personne qui entre en possession, soit sur les fonds de la bande, à la discrétion du ministre.

S.R., ch. I-6, art. 23.

Transfert de possession

24 Un Indien qui est légalement en possession d'une terre dans une réserve peut transférer à la bande, ou à un autre membre de celle-ci, le droit à la possession de la terre, mais aucun transfert ou accord en vue du transfert du droit à la possession de terres dans une réserve n'est valable tant qu'il n'est pas approuvé par le ministre.

S.R., ch. I-6, art. 24.

Indien qui cesse de résider sur la réserve

25 (1) Un Indien qui cesse d'avoir droit de résider sur une réserve peut, dans un délai de six mois ou dans tel délai prorogé que prescrit le ministre, transférer à la bande, ou à un autre membre de celle-ci, le droit à la possession de toute terre dans la réserve, dont il était légalement en possession.

Le droit de possession non transféré retourne à la bande

(2) Lorsqu'un Indien ne dispose pas de son droit de possession conformément au paragraphe (1), le droit à la possession de la terre retourne à la bande, sous réserve

Indian
Possession of Lands in Reserves
Sections 25-29

Indiens
Possession de terres dans des réserves
Articles 25-29

payment to the Indian who was lawfully in possession of the land, from the funds of the band, of such compensation for permanent improvements as the Minister may determine.

R.S., c. I-6, s. 25.

Correction of Certificate or Location Tickets

26 Whenever a Certificate of Possession or Occupation or a Location Ticket issued under *The Indian Act, 1880*, or any statute relating to the same subject-matter was, in the opinion of the Minister, issued to or in the name of the wrong person, through mistake, or contains any clerical error or misnomer or wrong description of any material fact therein, the Minister may cancel the Certificate or Location Ticket and issue a corrected Certificate in lieu thereof.

R.S., c. I-6, s. 26.

Cancellation of Certificates or Location Tickets

27 The Minister may, with the consent of the holder thereof, cancel any Certificate of Possession or Occupation or Location Ticket referred to in section 26, and may cancel any Certificate of Possession or Occupation or Location Ticket that in his opinion was issued through fraud or in error.

R.S., c. I-6, s. 27.

Grants, etc., of reserve lands void

28 (1) Subject to subsection (2), any deed, lease, contract, instrument, document or agreement of any kind, whether written or oral, by which a band or a member of a band purports to permit a person other than a member of that band to occupy or use a reserve or to reside or otherwise exercise any rights on a reserve is void.

Minister may issue permits

(2) The Minister may by permit in writing authorize any person for a period not exceeding one year, or with the consent of the council of the band for any longer period, to occupy or use a reserve or to reside or otherwise exercise rights on a reserve.

R.S., c. I-6, s. 28.

Exemption from seizure

29 Reserve lands are not subject to seizure under legal process.

R.S., c. I-6, s. 29.

du paiement, à l'Indien qui était légalement en possession de la terre, sur les fonds de la bande, de telle indemnité pour améliorations permanentes que fixe le ministre.

S.R., ch. I-6, art. 25.

Certificat corrigé; billet de location

26 Lorsqu'un certificat de possession ou d'occupation ou un billet de location délivré sous le régime de l'*Acte relatif aux Sauvages, 1880* ou de toute loi traitant du même sujet, a été, de l'avis du ministre, délivré par erreur à une personne à qui il n'était pas destiné ou au nom d'une telle personne, ou contient une erreur d'écriture ou une fausse appellation, ou une description erronée de quelque fait important, le ministre peut annuler le certificat ou billet de location et délivrer un certificat corrigé pour le remplacer.

S.R., ch. I-6, art. 26.

Certificat annulé; billet de location

27 Le ministre peut, avec le consentement de celui qui en est titulaire, annuler tout certificat de possession ou occupation ou billet de location mentionné à l'article 26, et peut annuler tout certificat de possession ou d'occupation ou billet de location qui, selon lui, a été délivré par fraude ou erreur.

S.R., ch. I-6, art. 27.

Nullité d'octrois, etc. de terre de réserve

28 (1) Sous réserve du paragraphe (2), est nul un acte, bail, contrat, instrument, document ou accord de toute nature, écrit ou oral, par lequel une bande ou un membre d'une bande est censé permettre à une personne, autre qu'un membre de cette bande, d'occuper ou utiliser une réserve ou de résider ou autrement exercer des droits sur une réserve.

Le ministre peut émettre des permis

(2) Le ministre peut, au moyen d'un permis par écrit, autoriser toute personne, pour une période maximale d'un an, ou, avec le consentement du conseil de la bande, pour toute période plus longue, à occuper ou utiliser une réserve, ou à résider ou autrement exercer des droits sur une réserve.

S.R., ch. I-6, art. 28.

Insaisissabilité

29 Les terres des réserves ne sont assujetties à aucune saisie sous le régime d'un acte judiciaire.

S.R., ch. I-6, art. 29.

Indian
Trespass on Reserves
Sections 30-33

Indiens
Violation du droit de propriété dans les réserves
Articles 30-33

Trespass on Reserves

Violation du droit de propriété dans les réserves

Penalty for trespass

30 A person who trespasses on a reserve is guilty of an offence and liable on summary conviction to a fine not exceeding fifty dollars or to imprisonment for a term not exceeding one month or to both.

R.S., c. I-6, s. 30.

Peine

30 Quiconque pénètre, sans droit ni autorisation, dans une réserve commet une infraction et encourt, sur déclaration de culpabilité par procédure sommaire, une amende maximale de cinquante dollars et un emprisonnement maximal d'un mois, ou l'une de ces peines.

S.R., ch. I-6, art. 30.

Information by Attorney General

31 (1) Without prejudice to section 30, where an Indian or a band alleges that persons other than Indians are or have been

(a) unlawfully in occupation or possession of,

(b) claiming adversely the right to occupation or possession of, or

(c) trespassing on

a reserve or part of a reserve, the Attorney General of Canada may exhibit an information in the Federal Court claiming, on behalf of the Indian or band, the relief or remedy sought.

Dénonciation par le procureur général

31 (1) Sans préjudice de l'article 30, lorsqu'un Indien ou une bande prétend que des personnes autres que des Indiens, selon le cas :

a) occupent ou possèdent illégalement, ou ont occupé ou possédé illégalement, une réserve ou une partie de réserve;

b) réclament ou ont réclamé sous forme d'opposition le droit d'occuper ou de posséder une réserve ou une partie de réserve;

c) pénètrent ou ont pénétré, sans droit ni autorisation, dans une réserve ou une partie de réserve,

le procureur général du Canada peut produire à la Cour fédérale une dénonciation réclamant, au nom de l'Indien ou de la bande, les mesures de redressement désirées.

Information deemed action by Crown

(2) An information exhibited under subsection (1) shall, for all purposes of the *Federal Courts Act*, be deemed to be a proceeding by the Crown within the meaning of that Act.

La dénonciation est réputée une action par la Couronne

(2) Une dénonciation produite sous le régime du paragraphe (1) est réputée, pour l'application de la *Loi sur les Cours fédérales*, une procédure engagée par la Couronne, au sens de cette loi.

Existing remedies preserved

(3) Nothing in this section shall be construed to impair, abridge or otherwise affect any right or remedy that, but for this section, would be available to Her Majesty or to an Indian or a band.

R.S., 1985, c. I-5, s. 31; 2002, c. 8, s. 182.

Les recours existants subsistent

(3) Le présent article n'a pas pour effet de porter atteinte aux droits ou recours que, en son absence, Sa Majesté, un Indien ou une bande pourrait exercer.

L.R. (1985), ch. I-5, art. 31; 2002, ch. 8, art. 182.

32 [Repealed, 2014, c. 38, s. 5]

33 [Repealed, 2014, c. 38, s. 5]

32 [Abrogé, 2014, ch. 38, art. 5]

33 [Abrogé, 2014, ch. 38, art. 5]

Indian
Roads and Bridges
Sections 34-35

Indiens
Routes et ponts
Articles 34-35

Roads and Bridges

Roads, bridges, etc.

34 (1) A band shall ensure that the roads, bridges, ditches and fences within the reserve occupied by that band are maintained in accordance with instructions issued from time to time by the superintendent.

Idem

(2) Where, in the opinion of the Minister, a band has not carried out the instructions of the superintendent issued under subsection (1), the Minister may cause the instructions to be carried out at the expense of the band or any member thereof and may recover the cost thereof from any amounts that are held by Her Majesty and are payable to the band or member.

R.S., c. I-6, s. 34.

Lands Taken for Public Purposes

Taking of lands by local authorities

35 (1) Where by an Act of Parliament or a provincial legislature Her Majesty in right of a province, a municipal or local authority or a corporation is empowered to take or to use lands or any interest therein without the consent of the owner, the power may, with the consent of the Governor in Council and subject to any terms that may be prescribed by the Governor in Council, be exercised in relation to lands in a reserve or any interest therein.

Procedure

(2) Unless the Governor in Council otherwise directs, all matters relating to compulsory taking or using of lands in a reserve under subsection (1) are governed by the statute by which the powers are conferred.

Grant in lieu of compulsory taking

(3) Whenever the Governor in Council has consented to the exercise by a province, a municipal or local authority or a corporation of the powers referred to in subsection (1), the Governor in Council may, in lieu of the province, authority or corporation taking or using the lands without the consent of the owner, authorize a transfer or grant of the lands to the province, authority or corporation, subject to any terms that may be prescribed by the Governor in Council.

Routes et ponts

Routes, ponts, etc.

34 (1) Une bande doit assurer l'entretien, en conformité avec les instructions du surintendant, des routes, ponts, fossés et clôtures dans la réserve qu'elle occupe.

Idem

(2) Lorsque, de l'avis du ministre, une bande n'a pas exécuté les instructions données par le surintendant en vertu du paragraphe (1), le ministre peut faire exécuter ces instructions aux frais de la bande ou de tout membre de cette dernière et en recouvrer les frais sur tout montant détenu par Sa Majesté et payable à la bande ou à ce membre.

S.R., ch. I-6, art. 34.

Terres prises pour cause d'utilité publique

Les autorités locales peuvent prendre des terres

35 (1) Lorsque, par une loi fédérale ou provinciale, Sa Majesté du chef d'une province, une autorité municipale ou locale, ou une personne morale, a le pouvoir de prendre ou d'utiliser des terres ou tout droit sur celles-ci sans le consentement du propriétaire, ce pouvoir peut, avec le consentement du gouverneur en conseil et aux conditions qu'il peut prescrire, être exercé relativement aux terres dans une réserve ou à tout droit sur celles-ci.

Procédures

(2) À moins que le gouverneur en conseil n'en ordonne autrement, toutes les questions concernant la prise ou l'utilisation obligatoire de terres dans une réserve, aux termes du paragraphe (1), doivent être régies par la loi qui confère les pouvoirs.

Octroi au lieu d'une prise obligatoire

(3) Lorsque le gouverneur en conseil a consenti à l'exercice des pouvoirs mentionnés au paragraphe (1) par une province, une autorité municipale ou locale ou une personne morale, il peut, au lieu que la province, l'autorité ou la personne morale prenne ou utilise les terres sans le consentement du propriétaire, permettre un transfert ou octroi de ces terres à la province, autorité ou personne morale, sous réserve des conditions qu'il fixe.

Indian
Lands Taken for Public Purposes
Sections 35-38

Indiens
Terres prises pour cause d'utilité publique
Articles 35-38

Payment

(4) Any amount that is agreed on or awarded in respect of the compulsory taking or using of land under this section or that is paid for a transfer or grant of land pursuant to this section shall be paid to the Receiver General for the use and benefit of the band or for the use and benefit of any Indian who is entitled to compensation or payment as a result of the exercise of the powers referred to in subsection (1).

R.S., c. I-6, s. 35.

Special Reserves

36 [Repealed, 2014, c. 38, s. 6]

Special reserves

36.1 Where lands the legal title to which is not vested in Her Majesty had been set apart for the use and benefit of a band before the coming into force of this section, the effect of section 36 of this Act, as it read immediately before the coming into force of this section, continues in respect of those lands and this Act applies as though the lands were a reserve within the meaning of this Act.

2014, c. 38, s. 6.

Surrenders and Designations

Sales

37 (1) Lands in a reserve shall not be sold nor title to them conveyed until they have been absolutely surrendered to Her Majesty pursuant to subsection 38(1) by the band for whose use and benefit in common the reserve was set apart.

Other transactions

(2) Except where this Act otherwise provides, lands in a reserve shall not be leased nor an interest in them granted until they have been designated under subsection 38(2) by the band for whose use and benefit in common the reserve was set apart.

R.S., 1985, c. I-5, s. 37; R.S., 1985, c. 17 (4th Supp.), s. 2; 2012, c. 31, s. 206.

Surrender to Her Majesty

38 (1) A band may absolutely surrender to Her Majesty, conditionally or unconditionally, all of the rights and interests of the band and its members in all or part of a reserve.

Designation

(2) A band may, conditionally or unconditionally, designate, by way of a surrender to Her Majesty that is not

Paiement

(4) Tout montant dont il est convenu ou qui est accordé à l'égard de la prise ou de l'utilisation obligatoire de terrains sous le régime du présent article ou qui est payé pour un transfert ou octroi de terre selon le présent article, doit être versé au receveur général à l'usage et au profit de la bande ou à l'usage et au profit de tout Indien qui a droit à l'indemnité ou au paiement du fait de l'exercice des pouvoirs mentionnés au paragraphe (1).

S.R., ch. I-6, art. 35.

Réserves spéciales

36 [Abrogé, 2014, ch. 38, art. 6]

Réserves spéciales

36.1 L'article 36, dans sa version antérieure à la date d'entrée en vigueur du présent article, continue d'avoir effet à l'égard des terres dont Sa Majesté n'est pas propriétaire ayant été mises de côté à l'usage et au profit d'une bande avant l'entrée en vigueur du présent article et la présente loi s'applique à l'égard de ces terres comme si elles étaient une réserve, au sens de la présente loi.

2014, ch. 38, art. 6.

Cession et désignation

Vente

37 (1) Les terres dans une réserve ne peuvent être vendues ou aliénées que si elles sont cédées à titre absolu conformément au paragraphe 38(1) à Sa Majesté par la bande à l'usage et au profit communs de laquelle la réserve a été mise de côté.

Opérations

(2) Sauf disposition contraire de la présente loi, les terres dans une réserve ne peuvent être données à bail ou faire l'objet d'un démembrement que si elles sont désignées en vertu du paragraphe 38(2) par la bande à l'usage et au profit communs de laquelle la réserve a été mise de côté.

L.R. (1985), ch. I-5, art. 37; L.R. (1985), ch. 17 (4e suppl.), art. 2; 2012, ch. 31, art. 206.

Cession à Sa Majesté

38 (1) Une bande peut céder à titre absolu à Sa Majesté, avec ou sans conditions, tous ses droits, et ceux de ses membres, portant sur tout ou partie d'une réserve.

Désignation

(2) Aux fins de les donner à bail ou de les démembrer, une bande peut désigner par voie de cession à Sa

Indian
Surrenders and Designations
Sections 38-39

Indiens
Cession et désignation
Articles 38-39

absolute, any right or interest of the band and its members in all or part of a reserve, for the purpose of its being leased or a right or interest therein being granted.

R.S., 1985, c. I-5, s. 38; R.S., 1985, c. 17 (4th Supp.), s. 2.

Conditions — surrender

39 (1) An absolute surrender is void unless

(a) it is made to Her Majesty;

(b) it is assented to by a majority of the electors of the band

(i) at a general meeting of the band called by the council of the band,

(ii) at a special meeting of the band called by the Minister for the purpose of considering a proposed absolute surrender, or

(iii) by a referendum as provided in the regulations; and

(c) it is accepted by the Governor in Council.

Minister may call meeting or referendum

(2) If a majority of the electors of a band did not vote at a meeting or referendum called under subsection (1), the Minister may, if the proposed absolute surrender was assented to by a majority of the electors who did vote, call another meeting by giving 30 days' notice of that other meeting or another referendum as provided in the regulations.

Assent of band

(3) If a meeting or referendum is called under subsection (2) and the proposed absolute surrender is assented to at the meeting or referendum by a majority of the electors voting, the surrender is deemed, for the purposes of this section, to have been assented to by a majority of the electors of the band.

Secret ballot

(4) The Minister may, at the request of the council of the band or whenever he considers it advisable, order that a vote at any meeting under this section shall be by secret ballot.

Majesté, avec ou sans conditions, autre qu'à titre absolu, tous droits de la bande, et ceux de ses membres, sur tout ou partie d'une réserve.

L.R. (1985), ch. I-5, art. 38; L.R. (1985), ch. 17 (4ᵉ suppl.), art. 2.

Conditions de validité : cession

39 (1) La cession à titre absolu n'est valide que si les conditions suivantes sont réunies :

a) elle est faite à Sa Majesté;

b) elle est sanctionnée par une majorité des électeurs de la bande :

(i) soit à une assemblée générale de la bande convoquée par son conseil,

(ii) soit à une assemblée spéciale de la bande convoquée par le ministre en vue d'examiner une proposition de cession à titre absolu,

(iii) soit au moyen d'un référendum comme le prévoient les règlements;

c) elle est acceptée par le gouverneur en conseil.

Assemblée de la bande ou référendum

(2) Lorsqu'une majorité des électeurs d'une bande n'ont pas voté à une assemblée convoquée, ou à un référendum tenu, au titre du paragraphe (1), le ministre peut, si la proposition de cession à titre absolu a reçu l'assentiment de la majorité des électeurs qui ont voté, convoquer une autre assemblée en en donnant un avis de trente jours, ou faire tenir un autre référendum comme le prévoient les règlements.

Assentiment de la bande

(3) Lorsqu'une assemblée est convoquée en vertu du paragraphe (2) ou qu'un référendum est tenu en vertu de ce paragraphe et que la proposition de cession à titre absolu est sanctionnée à l'assemblée ou lors du référendum par la majorité des électeurs votants, la cession est réputée, pour l'application du présent article, avoir été sanctionnée par une majorité des électeurs de la bande.

Scrutin secret

(4) Le ministre, à la demande du conseil de la bande ou chaque fois qu'il le juge opportun, peut ordonner qu'un vote, à toute assemblée prévue par le présent article, ait lieu au scrutin secret.

Indian
Surrenders and Designations
Sections 39-42

Indiens
Cession et désignation
Articles 39-42

Officials required

(5) Every meeting under this section shall be held in the presence of the superintendent or some other officer of the Department designated by the Minister.

R.S., 1985, c. I-5, s. 39; R.S., 1985, c. 17 (4th Supp.), s. 3; 2012, c. 31, s. 207.

Conditions — designation

39.1 A designation is valid if it is made to Her Majesty, is assented to by a majority of the electors of the band voting at a referendum held in accordance with the regulations, is recommended to the Minister by the council of the band and is accepted by the Minister.

2012, c. 31, s. 208.

Certification — surrender

40 A proposed absolute surrender that is assented to by the band in accordance with section 39 shall be certified on oath by the superintendent or other officer who attended the meeting and by the chief or a member of the council of the band and then submitted to the Governor in Council for acceptance or refusal.

R.S., 1985, c. I-5, s. 40; R.S., 1985, c. 17 (4th Supp.), s. 4; 2012, c. 31, s. 208.

Certification — designation

40.1 (1) A proposed designation that is assented to in accordance with section 39.1 shall be certified on oath by an officer of the Department and by the chief or a member of the council of the band.

Ministerial decision

(2) On the recommendation of the council of the band, the proposed designation shall be submitted to the Minister who may accept or reject it.

2012, c. 31, s. 208.

Effect of surrenders and designations

41 An absolute surrender or a designation shall be deemed to confer all rights that are necessary to enable Her Majesty to carry out the terms of the surrender or designation.

R.S., 1985, c. I-5, s. 41; R.S., 1985, c. 17 (4th Supp.), s. 4.

Descent of Property

Powers of Minister with respect to property of deceased Indians

42 (1) Subject to this Act, all jurisdiction and authority in relation to matters and causes testamentary, with respect to deceased Indians, is vested exclusively in the Minister and shall be exercised subject to and in accordance with regulations of the Governor in Council.

La présence de fonctionnaires est requise

(5) Chaque assemblée aux termes du présent article est tenue en présence du surintendant ou d'un autre fonctionnaire du ministère, que désigne le ministre.

L.R. (1985), ch. I-5, art. 39; L.R. (1985), ch. 17 (4ᵉ suppl.), art. 3; 2012, ch. 31, art. 207.

Conditions de validité : désignation

39.1 Est valide la désignation faite en faveur de Sa Majesté, sanctionnée par la majorité des électeurs de la bande ayant voté lors d'un référendum tenu conformément aux règlements, recommandée par le conseil de la bande au ministre et acceptée par celui-ci.

2012, ch. 31, art. 208.

Certificat : cession

40 La proposition de cession à titre absolu qui a été sanctionnée par la bande conformément à l'article 39 est attestée sous serment par le surintendant ou l'autre fonctionnaire qui a assisté à l'assemblée et par le chef ou un membre du conseil de la bande; elle est ensuite soumise au gouverneur en conseil pour acceptation ou rejet.

L.R. (1985), ch. I-5, art. 40; L.R. (1985), ch. 17 (4ᵉ suppl.), art. 4; 2012, ch. 31, art. 208.

Certificat : désignation

40.1 (1) La proposition de désignation qui a été sanctionnée conformément à l'article 39.1 est attestée sous serment par un fonctionnaire du ministère et par le chef ou un membre du conseil de la bande.

Décision ministérielle

(2) Sur la recommandation du conseil de la bande, la proposition de désignation est soumise au ministre qui peut l'accepter ou la rejeter.

2012, ch. 31, art. 208.

Effet de la cession et de la désignation

41 La cession à titre absolu ou la désignation est censée conférer tous les droits nécessaires pour permettre à Sa Majesté de donner effet aux conditions de la cession ou de la désignation.

L.R. (1985), ch. I-5, art. 41; L.R. (1985), ch. 17 (4ᵉ suppl.), art. 4.

Transmission de biens par droit de succession

Pouvoirs du ministre à l'égard des biens des Indiens décédés

42 (1) Sous réserve des autres dispositions de la présente loi, la compétence sur les questions testamentaires relatives aux Indiens décédés est attribuée exclusivement au ministre; elle est exercée en conformité avec les règlements pris par le gouverneur en conseil.

Indian
Descent of Property
Sections 42-44

Indiens
Transmission de biens par droit de succession
Articles 42-44

Regulations

(2) The Governor in Council may make regulations providing that a deceased Indian who at the time of his death was in possession of land in a reserve shall, in such circumstances and for such purposes as the regulations prescribe, be deemed to have been at the time of his death lawfully in possession of that land.

Application of regulations

(3) Regulations made under subsection (2) may be made applicable to estates of Indians who died before, on or after September 4, 1951.

R.S., c. I-6, s. 42.

Particular powers

43 Without restricting the generality of section 42, the Minister may

(a) appoint executors of wills and administrators of estates of deceased Indians, remove them and appoint others in their stead;

(b) authorize executors to carry out the terms of the wills of deceased Indians;

(c) authorize administrators to administer the property of Indians who die intestate;

(d) carry out the terms of wills of deceased Indians and administer the property of Indians who die intestate; and

(e) make or give any order, direction or finding that in his opinion it is necessary or desirable to make or give with respect to any matter referred to in section 42.

R.S., c. I-6, s. 43.

Courts may exercise jurisdiction with consent of Minister

44 (1) The court that would have jurisdiction if a deceased were not an Indian may, with the consent of the Minister, exercise, in accordance with this Act, the jurisdiction and authority conferred on the Minister by this Act in relation to testamentary matters and causes and any other powers, jurisdiction and authority ordinarily vested in that court.

Minister may refer a matter to the court

(2) The Minister may direct in any particular case that an application for the grant of probate of the will or letters of administration of a deceased shall be made to the court that would have jurisdiction if the deceased were not an Indian, and the Minister may refer to that court any question arising out of any will or the administration of any estate.

Règlements

(2) Le gouverneur en conseil peut prendre des règlements stipulant qu'un Indien décédé qui, au moment de son décès, était en possession de terres dans une réserve, sera réputé, en telles circonstances et à telles fins que prescrivent les règlements, avoir été légalement en possession de ces terres au moment de son décès.

Application des règlements

(3) Les règlements prévus par le paragraphe (2) peuvent être rendus applicables aux successions des Indiens morts avant ou après le 4 septembre 1951 ou à cette date.

S.R., ch. I-6, art. 42.

Pouvoirs particuliers

43 Sans que soit limitée la portée générale de l'article 42, le ministre peut :

a) nommer des exécuteurs testamentaires et des administrateurs de successions d'Indiens décédés, révoquer ces exécuteurs et administrateurs et les remplacer;

b) autoriser des exécuteurs à donner suite aux termes des testaments d'Indiens décédés;

c) autoriser des administrateurs à gérer les biens d'Indiens morts intestats;

d) donner effet aux testaments d'Indiens décédés et administrer les biens d'Indiens morts intestats;

e) prendre les arrêtés et donner les directives qu'il juge utiles à l'égard de quelque question mentionnée à l'article 42.

S.R., ch. I-6, art. 43.

Les tribunaux peuvent exercer leur compétence, avec le consentement du ministre

44 (1) Avec le consentement du ministre, le tribunal qui aurait compétence si la personne décédée n'était pas un Indien peut exercer, en conformité avec la présente loi, la compétence que la présente loi confère au ministre à l'égard des questions testamentaires, ainsi que tous autres pouvoirs et compétence ordinairement dévolus à ce tribunal.

Le ministre peut déférer des questions au tribunal

(2) Dans tout cas particulier, le ministre peut ordonner qu'une demande en vue d'obtenir l'homologation d'un testament ou l'émission de lettres d'administration soit présentée au tribunal qui aurait compétence si la personne décédée n'était pas un Indien. Il a la faculté de soumettre à ce tribunal toute question que peut faire surgir un testament ou l'administration d'une succession.

Indian
Descent of Property
Sections 44-46

Indiens
Transmission de biens par droit de succession
Articles 44-46

Orders relating to lands

(3) A court that is exercising any jurisdiction or authority under this section shall not without the consent in writing of the Minister enforce any order relating to real property on a reserve.

R.S., c. I-6, s. 44.

Wills

Indians may make wills

45 (1) Nothing in this Act shall be construed to prevent or prohibit an Indian from devising or bequeathing his property by will.

Form of will

(2) The Minister may accept as a will any written instrument signed by an Indian in which he indicates his wishes or intention with respect to the disposition of his property on his death.

Probate

(3) No will executed by an Indian is of any legal force or effect as a disposition of property until the Minister has approved the will or a court has granted probate thereof pursuant to this Act.

R.S., c. I-6, s. 45.

Minister may declare will void

46 (1) The Minister may declare the will of an Indian to be void in whole or in part if he is satisfied that

(a) the will was executed under duress or undue influence;

(b) the testator at the time of execution of the will lacked testamentary capacity;

(c) the terms of the will would impose hardship on persons for whom the testator had a responsibility to provide;

(d) the will purports to dispose of land in a reserve in a manner contrary to the interest of the band or contrary to this Act;

(e) the terms of the will are so vague, uncertain or capricious that proper administration and equitable distribution of the estate of the deceased would be difficult or impossible to carry out in accordance with this Act; or

(f) the terms of the will are against the public interest.

Ordonnances visant des terres

(3) Un tribunal qui exerce sa compétence sous le régime du présent article ne peut, sans le consentement écrit du ministre, faire exécuter une ordonnance visant des biens immeubles sur une réserve.

S.R., ch. I-6, art. 44.

Testaments

Les Indiens peuvent tester

45 (1) La présente loi n'a pas pour effet d'empêcher un Indien, ou de lui interdire, de transmettre ses biens par testament.

Forme de testaments

(2) Le ministre peut accepter comme testament tout document écrit signé par un Indien dans lequel celui-ci indique ses désirs ou intentions à l'égard de la disposition de ses biens lors de son décès.

Homologation

(3) Nul testament fait par un Indien n'a d'effet juridique comme disposition de biens tant qu'il n'a pas été approuvé par le ministre ou homologué par un tribunal en conformité avec la présente loi.

S.R., ch. I-6, art. 45.

Le ministre peut déclarer nul un testament

46 (1) Le ministre peut déclarer nul, en totalité ou en partie, le testament d'un Indien, s'il est convaincu de l'existence de l'une des circonstances suivantes :

a) le testament a été établi sous l'effet de la contrainte ou d'une influence indue;

b) au moment où il a fait ce testament, le testateur n'était pas habile à tester;

c) les clauses du testament seraient la cause de privations pour des personnes auxquelles le testateur était tenu de pourvoir;

d) le testament vise à disposer d'un terrain, situé dans une réserve, d'une façon contraire aux intérêts de la bande ou aux dispositions de la présente loi;

e) les clauses du testament sont si vagues, si incertaines ou si capricieuses que la bonne administration et la distribution équitable des biens de la personne décédée seraient difficiles ou impossibles à effectuer suivant la présente loi;

f) les clauses du testament sont contraires à l'intérêt public.

Indian
Wills
Sections 46-48

Indiens
Testaments
Articles 46-48

Where will declared void

(2) Where a will of an Indian is declared by the Minister or by a court to be wholly void, the person executing the will shall be deemed to have died intestate, and where the will is so declared to be void in part only, any bequest or devise affected thereby, unless a contrary intention appears in the will, shall be deemed to have lapsed.

R.S., c. I-6, s. 46.

Appeals

Appeal to Federal Court

47 A decision of the Minister made in the exercise of the jurisdiction or authority conferred on him by section 42, 43 or 46 may, within two months from the date thereof, be appealed by any person affected thereby to the Federal Court, if the amount in controversy in the appeal exceeds five hundred dollars or if the Minister consents to an appeal.

R.S., c. I-6, s. 47; R.S., c. 10(2nd Supp.), ss. 64, 65.

Distribution of Property on Intestacy

Surviving spouse's share

48 (1) Where the net value of the estate of an intestate does not, in the opinion of the Minister, exceed seventy-five thousand dollars or such other amount as may be fixed by order of the Governor in Council, the estate shall go to the survivor.

Idem

(2) Where the net value of the estate of an intestate, in the opinion of the Minister, exceeds seventy-five thousand dollars, or such other amount as may be fixed by order of the Governor in Council, seventy-five thousand dollars, or such other amount as may be fixed by order of the Governor in Council, shall go to the survivor, and

(a) if the intestate left no issue, the remainder shall go to the survivor,

(b) if the intestate left one child, one-half of the remainder shall go to the survivor, and

(c) if the intestate left more than one child, one-third of the remainder shall go to the survivor,

and where a child has died leaving issue and that issue is alive at the date of the intestate's death, the survivor shall take the same share of the estate as if the child had been living at that date.

Cas de nullité

(2) Lorsque le testament d'un Indien est déclaré entièrement nul par le ministre ou par un tribunal, la personne qui a fait ce testament est censée être morte intestat, et, lorsque le testament est ainsi déclaré nul en partie seulement, sauf indication d'une intention contraire y énoncée, tout legs de biens meubles ou immeubles visé de la sorte est réputé caduc.

S.R., ch. I-6, art. 46.

Appels

Appels à la Cour fédérale

47 Une décision rendue par le ministre dans l'exercice de la compétence que lui confère l'article 42, 43 ou 46 peut être portée en appel devant la Cour fédérale dans les deux mois de cette décision, par toute personne y intéressée, si la somme en litige dans l'appel dépasse cinq cents dollars ou si le ministre y consent.

S.R., ch. I-6, art. 47; S.R., ch. 10(2ᵉ suppl.), art. 64 et 65.

Distribution des biens ab intestat

Part du survivant

48 (1) Lorsque, de l'avis du ministre, la valeur nette de la succession d'un intestat n'excède pas soixante-quinze mille dollars ou tout autre montant fixé par décret du gouverneur en conseil, la succession est dévolue au survivant.

Idem

(2) Lorsque la valeur nette de la succession d'un intestat excède, de l'avis du ministre, soixante-quinze mille dollars ou tout autre montant fixé par décret du gouverneur en conseil, une somme de soixante-quinze mille dollars ou toute autre somme fixée par décret du gouverneur en conseil est dévolue au survivant et le reste est attribué de la façon suivante :

a) si l'intestat n'a pas laissé de descendant, le solde est dévolu au survivant;

b) si l'intestat a laissé un enfant, la moitié du solde est dévolue au survivant;

c) si l'intestat a laissé plus d'un enfant, le tiers du solde est dévolu au survivant,

et lorsqu'un enfant est décédé laissant des descendants et que ceux-ci sont vivants à la date du décès de l'intestat, le

Indian
Distribution of Property on Intestacy
Section 48

Indiens
Distribution des biens ab intestat
Article 48

survivant reçoit la même partie de la succession que si l'enfant avait vécu à cette date.

Where children not provided for

(3) Notwithstanding subsections (1) and (2),

(a) where in any particular case the Minister is satisfied that any children of the deceased will not be adequately provided for, he may direct that all or any part of the estate that would otherwise go to the survivor shall go to the children; and

(b) the Minister may direct that the survivor shall have the right to occupy any lands in a reserve that were occupied by the deceased at the time of death.

Distribution to issue

(4) Where an intestate dies leaving issue, his estate shall be distributed, subject to the rights of the survivor, if any, *per stirpes* among such issue.

Distribution to parents

(5) Where an intestate dies leaving no survivor or issue, the estate shall go to the parents of the deceased in equal shares if both are living, but if either of them is dead the estate shall go to the surviving parent.

Distribution to brothers, sisters and their issue

(6) Where an intestate dies leaving no survivor or issue or father or mother, his estate shall be distributed among his brothers and sisters in equal shares, and where any brother or sister is dead the children of the deceased brother or sister shall take the share their parent would have taken if living, but where the only persons entitled are children of deceased brothers and sisters, they shall take per capita.

Next-of-kin

(7) Where an intestate dies leaving no survivor, issue, father, mother, brother or sister, and no children of any deceased brother or sister, his estate shall go to his next-of-kin.

Distribution among next-of-kin

(8) Where an estate goes to the next-of-kin, it shall be distributed equally among the next-of-kin of equal degree of consanguinity to the intestate and those who legally represent them, but in no case shall representation be admitted after brothers' and sisters' children, and any interest in land in a reserve shall vest in Her Majesty

Cas où il n'est pas pourvu aux besoins des enfants

(3) Par dérogation aux paragraphes (1) et (2) :

a) si, dans un cas particulier, le ministre est convaincu qu'il ne sera pas suffisamment pourvu aux besoins de tout enfant du défunt, il peut ordonner que la totalité ou toute partie de la succession qui autrement irait au survivant soit dévolue à l'enfant;

b) le ministre peut ordonner que le survivant ait le droit d'occuper toutes terres situées dans une réserve que la personne décédée occupait au moment de son décès.

Distribution aux descendants

(4) Lorsqu'un intestat laisse à son décès des descendants, sa succession est, sous réserve des droits du survivant, s'il en est, distribuée par souche entre ces descendants.

Distribution aux parents

(5) Lorsqu'un intestat ne laisse à sa mort ni survivant ni descendant, sa succession est dévolue à ses parents en parts égales si tous deux sont vivants, ou au parent survivant si l'un des deux est décédé.

Distribution aux frères, sœurs et descendants de frères et sœurs

(6) Lorsqu'un intestat ne laisse à sa mort ni survivant, ni descendant, ni père, ni mère, sa succession est dévolue à ses frères et sœurs en parts égales, et, si l'un de ses frères ou sœurs est décédé, les enfants du frère ou de la sœur décédé reçoivent la part que leur père ou mère aurait reçue s'il avait été vivant, mais, lorsque les seuls ayants droit sont les enfants de frères et sœurs décédés, les biens leur sont distribués par tête.

Plus proche parent

(7) Lorsqu'un intestat ne laisse à sa mort ni survivant, ni descendant, ni père, ni mère, ni frère, ni sœur, ni enfant d'un frère décédé ou d'une sœur décédée, la succession est dévolue à son plus proche parent.

Distribution aux plus proches parents

(8) Lorsque la succession est dévolue aux plus proches parents, elle doit être distribuée en parts égales entre tous les plus proches parents à un même degré de consanguinité avec l'intestat et leurs représentants légaux, mais dans aucun cas la représentation ne peut être admise après les enfants des frères et sœurs, et tout droit sur un bien-fonds situé dans une réserve est dévolu à Sa

Indian
Distribution of Property on Intestacy
Sections 48-50

Indiens
Distribution des biens ab intestat
Articles 48-50

for the benefit of the band if the nearest of kin of the intestate is more remote than a brother or sister.

Degrees of kindred

(9) For the purposes of this section, degrees of kindred shall be computed by counting upward from the intestate to the nearest common ancestor and then downward to the relative, and the kindred of the half-blood shall inherit equally with those of the whole-blood in the same degree.

Descendants and relatives born after intestate's death

(10) Descendants and relatives of an intestate begotten before his death but born thereafter shall inherit as if they had been born in the lifetime of the intestate and had survived him.

Estate not disposed of by will

(11) All such estate as is not disposed of by will shall be distributed as if the testator had died intestate and had left no other estate.

No community of property

(12) There is no community of real or personal property situated in a reserve.

(13) and (14) [Repealed, R.S., 1985, c. 32 (1st Supp.), s. 9]

Equal application to men and women

(15) This section applies in respect of an intestate woman as it applies in respect of an intestate man.

(16) [Repealed, R.S., 1985, c. 32 (1st Supp.), s. 9]

R.S., 1985, c. I-5, s. 48; R.S., 1985, c. 32 (1st Supp.), s. 9, c. 48 (4th Supp.), s. 2; 2000, c. 12, ss. 149, 151.

Devisee's entitlement

49 A person who claims to be entitled to possession or occupation of lands in a reserve by devise or descent shall be deemed not to be in lawful possession or occupation of those lands until the possession is approved by the Minister.

R.S., c. I-6, s. 49.

Non-resident of reserve

50 (1) A person who is not entitled to reside on a reserve does not by devise or descent acquire a right to possession or occupation of land in that reserve.

Majesté au bénéfice de la bande si le plus proche parent de l'intestat est plus éloigné qu'un frère ou une sœur.

Degré de parenté

(9) Pour l'application du présent article, les degrés de parenté sont établis en remontant les générations à partir de l'intestat jusqu'au plus proche auteur commun et en redescendant jusqu'au parent en question; les parents d'un seul côté héritent à parts égales avec les parents des deux côtés au même degré.

Descendants et parents nés après la mort de l'intestat

(10) Les descendants et parents de l'intestat engendrés avant la mort de ce dernier mais nés ensuite héritent au même titre que s'ils étaient nés du vivant de l'intestat et lui avaient survécu.

Biens non aliénés par testament

(11) Tous les biens dont il n'est pas disposé par testament sont distribués comme si le testateur était mort intestat et n'avait laissé aucun autre bien.

Absence de communauté de biens

(12) Il n'y a aucune communauté de biens meubles ou immeubles situés dans une réserve.

(13) et (14) [Abrogés, L.R. (1985), ch. 32 (1er suppl.), art. 9]

Application aux personnes des deux sexes

(15) Le présent article s'applique à l'égard d'une femme intestat de la même manière qu'à l'égard d'un homme intestat.

(16) [Abrogé, L.R. (1985), ch. 32 (1er suppl.), art. 9]

L.R. (1985), ch. I-5, art. 48; L.R. (1985), ch. 32 (1er suppl.), art. 9, ch. 48 (4e suppl.), art. 2; 2000, ch. 12, art. 149 et 151.

Droit du légataire

49 Une personne qui prétend avoir droit à la possession ou à l'occupation de terres situées dans une réserve en raison d'un legs ou d'une transmission par droit de succession est censée ne pas en avoir la possession ou l'occupation légitime tant que le ministre n'a pas approuvé cette possession.

S.R., ch. I-6, art. 49.

Non-résident d'une réserve

50 (1) Une personne non autorisée à résider dans une réserve n'acquiert pas, par legs ou transmission sous forme de succession, le droit de posséder ou d'occuper une terre dans cette réserve.

Indian
Distribution of Property on Intestacy
Sections 50-51

Indiens
Distribution des biens ab intestat
Articles 50-51

Sale by superintendent

(2) Where a right to possession or occupation of land in a reserve passes by devise or descent to a person who is not entitled to reside on a reserve, that right shall be offered for sale by the superintendent to the highest bidder among persons who are entitled to reside on the reserve and the proceeds of the sale shall be paid to the devisee or descendant, as the case may be.

Unsold lands revert to band

(3) Where no tender is received within six months or such further period as the Minister may direct after the date when the right to possession or occupation of land is offered for sale under subsection (2), the right shall revert to the band free from any claim on the part of the devisee or descendant, subject to the payment, at the discretion of the Minister, to the devisee or descendant, from the funds of the band, of such compensation for permanent improvements as the Minister may determine.

Approval required

(4) The purchaser of a right to possession or occupation of land under subsection (2) shall be deemed not to be in lawful possession or occupation of the land until the possession is approved by the Minister.

R.S., c. I-6, s. 50.

Regulations

50.1 The Governor in Council may make regulations respecting circumstances where more than one person qualifies as a survivor of an intestate under section 48.

2000, c. 12, s. 150.

Mentally Incompetent Indians

Powers of Minister generally

51 (1) Subject to this section, all jurisdiction and authority in relation to the property of mentally incompetent Indians is vested exclusively in the Minister.

Particular powers

(2) Without restricting the generality of subsection (1), the Minister may

(a) appoint persons to administer the estates of mentally incompetent Indians;

Vente par le surintendant

(2) Lorsqu'un droit à la possession ou à l'occupation de terres dans une réserve est dévolu, par legs ou transmission sous forme de succession, à une personne non autorisée à y résider, ce droit doit être offert en vente par le surintendant au plus haut enchérisseur entre les personnes habiles à résider dans la réserve et le produit de la vente doit être versé au légataire ou au descendant, selon le cas.

Les terres non vendues retournent à la bande

(3) Si, dans les six mois ou tout délai supplémentaire que peut déterminer le ministre, à compter de la mise en vente du droit à la possession ou occupation d'une terre, en vertu du paragraphe (2), il n'est reçu aucune soumission, le droit retourne à la bande, libre de toute réclamation de la part du légataire ou descendant, sous réserve du versement, à la discrétion du ministre, au légataire ou descendant, sur les fonds de la bande, de l'indemnité pour améliorations permanentes que le ministre peut déterminer.

Approbation requise

(4) L'acheteur d'un droit à la possession ou occupation d'une terre sous le régime du paragraphe (2) n'est pas censé avoir la possession ou l'occupation légitime de la terre tant que le ministre n'a pas approuvé la possession.

S.R., ch. I-6, art. 50.

Pouvoir réglementaire

50.1 Le gouverneur en conseil peut, par règlement, régir les cas où il existe plus d'un survivant à l'égard du même intestat visé à l'article 48.

2000, ch. 12, art. 150.

Indiens mentalement incapables

Pouvoirs du ministre, en général

51 (1) Sous réserve des autres dispositions du présent article, la compétence à l'égard des biens des Indiens mentalement incapables est attribuée exclusivement au ministre.

Pouvoirs particuliers

(2) Sans que soit limitée la portée générale du paragraphe (1), le ministre peut :

a) nommer des personnes pour administrer les biens des Indiens mentalement incapables;

b) ordonner que tout bien d'un Indien mentalement incapable soit vendu, loué, aliéné, hypothéqué, qu'il en

Indian
Mentally Incompetent Indians
Sections 51-52.1

Indiens
Indiens mentalement incapables
Articles 51-52.1

(b) order that any property of a mentally incompetent Indian shall be sold, leased, alienated, mortgaged, disposed of or otherwise dealt with for the purpose of

    (i) paying his debts or engagements,

    (ii) discharging encumbrances on his property,

    (iii) paying debts or expenses incurred for his maintenance or otherwise for his benefit, or

    (iv) paying or providing for the expenses of future maintenance; and

(c) make such orders and give such directions as he considers necessary to secure the satisfactory management of the estates of mentally incompetent Indians.

Property off reserve

(3) The Minister may order that any property situated off a reserve and belonging to a mentally incompetent Indian shall be dealt with under the laws of the province in which the property is situated.
R.S., c. I-6, s. 51.

Guardianship

Property of infant children

52 The Minister may administer or provide for the administration of any property to which infant children of Indians are entitled, and may appoint guardians for that purpose.
R.S., c. I-6, s. 52.

Money of Infant Children

Distributions of capital

52.1 (1) The council of a band may determine that the payment of not more than three thousand dollars, or such other amount as may be fixed by order of the Governor in Council, in a year of the share of a distribution under paragraph 64(1)(a) that belongs to an infant child who is a member of the band is necessary or proper for the maintenance, advancement or other benefit of the child.

Procedure

(2) Before making a determination under subsection (1), the council of the band must

    (a) post in a conspicuous place on the reserve fourteen days before the determination is made a notice that it proposes to make such a determination; and

soit disposé ou que d'autres mesures soient prises à son égard aux fins, selon le cas :

    (i) d'acquitter ses dettes ou engagements,

    (ii) de dégrever ses biens,

    (iii) d'acquitter les dettes ou les dépenses subies pour son entretien ou autrement à son avantage,

    (iv) d'acquitter les frais de l'entretien ultérieur ou d'y pourvoir;

c) prendre les arrêtés et donner les instructions qu'il juge nécessaires pour assurer l'administration satisfaisante des biens des Indiens mentalement incapables.

Biens situés en dehors d'une réserve

(3) Le ministre peut ordonner que tout bien situé en dehors d'une réserve et appartenant à un Indien mentalement incapable soit traité selon la législation de la province où le bien est situé.
S.R., ch. I-6, art. 51.

Tutelle

Biens d'enfants mineurs

52 Le ministre peut administrer tous biens auxquels les enfants mineurs d'Indiens ont droit, ou en assurer l'administration, et il peut nommer des tuteurs à cette fin.
S.R., ch. I-6, art. 52.

Fonds des mineurs

Versement

52.1 (1) Le conseil d'une bande peut statuer que le versement de la fraction dévolue, à la suite du partage visé à l'alinéa 64(1)a), à un enfant mineur qui est membre de la bande est dans l'intérêt de l'enfant, notamment pour son entretien ou son épanouissement. Ce versement ne peut toutefois excéder trois mille dollars par an ou le montant fixé par décret du gouverneur en conseil.

Procédure

(2) Le cas échéant, le conseil affiche un avis de son intention, en un lieu bien en évidence dans la réserve, quatorze jours avant de prendre sa décision et donne aux membres de la bande la possibilité de présenter leurs observations lors d'une assemblée générale tenue avant la prise de la décision.

Indian
Money of Infant Children
Sections 52.1-52.3

Indiens
Fonds des mineurs
Articles 52.1-52.3

(b) give the members of the band a reasonable opportunity to be heard at a general meeting of the band held before the determination is made.

Minister's duty

(3) Where the council of the band makes a determination under subsection (1) and notifies the Minister, at the time it gives its consent to the distribution pursuant to paragraph 64(1)(a), that it has made that determination and that, before making it, it complied with subsection (2), the Minister shall make a payment described in subsection (1) for the maintenance, advancement or other benefit of the child to a parent or person who is responsible for the care and custody of the child or, if so requested by the council on giving its consent to that distribution, to the council.

R.S., 1985, c. 48 (4th Supp.), s. 3.

Money of infant children of Indians

52.2 The Minister may, regardless of whether a payment is made under section 52.1, pay all or part of any money administered by the Minister under section 52 that belongs to an infant child of an Indian to a parent or person who is responsible for the care and custody of the child or otherwise apply all or part of that money if

(a) the Minister is requested in writing to do so by the parent or the person responsible; and

(b) in the opinion of the Minister, the payment or application is necessary or proper for the maintenance, advancement or other benefit of the child.

R.S., 1985, c. 48 (4th Supp.), s. 3.

Attaining majority

52.3 (1) Where a child of an Indian attains the age of majority, the Minister shall pay any money administered by the Minister under section 52 to which the child is entitled to that child in one lump sum.

Exception

(2) Notwithstanding subsection (1), where requested in writing to do so before a child of an Indian attains the age of majority by a parent or a person who is responsible for the care and custody of the child or by the council of the band of which the child is a member, the Minister may, instead of paying the money in one lump sum, pay it in instalments during a period beginning on the day the child attains the age of majority and ending not later than the day that is three years after that day.

R.S., 1985, c. 48 (4th Supp.), s. 3.

Versement obligatoire

(3) Le ministre est tenu d'effectuer le versement mentionné au paragraphe (1) soit à un parent ou au détenteur de l'autorité parentale, soit, s'il le demande, au conseil de la bande lorsque celui-ci a d'une part, statué dans le sens prévu à ce paragraphe et, d'autre part, certifié au ministre, lors de l'acceptation du partage visé à l'alinéa 64(1)a), la conformité de cette décision à la procédure établie.

L.R. (1985), ch. 48 (4ᵉ suppl.), art. 3.

Fonds des mineurs

52.2 Sur demande écrite d'un parent ou du détenteur de l'autorité parentale, le ministre peut, sans qu'il soit tenu compte de tout versement effectué au titre de l'article 52.1, soit lui verser, en tout ou en partie, les sommes d'argent gérées par lui conformément à l'article 52 et appartenant aux enfants mineurs d'Indiens s'il l'estime être dans leur intérêt, notamment pour leur entretien ou leur épanouissement, soit les verser pour leur compte.

L.R. (1985), ch. 48 (4ᵉ suppl.), art. 3.

Paiement à la majorité

52.3 (1) Le ministre est tenu de remettre, en un versement unique, toute somme d'argent gérée au titre de l'article 52 à l'Indien qui y a droit et a atteint sa majorité.

Exception

(2) Sur demande écrite — avant que l'Indien atteigne sa majorité — d'un parent ou du détenteur de l'autorité parentale ou du conseil de la bande dont l'intéressé est membre, le ministre peut toutefois payer la somme en versements échelonnés à compter de la date de la majorité pendant au plus trois ans après celle-ci.

L.R. (1985), ch. 48 (4ᵉ suppl.), art. 3.

Indian
Money of Infant Children
Sections 52.4-53

Indiens
Fonds des mineurs
Articles 52.4-53

Relief

52.4 Where, in a proceeding in respect of the share of a distribution under paragraph 64(1)(a) or of money belonging to an infant child that was paid pursuant to section 52.1, 52.2 or 52.3, it appears to the court that the Minister, the band, its council or a member of that council acted honestly and reasonably and ought fairly to be relieved from liability in respect of the payment, the court may relieve the Minister, band, council or member, either in whole or in part, from liability in respect of the payment.

R.S., 1985, c. 48 (4th Supp.), s. 3; 1992, c. 1, s. 144(F).

Effect of payment

52.5 (1) The receipt in writing from a parent or person who is responsible for the care and custody of an infant child for a payment made pursuant to section 52.1 or 52.2

(a) discharges the duty of the Minister, the band, its council and each member of that council to make the payment to the extent of the amount paid; and

(b) discharges the Minister, the band, its council and each member of that council from seeing to its application or being answerable for its loss or misapplication.

Idem

(2) The receipt in writing from the council of the band of which an infant child is a member for a payment made pursuant to section 52.1

(a) discharges the duty of the Minister to make the payment to the extent of the amount paid; and

(b) discharges the Minister from seeing to the application of the amount paid or being answerable for its loss or misapplication.

R.S., 1985, c. 48 (4th Supp.), s. 3.

Management of Reserves and Surrendered and Designated Lands

Transactions re surrendered and designated lands

53 (1) The Minister or a person appointed by the Minister for the purpose may, in accordance with this Act and the terms of the absolute surrender or designation, as the case may be,

(a) manage or sell absolutely surrendered lands; or

Libération

52.4 Le tribunal peut, dans toute affaire relative au versement d'une fraction dévolue à un enfant mineur dans le cadre du partage visé à l'alinéa 64(1)a) et effectué en application des articles 52.1, 52.2 ou 52.3, libérer, en tout ou en partie, le ministre, la bande, son conseil ou les membres de celui-ci de toute responsabilité à cet égard lorsqu'il lui apparaît que tel d'entre eux, ayant agi honnêtement et raisonnablement, devrait, en toute justice, l'être.

L.R. (1985), ch. 48 (4ᵉ suppl.), art. 3; 1992, ch. 1, art. 144(F).

Effet du versement

52.5 (1) L'accusé de réception transmis par le destinataire — parent ou détenteur de l'autorité parentale — du versement visé à l'article 52.1 ou 52.2 libère le ministre, la bande, son conseil et les membres de celui-ci, à concurrence du montant versé, de son obligation, ainsi que de toute responsabilité à l'égard de celui-ci ou de son éventuel détournement.

Idem

(2) L'accusé de réception transmis par le destinataire — conseil de la bande dont l'enfant est membre — du versement visé à l'article 52.1 libère le ministre, à concurrence du montant versé, de son obligation, ainsi que de toute responsabilité à l'égard de celui-ci ou de son éventuel détournement.

L.R. (1985), ch. 48 (4ᵉ suppl.), art. 3.

Administration des réserves et des terres cédées ou désignées

Opérations concernant les terres cédées ou désignées

53 (1) Le ministre ou son délégué peut, conformément à la présente loi et aux conditions de la cession à titre absolu ou de la désignation :

a) administrer ou vendre les terres cédées à titre absolu;

Indian
Management of Reserves and Surrendered and Designated Lands
Sections 53-55

Indiens
Administration des réserves et des terres cédées ou désignées
Articles 53-55

(b) manage, lease or carry out any other transaction affecting designated lands.

Grant where original purchaser dead

(2) Where the original purchaser of surrendered lands is dead and the heir, assignee or devisee of the original purchaser applies for a grant of the lands, the Minister may, on receipt of proof in such manner as he directs and requires in support of any claim for the grant and on being satisfied that the claim has been equitably and justly established, allow the claim and authorize a grant to issue accordingly.

Departmental employees

(3) No person who is appointed pursuant to subsection (1) or who is an officer or a servant of Her Majesty employed in the Department may, except with the approval of the Governor in Council, acquire directly or indirectly any interest in absolutely surrendered or designated lands.

R.S., 1985, c. I-5, s. 53; R.S., 1985, c. 17 (4th Supp.), s. 5.

Assignments

54 Where absolutely surrendered lands are agreed to be sold and letters patent relating thereto have not issued, or where designated lands are leased or an interest in them granted, the purchaser, lessee or other person who has an interest in the absolutely surrendered or designated lands may, with the approval of the Minister, assign all or part of that interest to any other person.

R.S., 1985, c. I-5, s. 54; R.S., 1985, c. 17 (4th Supp.), s. 6.

Surrendered and Designated Lands Register

55 (1) There shall be maintained in the Department a register, to be known as the Surrendered and Designated Lands Register, in which shall be recorded particulars in connection with any transaction affecting absolutely surrendered or designated lands.

Conditional assignment

(2) A conditional assignment shall not be registered.

Proof of execution

(3) Registration of an assignment may be refused until proof of its execution has been furnished.

Concession lorsque l'acquéreur initial est décédé

(2) Lorsque l'acquéreur initial de terres cédées est mort et que l'héritier, cessionnaire ou légataire de l'acquéreur initial demande une concession des terres, le ministre peut, sur réception d'une preuve d'après la manière qu'il ordonne et exige à l'appui de toute demande visant cette concession et lorsqu'il est convaincu que la demande a été établie de façon juste et équitable, agréer la demande et autoriser la délivrance d'une concession en conséquence.

Fonctionnaires du ministère

(3) La personne qui est nommée à titre de délégué conformément au paragraphe (1), ou qui est un fonctionnaire ou préposé de Sa Majesté à l'emploi du ministère, ne peut, sauf approbation du gouverneur en conseil, acquérir directement ou indirectement d'intérêts dans des terres cédées à titre absolu ou désignées.

L.R. (1985), ch. I-5, art. 53; L.R. (1985), ch. 17 (4ᵉ suppl.), art. 5.

Transfert

54 Lorsqu'il a été convenu de la vente de terres cédées à titre absolu et que des lettres patentes n'ont pas été délivrées à leur égard, ou lorsque des terres désignées ont été données à bail ou ont fait l'objet d'un démembrement, l'acheteur, le locataire ou toute autre personne ayant un droit sur ces terres peut, avec l'approbation du ministre, transférer à toute autre personne tout ou partie de son droit.

L.R. (1985), ch. I-5, art. 54; L.R. (1985), ch. 17 (4ᵉ suppl.), art. 6.

Registre des terres cédées ou désignées

55 (1) Est tenu au ministère un registre, appelé Registre des terres cédées ou désignées, dans lequel sont consignés tous les détails relatifs à toute opération touchant les terres cédées à titre absolu ou désignées.

Transfert conditionnel

(2) Un transfert conditionnel n'est pas enregistré.

Preuve de souscription

(3) L'inscription d'un transfert peut être refusée tant que la preuve de l'établissement de cet acte n'a pas été fournie.

Indian
Management of Reserves and Surrendered and Designated Lands
Sections 55-58

Indiens
Administration des réserves et des terres cédées ou désignées
Articles 55-58

Effect of registration

(4) An assignment registered under this section is valid against an unregistered assignment or an assignment subsequently registered.

R.S., 1985, c. I-5, s. 55; R.S., 1985, c. 17 (4th Supp.), s. 7.

Certificate of registration

56 Where an assignment is registered, there shall be endorsed on the original copy thereof a certificate of registration signed by the Minister or by an officer of the Department authorized by the Minister to sign such certificates.

R.S., c. I-6, s. 56.

Regulations

57 The Governor in Council may make regulations

(a) authorizing the Minister to grant licences to cut timber on surrendered lands, or, with the consent of the council of the band, on reserve lands;

(b) imposing terms, conditions and restrictions with respect to the exercise of rights conferred by licences granted under paragraph (a);

(c) providing for the disposition of surrendered mines and minerals underlying lands in a reserve;

(d) prescribing the punishment, not exceeding one hundred dollars or imprisonment for a term not exceeding three months or both, that may be imposed on summary conviction for contravention of any regulation made under this section; and

(e) providing for the seizure and forfeiture of any timber or minerals taken in contravention of any regulation made under this section.

R.S., c. I-6, s. 57.

Uncultivated or unused lands

58 (1) Where land in a reserve is uncultivated or unused, the Minister may, with the consent of the council of the band,

(a) improve or cultivate that land and employ persons therefor, and authorize and direct the expenditure of such amount of the capital funds of the band as he considers necessary for that improvement or cultivation including the purchase of such stock, machinery or material or for the employment of such labour as the Minister considers necessary;

Effet de l'inscription

(4) Un transfert enregistré selon le présent article est valide à l'encontre d'un transfert non enregistré ou d'un transfert enregistré subséquemment.

L.R. (1985), ch. I-5, art. 55; L.R. (1985), ch. 17 (4ᵉ suppl.), art. 7.

Certificat d'enregistrement

56 Lorsqu'un transfert est enregistré, on appose sur la copie originale de l'acte un certificat d'enregistrement signé par le ministre ou par un fonctionnaire du ministère que le ministre autorise à signer.

S.R., ch. I-6, art. 56.

Règlements

57 Le gouverneur en conseil peut prendre des règlements :

a) autorisant le ministre à accorder des permis de couper du bois sur des terres cédées ou, avec le consentement du conseil de la bande, sur des terres de réserve;

b) établissant des conditions et des restrictions à l'égard de l'exercice des droits conférés par les permis accordés sous le régime de l'alinéa a);

c) pourvoyant à l'aliénation de mines et minéraux cédés dans le sous-sol d'une réserve;

d) prescrivant l'amende maximale de cent dollars et l'emprisonnement maximal de trois mois, ou l'une de ces peines, qui peuvent être infligés, sur déclaration de culpabilité par procédure sommaire, pour infraction à l'un des règlements prévus au présent article;

e) prévoyant la saisie et la confiscation du bois ou des minéraux pris en violation d'un règlement pris en vertu du présent article.

S.R., ch. I-6, art. 57.

Terrains incultes ou inutilisés

58 (1) Lorsque, dans une réserve, un terrain est inculte ou inutilisé, le ministre peut, avec le consentement du conseil de la bande :

a) améliorer ou cultiver le terrain et employer des personnes à cette fin, autoriser et prescrire la dépense de telle partie des fonds en capital de la bande qu'il juge nécessaire à l'amélioration ou à la culture, y compris l'achat du bétail, des machines ou du matériel ou l'emploi de la main-d'œuvre qu'il estime nécessaire;

b) si le terrain est en la possession légitime d'un particulier, accorder la location de ce terrain à des fins de

(b) where the land is in the lawful possession of any individual, grant a lease of that land for agricultural or grazing purposes or for any purpose that is for the benefit of the person in possession of the land; and

(c) where the land is not in the lawful possession of any individual, grant for the benefit of the band a lease of that land for agricultural or grazing purposes.

Distribution of proceeds

(2) Out of the proceeds derived from the improvement or cultivation of lands pursuant to paragraph (1)(b), a reasonable rent shall be paid to the individual in lawful possession of the lands or any part thereof and the remainder of the proceeds shall be placed to the credit of the band, but if improvements are made on the lands occupied by an individual, the Minister may deduct the value of the improvements from the rent payable to the individual under this subsection.

Lease at request of occupant

(3) The Minister may lease for the benefit of any Indian, on application of that Indian for that purpose, the land of which the Indian is lawfully in possession without the land being designated.

Disposition of grass, timber, non-metallic substances, etc.

(4) Notwithstanding anything in this Act, the Minister may, without an absolute surrender or a designation

(a) dispose of wild grass or dead or fallen timber; and

(b) with the consent of the council of the band, dispose of sand, gravel, clay and other non-metallic substances on or under lands in a reserve, or, where that consent cannot be obtained without undue difficulty or delay, may issue temporary permits for the taking of sand, gravel, clay and other non-metallic substances on or under lands in a reserve, renewable only with the consent of the council of the band.

Proceeds

(5) The proceeds of the transactions referred to in subsection (4) shall be credited to band funds or shall be divided between the band and the individual Indians in lawful possession of the lands in such shares as the Minister may determine.

R.S., 1985, c. I-5, s. 58; R.S., 1985, c. 17 (4th Supp.), s. 8.

culture ou de pâturage ou à toute fin se trouvant au profit de la personne qui en a la possession;

c) si le terrain n'est pas en la possession légitime d'un particulier, accorder la location du terrain, au profit de la bande, à des fins de culture ou de pâturage.

Distribution du produit

(2) Sur les montants provenant de l'amélioration ou de la culture de terrains selon l'alinéa (1)b), un loyer raisonnable est versé au particulier en possession légitime des terrains ou une partie de ceux-ci, et le solde est porté au crédit de la bande. Toutefois, lorsque des améliorations sont apportées à des terrains occupés par un particulier, le ministre peut déduire, du loyer payable à celui-ci sous le régime du présent paragraphe, la valeur de ces améliorations.

Location à la demande de l'occupant

(3) Le ministre peut louer au profit de tout Indien, à la demande de celui-ci, la terre dont ce dernier est en possession légitime sans que celle-ci soit désignée.

Aliénation d'herbes, de bois et de substances non métalliques, etc.

(4) Nonobstant toute autre disposition de la présente loi, le ministre peut, sans cession à titre absolu ou désignation :

a) disposer des herbes sauvages ou du bois mort sur pied ou du chablis;

b) avec le consentement du conseil de la bande, disposer du sable, du gravier, de la glaise et des autres substances non métalliques se trouvant sur des terres ou dans le sous-sol d'une réserve, ou lorsque ce consentement ne peut être obtenu sans obstacle ou retard indu, peut délivrer des permis temporaires pour la prise du sable, du gravier, de la glaise et d'autres substances non métalliques sur des terres ou dans le sous-sol d'une réserve, renouvelables avec le consentement du conseil de la bande seulement.

Produit

(5) Le produit de ces opérations doit être porté au crédit des fonds de bande ou partagé entre la bande et les Indiens particuliers en possession légitime des terres selon les proportions que le ministre peut déterminer.

L.R. (1985), ch. I-5, art. 58; L.R. (1985), ch. 17 (4e suppl.), art. 8.

Indian
Management of Reserves and Surrendered and Designated Lands
Sections 59-62

Indiens
Administration des réserves et des terres cédées ou désignées
Articles 59-62

Adjustment of contracts

59 The Minister may, with the consent of the council of a band,

(a) reduce or adjust the amount payable to Her Majesty in respect of a transaction affecting absolutely surrendered lands, designated lands or other lands in a reserve or the rate of interest payable thereon; and

(b) reduce or adjust the amount payable to the band by an Indian in respect of a loan made to the Indian from band funds.

R.S., 1985, c. I-5, s. 59; R.S., 1985, c. 17 (4th Supp.), s. 9.

Control over lands

60 (1) The Governor in Council may at the request of a band grant to the band the right to exercise such control and management over lands in the reserve occupied by that band as the Governor in Council considers desirable.

Withdrawal

(2) The Governor in Council may at any time withdraw from a band a right conferred on the band under subsection (1).

R.S., c. I-6, s. 60.

Management of Indian Moneys

Indian moneys to be held for use and benefit

61 (1) Indian moneys shall be expended only for the benefit of the Indians or bands for whose use and benefit in common the moneys are received or held, and subject to this Act and to the terms of any treaty or surrender, the Governor in Council may determine whether any purpose for which Indian moneys are used or are to be used is for the use and benefit of the band.

Interest

(2) Interest on Indian moneys held in the Consolidated Revenue Fund shall be allowed at a rate to be fixed from time to time by the Governor in Council.

R.S., c. I-6, s. 61.

Capital and revenue

62 All Indian moneys derived from the sale of surrendered lands or the sale of capital assets of a band shall be deemed to be capital moneys of the band and all Indian moneys other than capital moneys shall be deemed to be revenue moneys of the band.

R.S., c. I-6, s. 62.

Ajustement de contrats

59 Avec le consentement du conseil d'une bande, le ministre peut :

a) réduire ou ajuster le montant payable à Sa Majesté à l'égard de toute opération touchant des terres cédées à titre absolu, des terres désignées ou toute autre terre située dans une réserve, ou le taux d'intérêt payable à cet égard;

b) réduire ou ajuster le montant qu'un Indien doit payer à la bande pour un prêt consenti à cet Indien sur les fonds de la bande.

L.R. (1985), ch. I-5, art. 59; L.R. (1985), ch. 17 (4ᵉ suppl.), art. 9.

Contrôle sur des terres

60 (1) À la demande d'une bande, le gouverneur en conseil peut lui accorder le droit d'exercer, sur des terres situées dans une réserve qu'elle occupe, le contrôle et l'administration qu'il estime désirables.

Retrait

(2) Le gouverneur en conseil peut retirer à une bande un droit qui lui a été conféré sous le régime du paragraphe (1).

S.R., ch. I-6, art. 60.

Administration de l'argent des indiens

L'argent des Indiens est détenu pour usage et profit

61 (1) L'argent des Indiens ne peut être dépensé qu'au bénéfice des Indiens ou des bandes à l'usage et au profit communs desquels il est reçu ou détenu, et, sous réserve des autres dispositions de la présente loi et des clauses de tout traité ou cession, le gouverneur en conseil peut décider si les fins auxquelles l'argent des Indiens est employé ou doit l'être, est à l'usage et au profit de la bande.

Intérêts

(2) Les intérêts sur l'argent des Indiens détenu au Trésor sont alloués au taux que fixe le gouverneur en conseil.

S.R., ch. I-6, art. 61.

Capital et revenu

62 L'argent des Indiens qui provient de la vente de terres cédées ou de biens de capital d'une bande est réputé appartenir au compte en capital de la bande; les autres sommes d'argent des Indiens sont réputées appartenir au compte de revenu de la bande.

S.R., ch. I-6, art. 62.

Indian
Management of Indian Moneys
Sections 63-64

Indiens
Administration de l'argent des indiens
Articles 63-64

Payments to Indians

63 Notwithstanding the *Financial Administration Act*, where moneys to which an Indian is entitled are paid to a superintendent under any lease or agreement made under this Act, the superintendent may pay the moneys to the Indian.

R.S., c. I-6, s. 63.

Expenditure of capital moneys with consent

64 (1) With the consent of the council of a band, the Minister may authorize and direct the expenditure of capital moneys of the band

(a) to distribute per capita to the members of the band an amount not exceeding fifty per cent of the capital moneys of the band derived from the sale of surrendered lands;

(b) to construct and maintain roads, bridges, ditches and watercourses on reserves or on surrendered lands;

(c) to construct and maintain outer boundary fences on reserves;

(d) to purchase land for use by the band as a reserve or as an addition to a reserve;

(e) to purchase for the band the interest of a member of the band in lands on a reserve;

(f) to purchase livestock and farm implements, farm equipment or machinery for the band;

(g) to construct and maintain on or in connection with a reserve such permanent improvements or works as in the opinion of the Minister will be of permanent value to the band or will constitute a capital investment;

(h) to make to members of the band, for the purpose of promoting the welfare of the band, loans not exceeding one-half of the total value of

(i) the chattels owned by the borrower, and

(ii) the land with respect to which he holds or is eligible to receive a Certificate of Possession,

and may charge interest and take security therefor;

(i) to meet expenses necessarily incidental to the management of lands on a reserve, surrendered lands and any band property;

Versements aux Indiens

63 Par dérogation à la *Loi sur la gestion des finances publiques*, lorsque des sommes d'argent auxquelles un Indien a droit sont versées à un surintendant en vertu d'un bail ou d'une entente passé sous le régime de la présente loi, le surintendant peut remettre ces sommes à l'Indien.

S.R., ch. I-6, art. 63.

Dépense de sommes d'argent au compte en capital avec consentement

64 (1) Avec le consentement du conseil d'une bande, le ministre peut autoriser et prescrire la dépense de sommes d'argent au compte en capital de la bande :

a) pour distribuer *per capita* aux membres de la bande un montant maximal de cinquante pour cent des sommes d'argent au compte en capital de la bande, provenant de la vente de terres cédées;

b) pour construire et entretenir des routes, ponts, fossés et cours d'eau dans des réserves ou sur des terres cédées;

c) pour construire et entretenir des clôtures de délimitation extérieure sur les réserves;

d) pour acheter des terrains que la bande emploiera comme réserve ou comme addition à une réserve;

e) pour acheter pour la bande les droits d'un membre de la bande sur des terrains sur une réserve;

f) pour acheter des animaux, des instruments ou de l'outillage de ferme ou des machines pour la bande;

g) pour établir et entretenir dans une réserve ou à l'égard d'une réserve les améliorations ou ouvrages permanents qui, de l'avis du ministre, seront d'une valeur permanente pour la bande ou constitueront un placement en capital;

h) pour consentir aux membres de la bande, en vue de favoriser son bien-être, des prêts n'excédant pas la moitié de la valeur globale des éléments suivants :

(i) les biens meubles appartenant à l'emprunteur,

(ii) la terre concernant laquelle il détient ou a le droit de recevoir un certificat de possession,

et percevoir des intérêts et recevoir des gages à cet égard;

Indian
Management of Indian Moneys
Sections 64-64.1

Indiens
Administration de l'argent des indiens
Articles 64-64.1

(j) to construct houses for members of the band, to make loans to members of the band for building purposes with or without security and to provide for the guarantee of loans made to members of the band for building purposes; and

(k) for any other purpose that in the opinion of the Minister is for the benefit of the band.

Expenditure of capital moneys in accordance with by-laws

(2) The Minister may make expenditures out of the capital moneys of a band in accordance with by-laws made pursuant to paragraph 81(1)(p.3) for the purpose of making payments to any person whose name was deleted from the Band List of the band in an amount not exceeding one per capita share of the capital moneys.

R.S., 1985, c. I-5, s. 64; R.S., 1985, c. 32 (1st Supp.), s. 10.

Expenditure of capital moneys with consent

64.1 (1) A person who has received an amount that exceeds $1,000 under paragraph 15(1)(a), as it read immediately before April 17, 1985, or under any former provision of this Act relating to the same subject matter as that paragraph, by reason of ceasing to be a member of a band in the circumstances set out in paragraph 6(1)(a.1), (d) or (e) is not entitled to receive an amount under paragraph 64(1)(a) until such time as the aggregate of all amounts that the person would, but for this subsection, have received under paragraph 64(1)(a) is equal to the amount by which the amount that the person received under paragraph 15(1)(a), as it read immediately before April 17, 1985, or under any former provision of this Act relating to the same subject matter as that paragraph, exceeds $1,000, together with any interest.

Expenditure of capital moneys in accordance with by-laws

(2) If the council of a band makes a by-law under paragraph 81(1)(p.4) bringing this subsection into effect, a person who has received an amount that exceeds $1,000 under paragraph 15(1)(a), as it read immediately before April 17, 1985, or under any former provision of this Act relating to the same subject matter as that paragraph, by reason of ceasing to be a member of the band in the circumstances set out in paragraph 6(1)(a.1), (d) or (e) is not entitled to receive any benefit afforded to members of the band as individuals as a result of the expenditure of

i) pour subvenir aux frais nécessairement accessoires à la gestion de terres situées sur une réserve, de terres cédées et de tout bien appartenant à la bande;

j) pour construire des maisons destinées aux membres de la bande, pour consentir des prêts aux membres de la bande aux fins de construction, avec ou sans garantie, et pour prévoir la garantie des prêts consentis aux membres de la bande en vue de la construction;

k) pour toute autre fin qui, d'après le ministre, est à l'avantage de la bande.

Dépenses sur les sommes d'argent au compte de capital

(2) Le ministre peut effectuer des dépenses sur les sommes d'argent au compte de capital d'une bande conformément aux règlements administratifs pris en vertu de l'alinéa 81(1)p.3) en vue de faire des paiements à toute personne dont le nom a été retranché de la liste de la bande pour un montant ne dépassant pas une part *per capita* de ces sommes.

L.R. (1985), ch. I-5, art. 64; L.R. (1985), ch. 32 (1ᵉʳ suppl.), art. 10.

Dépense de sommes d'argent au compte en capital avec consentement

64.1 (1) Une personne qui a reçu un montant supérieur à mille dollars en vertu de l'alinéa 15(1)a), dans sa version antérieure au 17 avril 1985, ou en vertu de toute disposition antérieure de la présente loi portant sur le même sujet que celui de cet alinéa, du fait qu'elle a cessé d'être membre d'une bande dans les circonstances prévues aux alinéas 6(1)a.1), d) ou e) n'a pas le droit de recevoir de montant en vertu de l'alinéa 64(1)a) jusqu'à ce que le total de tous les montants qu'elle aurait reçus en vertu de l'alinéa 64(1)a), n'eût été le présent paragraphe, soit égal à l'excédent du montant qu'elle a reçu en vertu de l'alinéa 15(1)a), dans sa version antérieure au 17 avril 1985, ou en vertu de toute disposition antérieure de la présente loi portant sur le même sujet que celui de cet alinéa, sur mille dollars, y compris les intérêts.

Dépenses sur les sommes d'argent au compte de capital

(2) Lorsque le conseil d'une bande prend, en vertu de l'alinéa 81(1)p.4), des règlements administratifs mettant en vigueur le présent paragraphe, la personne qui a reçu un montant supérieur à mille dollars en vertu de l'alinéa 15(1)a) dans sa version antérieure au 17 avril 1985, ou en vertu de toute autre disposition antérieure de la présente loi portant sur le même sujet que celui de cet alinéa, parce qu'elle a cessé d'être membre de la bande dans les circonstances prévues aux alinéas 6(1)a.1), d) ou e) n'a le droit de recevoir aucun des avantages offerts aux

Indian
Management of Indian Moneys
Sections 64.1-66

Indiens
Administration de l'argent des indiens
Articles 64.1-66

Indian moneys under paragraphs 64(1)(b) to (k), subsection 66(1) or subsection 69(1) until the amount by which the amount so received exceeds $1,000, together with any interest, has been repaid to the band.

Regulations

(3) The Governor in Council may make regulations prescribing the manner of determining interest for the purpose of subsections (1) and (2).

R.S., 1985, c. 32 (1st Supp.), s. 11; 2017, c. 25, s. 3.2.

Expenditure of capital

65 The Minister may pay from capital moneys

(a) compensation to an Indian in an amount that is determined in accordance with this Act to be payable to him in respect of land compulsorily taken from him for band purposes; and

(b) expenses incurred to prevent or suppress grass or forest fires or to protect the property of Indians in cases of emergency.

R.S., c. I-6, s. 65.

Expenditure of revenue moneys with consent of band

66 (1) With the consent of the council of a band, the Minister may authorize and direct the expenditure of revenue moneys for any purpose that in the opinion of the Minister will promote the general progress and welfare of the band or any member of the band.

Minister may direct expenditure

(2) The Minister may make expenditures out of the revenue moneys of the band to assist sick, disabled, aged or destitute Indians of the band, to provide for the burial of deceased indigent members of the band and to provide for the payment of contributions under the *Employment Insurance Act* on behalf of employed persons who are paid in respect of their employment out of moneys of the band.

Idem

(2.1) The Minister may make expenditures out of the revenue moneys of a band in accordance with by-laws made pursuant to paragraph 81(1)(p.3) for the purpose of making payments to any person whose name was deleted from the Band List of the band in an amount not exceeding one per capita share of the revenue moneys.

membres de la bande à titre individuel résultant de la dépense d'argent des Indiens au titre des alinéas 64(1)b) à k), du paragraphe 66(1) ou du paragraphe 69(1) jusqu'à ce que l'excédent du montant ainsi reçu sur mille dollars, y compris l'intérêt sur celui-ci, ait été remboursé à la bande.

Règlements

(3) Le gouverneur en conseil peut prendre des règlements prévoyant la façon de déterminer les intérêts pour l'application des paragraphes (1) et (2).

L.R. (1985), ch. 32 (1er suppl.), art. 11; 2017, ch. 25, art. 3.2.

Dépenses de capital

65 Le ministre peut payer, sur les sommes d'argent au compte en capital :

a) une indemnité à un Indien, au montant déterminé en conformité avec la présente loi comme lui étant payable à l'égard de terres qui lui ont été enlevées obligatoirement pour les fins de la bande;

b) les dépenses subies afin de prévenir ou maîtriser les incendies d'herbes ou de forêts ou pour protéger les biens des Indiens en cas d'urgence.

S.R., ch. I-6, art. 65.

Dépense des sommes d'argent du compte de revenu avec le consentement de la bande

66 (1) Avec le consentement du conseil d'une bande, le ministre peut autoriser et ordonner la dépense de sommes d'argent du compte de revenu à toute fin qui, d'après lui, favorisera le progrès général et le bien-être de la bande ou d'un de ses membres.

Le ministre peut déterminer les dépenses

(2) Le ministre peut dépenser l'argent du compte de revenu de la bande en vue d'aider les Indiens malades, invalides, âgés ou indigents de la bande et pour pourvoir aux funérailles des membres indigents de celle-ci, de même qu'en vue de pourvoir au versement des contributions sous le régime de la *Loi sur l'assurance-emploi* pour le compte de personnes employées qui sont payées, à l'égard de leur emploi, sur l'argent de la bande.

Idem

(2.1) Le ministre peut effectuer des dépenses sur les sommes d'argent de revenu de la bande conformément aux règlements administratifs visés à l'alinéa 81(1)p.3) en vue d'effectuer des paiements à une personne dont le nom a été retranché de la liste de bande jusqu'à concurrence d'un montant n'excédant pas une part *per capita* de ces sommes.

Indian
Management of Indian Moneys
Sections 66-68

Indiens
Administration de l'argent des indiens
Articles 66-68

Expenditure of revenue moneys with authority of Minister

(3) The Minister may authorize the expenditure of revenue moneys of the band for all or any of the following purposes, namely,

(a) for the destruction of noxious weeds and the prevention of the spreading or prevalence of insects, pests or diseases that may destroy or injure vegetation on Indian reserves;

(b) to prevent, mitigate and control the spread of diseases on reserves, whether or not the diseases are infectious or communicable;

(c) to provide for the inspection of premises on reserves and the destruction, alteration or renovation thereof;

(d) to prevent overcrowding of premises on reserves used as dwellings;

(e) to provide for sanitary conditions in private premises on reserves as well as in public places on reserves; and

(f) for the construction and maintenance of boundary fences.

R.S., 1985, c. I-5, s. 66; R.S., 1985, c. 32 (1st Supp.), s. 12; 1996, c. 23, s. 187.

Recovery of certain expenses

67 Where money is expended by Her Majesty for the purpose of raising or collecting Indian moneys, the Minister may authorize the recovery of the amount so expended from the moneys of the band.

R.S., c. I-6, s. 67.

Maintenance of dependants

68 Where the Minister is satisfied that an Indian

(a) has deserted his spouse or common-law partner or family without sufficient cause,

(b) has conducted himself in such a manner as to justify the refusal of his spouse or common-law partner or family to live with him, or

(c) has been separated by imprisonment from his spouse or common-law partner and family,

the Minister may order that payments of any annuity or interest money to which that Indian is entitled shall be applied to the support of the spouse or common-law

Le ministre peut autoriser la dépense de sommes d'argent du compte de revenu

(3) Le ministre peut autoriser la dépense de sommes d'argent du compte de revenu de la bande pour l'ensemble ou l'un des objets suivants :

a) la destruction des herbes nuisibles et la prévention de la propagation ou de la présence généralisée des insectes, parasites ou maladies susceptibles de ruiner ou d'endommager la végétation dans les réserves indiennes;

b) la prophylaxie des maladies infectieuses ou contagieuses, ou non, sur les réserves;

c) l'inspection des locaux sur les réserves et la destruction, la modification ou la rénovation de ces locaux;

d) l'adoption de mesures préventives contre le surpeuplement des locaux utilisés comme logements sur les réserves;

e) la salubrité dans les locaux privés comme dans les endroits publics, sur les réserves;

f) la construction et l'entretien de clôtures de délimitation.

L.R. (1985), ch. I-5, art. 66; L.R. (1985), ch. 32 (1er suppl.), art. 12; 1996, ch. 23, art. 187.

Recouvrement de certaines dépenses

67 Lorsqu'une somme d'argent est dépensée par Sa Majesté pour procurer ou percevoir des sommes d'argent destinées aux Indiens, le ministre peut autoriser le recouvrement du montant ainsi dépensé sur l'argent de la bande.

S.R., ch. I-6, art. 67.

Entretien des personnes à charge

68 Le ministre peut ordonner que les paiements de rentes ou d'intérêts auxquels un Indien a droit soient appliqués au soutien de l'époux ou conjoint de fait ou de la famille de celui-ci, ou des deux, lorsqu'il est convaincu que cet Indien, selon le cas :

a) a abandonné son époux ou conjoint de fait ou sa famille sans raison suffisante;

b) s'est conduit de façon à justifier le refus de son époux ou conjoint de fait ou de sa famille de vivre avec lui;

c) a été séparé de son époux ou conjoint de fait et de sa famille par emprisonnement.

L.R. (1985), ch. I-5, art. 68; L.R. (1985), ch. 32 (1er suppl.), art. 13; 2000, ch. 12, art. 152.

Indian
Management of Indian Moneys
Sections 68-70

Indiens
Administration de l'argent des indiens
Articles 68-70

partner or family or both the spouse or common-law partner and family of that Indian.

R.S., 1985, c. I-5, s. 68; R.S., 1985, c. 32 (1st Supp.), s. 13; 2000, c. 12, s. 152.

Management of revenue moneys by band

69 (1) The Governor in Council may by order permit a band to control, manage and expend in whole or in part its revenue moneys and may amend or revoke any such order.

Regulations

(2) The Governor in Council may make regulations to give effect to subsection (1) and may declare therein the extent to which this Act and the *Financial Administration Act* shall not apply to a band to which an order made under subsection (1) applies.

R.S., c. I-6, s. 69.

Loans to Indians

Loans to Indians

70 (1) The Minister of Finance may authorize advances to the Minister out of the Consolidated Revenue Fund of such sums of money as the Minister may require to enable him

(a) to make loans to bands, groups of Indians or individual Indians for the purchase of farm implements, machinery, livestock, motor vehicles, fishing equipment, seed grain, fencing materials, materials to be used in native handicrafts, any other equipment, and gasoline and other petroleum products, or for the making of repairs or the payment of wages, or for the clearing and breaking of land within reserves;

(b) to expend or to lend money for the carrying out of cooperative projects on behalf of Indians; or

(c) to provide for any other matter prescribed by the Governor in Council.

Regulations

(2) The Governor in Council may make regulations to give effect to subsection (1).

Accounting

(3) Expenditures that are made under subsection (1) shall be accounted for in the same manner as public moneys.

Administration des sommes d'argent du compte de revenu par la bande

69 (1) Le gouverneur en conseil peut, par décret, permettre à une bande de contrôler, administrer et dépenser la totalité ou une partie de l'argent de son compte de revenu; il peut aussi modifier ou révoquer un tel décret.

Règlements

(2) Le gouverneur en conseil peut prendre des règlements pour donner effet au paragraphe (1) et y déclarer dans quelle mesure la présente loi et la *Loi sur la gestion des finances publiques* ne s'appliquent pas à une bande visée par un décret pris sous le régime du paragraphe (1).

S.R., ch. I-6, art. 69.

Prêts aux indiens

Prêts aux Indiens

70 (1) Le ministre des Finances peut autoriser l'avance au ministre, sur le Trésor, des sommes d'argent dont ce dernier a besoin pour être en mesure :

a) soit de consentir des prêts à des bandes ou à des groupes d'Indiens ou à des Indiens individuellement, pour l'achat d'instruments agricoles, de machines, d'animaux de ferme, de véhicules à moteur, d'agrès de pêche, de graines de semence, de matériaux à clôture, de matériaux destinés aux arts et métiers indigènes, de tout autre équipement, d'essence et d'autres produits du pétrole, ou pour des réparations ou le paiement de salaires, ou pour défricher et déblayer les terres à l'intérieur des réserves;

b) soit de dépenser ou de prêter des fonds en vue de l'exécution de projets coopératifs pour le compte d'Indiens;

c) soit de pourvoir à toute autre question prévue par le gouverneur en conseil.

Règlements

(2) Le gouverneur en conseil peut prendre des règlements pour l'application du paragraphe (1).

Comptabilité

(3) Il doit être rendu compte des fonds dépensés sous le régime du paragraphe (1) de la même manière que des deniers publics.

Indian
Loans to Indians
Sections 70-72

Indiens
Prêts aux indiens
Articles 70-72

Repayment

(4) The Minister shall pay to the Receiver General all moneys that he receives from bands, groups of Indians or individual Indians by way of repayments of loans made under subsection (1).

Limitation

(5) The total amount of outstanding advances to the Minister under this section shall not at any one time exceed six million and fifty thousand dollars.

Report to Parliament

(6) The Minister shall within fifteen days after the termination of each fiscal year or, if Parliament is not then in session, within fifteen days after the commencement of the next ensuing session, lay before Parliament a report setting out the total number and amount of loans made under subsection (1) during that year.

R.S., c. I-6, s. 70.

Farms

Minister may operate farms

71 (1) The Minister may operate farms on reserves and may employ such persons as he considers necessary to instruct Indians in farming and may purchase and distribute without charge pure seed to Indian farmers.

Application of profits

(2) The Minister may apply any profits that result from the operation of farms pursuant to subsection (1) on reserves to extend farming operations on the reserves or to make loans to Indians to enable them to engage in farming or other agricultural operations or he may apply those profits in any way that he considers to be desirable to promote the progress and development of the Indians.

R.S., c. I-6, s. 71.

Treaty Money

Treaty money payable out of C.R.F.

72 Moneys that are payable to Indians or to Indian bands under a treaty between Her Majesty and a band and for the payment of which the Government of Canada is responsible may be paid out of the Consolidated Revenue Fund.

R.S., c. I-6, s. 72.

Remboursement

(4) Le ministre doit verser au receveur général tout l'argent qu'il reçoit des bandes, groupes d'Indiens ou Indiens pris individuellement, en remboursement des prêts consentis en vertu du paragraphe (1).

Limitation

(5) Le total non remboursé des avances consenties au ministre sous le régime du présent article ne peut dépasser six millions cinquante mille dollars.

Rapport au Parlement

(6) Le ministre doit, dans les quinze jours qui suivent la fin de chaque exercice ou, si le Parlement n'est pas alors en session, dans les quinze premiers jours de la session suivante, présenter au Parlement un rapport indiquant le nombre total et le chiffre global des prêts consentis au cours de l'exercice sous le régime du paragraphe (1).

S.R., ch. I-6, art. 70.

Fermes

Le ministre peut exploiter des fermes

71 (1) Le ministre peut exploiter des fermes dans les réserves et employer les personnes qu'il juge nécessaires pour enseigner l'agriculture aux Indiens. Il peut aussi acheter et gratuitement distribuer des semences pures aux cultivateurs indiens.

Emploi des bénéfices

(2) Le ministre peut employer les bénéfices provenant de l'exploitation de fermes dans les réserves, en conformité avec le paragraphe (1), à l'expansion des exploitations agricoles sur ces réserves, ou à effectuer des prêts aux Indiens pour leur permettre de s'adonner à la culture ou à d'autres travaux agricoles, ou de toute manière qu'il croit propre à favoriser le progrès et le développement des Indiens.

S.R., ch. I-6, art. 71.

Sommes payables en vertu d'un traité

Les sommes visées par des traités sont payables sur le Trésor

72 Les sommes payables à des Indiens ou à des bandes d'Indiens en vertu d'un traité entre Sa Majesté et la bande, et dont le paiement incombe au gouvernement du Canada, peuvent être prélevées sur le Trésor.

S.R., ch. I-6, art. 72.

Indian
Regulations
Section 73

Indiens
Règlements
Article 73

Regulations

Regulations

73 (1) The Governor in Council may make regulations

(a) for the protection and preservation of fur-bearing animals, fish and other game on reserves;

(b) for the destruction of noxious weeds and the prevention of the spreading or prevalence of insects, pests or diseases that may destroy or injure vegetation on Indian reserves;

(c) for the control of the speed, operation and parking of vehicles on roads within reserves;

(d) for the taxation, control and destruction of dogs and for the protection of sheep on reserves;

(e) for the operation, supervision and control of pool rooms, dance halls and other places of amusement on reserves;

(f) to prevent, mitigate and control the spread of diseases on reserves, whether or not the diseases are infectious or communicable;

(g) to provide medical treatment and health services for Indians;

(h) to provide compulsory hospitalization and treatment for infectious diseases among Indians;

(i) to provide for the inspection of premises on reserves and the destruction, alteration or renovation thereof;

(j) to prevent overcrowding of premises on reserves used as dwellings;

(k) to provide for sanitary conditions in private premises on reserves as well as in public places on reserves;

(l) for the construction and maintenance of boundary fences; and

(m) for empowering and authorizing the council of a band to borrow money for band projects or housing purposes and providing for the making of loans out of moneys so borrowed to members of the band for housing purposes.

Règlements

Règlements

73 (1) Le gouverneur en conseil peut prendre des règlements concernant :

a) la protection et la conservation des animaux à fourrure, du poisson et du gibier de toute sorte dans les réserves;

b) la destruction des herbes nuisibles et la prévention de la propagation ou de la présence généralisée des insectes, parasites ou maladies susceptibles de ruiner ou d'endommager la végétation dans les réserves indiennes;

c) le contrôle de la vitesse, de la conduite et du stationnement des véhicules sur les routes dans les réserves;

d) la taxation et la surveillance relatives aux chiens et leur destruction, ainsi que la protection des moutons dans les réserves;

e) le fonctionnement, la surveillance et le contrôle des salles de billard, des salles de danse et autres endroits d'amusement dans les réserves;

f) la prophylaxie des maladies infectieuses ou contagieuses, ou non, sur les réserves;

g) les traitements médicaux et les services d'hygiène destinés aux Indiens;

h) l'hospitalisation et le traitement obligatoires des Indiens atteints de maladies infectieuses;

i) l'inspection des locaux sur les réserves et la destruction, la modification ou la rénovation de ces locaux;

j) l'adoption de mesures préventives contre le surpeuplement des locaux utilisés comme logements sur les réserves;

k) la salubrité dans les locaux privés comme dans les endroits publics, sur les réserves;

l) la construction et l'entretien de clôtures de délimitation;

m) l'octroi, au conseil d'une bande, du pouvoir et de l'autorisation d'emprunter de l'argent pour des entreprises de la bande ou à des fins d'habitation, et prévoyant l'octroi de prêts, sur l'argent ainsi emprunté, aux membres de la bande, à des fins d'habitation.

Indian
Regulations
Sections 73-74

Indiens
Règlements
Articles 73-74

Punishment

(2) The Governor in Council may prescribe the punishment, not exceeding a fine of one hundred dollars or imprisonment for a term not exceeding three months or both, that may be imposed on summary conviction for contravention of a regulation made under subsection (1).

Orders and regulations

(3) The Governor in Council may make orders and regulations to carry out the purposes and provisions of this Act.

R.S., c. I-6, s. 73.

Elections of Chiefs and Band Councils

Elected councils

74 (1) Whenever he deems it advisable for the good government of a band, the Minister may declare by order that after a day to be named therein the council of the band, consisting of a chief and councillors, shall be selected by elections to be held in accordance with this Act.

Composition of council

(2) Unless otherwise ordered by the Minister, the council of a band in respect of which an order has been made under subsection (1) shall consist of one chief, and one councillor for every one hundred members of the band, but the number of councillors shall not be less than two nor more than twelve and no band shall have more than one chief.

Regulations

(3) The Governor in Council may, for the purposes of giving effect to subsection (1), make orders or regulations to provide

(a) that the chief of a band shall be elected by

(i) a majority of the votes of the electors of the band, or

(ii) a majority of the votes of the elected councillors of the band from among themselves,

but the chief so elected shall remain a councillor; and

(b) that the councillors of a band shall be elected by

(i) a majority of the votes of the electors of the band, or

Peine

(2) Le gouverneur en conseil peut prescrire l'amende maximale de cent dollars et l'emprisonnement maximal de trois mois, ou l'une de ces peines, qui peuvent être infligés, sur déclaration de culpabilité par procédure sommaire, pour infraction à un règlement pris sous le régime du paragraphe (1).

Décrets et règlements

(3) Le gouverneur en conseil peut prendre des décrets et règlements en vue de l'application de la présente loi.

S.R., ch. I-6, art. 73.

Élection des chefs et des conseils de bande

Conseils élus

74 (1) Lorsqu'il le juge utile à la bonne administration d'une bande, le ministre peut déclarer par arrêté qu'à compter d'un jour qu'il désigne le conseil d'une bande, comprenant un chef et des conseillers, sera constitué au moyen d'élections tenues selon la présente loi.

Composition du conseil

(2) Sauf si le ministre en ordonne autrement, le conseil d'une bande ayant fait l'objet d'un arrêté prévu par le paragraphe (1) se compose d'un chef, ainsi que d'un conseiller par cent membres de la bande, mais le nombre des conseillers ne peut être inférieur à deux ni supérieur à douze. Une bande ne peut avoir plus d'un chef.

Règlements

(3) Pour l'application du paragraphe (1), le gouverneur en conseil peut prendre des décrets ou règlements prévoyant :

a) que le chef d'une bande doit être élu :

(i) soit à la majorité des votes des électeurs de la bande,

(ii) soit à la majorité des votes des conseillers élus de la bande désignant un d'entre eux,

le chef ainsi élu devant cependant demeurer conseiller;

b) que les conseillers d'une bande doivent être élus :

(i) soit à la majorité des votes des électeurs de la bande,

Indian
Elections of Chiefs and Band Councils
Sections 74-76

Indiens
Élection des chefs et des conseils de bande
Articles 74-76

(ii) a majority of the votes of the electors of the band in the electoral section in which the candidate resides and that he proposes to represent on the council of the band.

Electoral sections

(4) A reserve shall for voting purposes consist of one electoral section, except that where the majority of the electors of a band who were present and voted at a referendum or a special meeting held and called for the purpose in accordance with the regulations have decided that the reserve should for voting purposes be divided into electoral sections and the Minister so recommends, the Governor in Council may make orders or regulations to provide for the division of the reserve for voting purposes into not more than six electoral sections containing as nearly as may be an equal number of Indians eligible to vote and to provide for the manner in which electoral sections so established are to be distinguished or identified.

R.S., c. I-6, s. 74.

Eligibility

75 (1) No person other than an elector who resides in an electoral section may be nominated for the office of councillor to represent that section on the council of the band.

Nomination

(2) No person may be a candidate for election as chief or councillor of a band unless his nomination is moved and seconded by persons who are themselves eligible to be nominated.

R.S., c. I-6, s. 75.

Regulations governing elections

76 (1) The Governor in Council may make orders and regulations with respect to band elections and, without restricting the generality of the foregoing, may make regulations with respect to

(a) meetings to nominate candidates;

(b) the appointment and duties of electoral officers;

(c) the manner in which voting is to be carried out;

(d) election appeals; and

(e) the definition of *residence* for the purpose of determining the eligibility of voters.

(ii) soit à la majorité des votes des électeurs de la bande demeurant dans la section électorale que le candidat habite et qu'il projette de représenter au conseil de la bande.

Sections électorales

(4) Aux fins de votation, une réserve se compose d'une section électorale; toutefois, lorsque la majorité des électeurs d'une bande qui étaient présents et ont voté lors d'un référendum ou à une assemblée spéciale tenue et convoquée à cette fin en conformité avec les règlements, a décidé que la réserve devrait, aux fins de votation, être divisée en sections électorales et que le ministre le recommande, le gouverneur en conseil peut prendre des décrets ou règlements stipulant qu'aux fins de votation la réserve doit être divisée en six sections électorales au plus, contenant autant que possible un nombre égal d'Indiens habilités à voter et décrétant comment les sections électorales ainsi établies doivent se distinguer ou s'identifier.

S.R., ch. I-6, art. 74.

Éligibilité

75 (1) Seul un électeur résidant dans une section électorale peut être présenté au poste de conseiller pour représenter cette section au conseil de la bande.

Présentation de candidats

(2) Nul ne peut être candidat à une élection au poste de chef ou de conseiller d'une bande, à moins que sa candidature ne soit proposée et appuyée par des personnes habiles elles-mêmes à être présentées.

S.R., ch. I-6, art. 75.

Règlements régissant les élections

76 (1) Le gouverneur en conseil peut prendre des décrets et règlements sur les élections au sein des bandes et, notamment, des règlements concernant :

a) les assemblées pour la présentation de candidats;

b) la nomination et les fonctions des préposés aux élections;

c) la manière dont la votation doit avoir lieu;

d) les appels en matière électorale;

e) la définition de *résidence* aux fins de déterminer si une personne est habile à voter.

Indian
Elections of Chiefs and Band Councils
Sections 76-78

Indiens
Élection des chefs et des conseils de bande
Articles 76-78

Secrecy of voting

(2) The regulations made under paragraph (1)(c) shall provide for secrecy of voting.

R.S., c. I-6, s. 76.

Eligibility of voters for chief

77 (1) A member of a band who has attained the age of eighteen years and is ordinarily resident on the reserve is qualified to vote for a person nominated to be chief of the band and, where the reserve for voting purposes consists of one section, to vote for persons nominated as councillors.

Councillor

(2) A member of a band who is of the full age of eighteen years and is ordinarily resident in a section that has been established for voting purposes is qualified to vote for a person nominated to be councillor to represent that section.

R.S., 1985, c. I-5, s. 77; R.S., 1985, c. 32 (1st Supp.), s. 14.

Tenure of office

78 (1) Subject to this section, the chief and councillors of a band hold office for two years.

Vacancy

(2) The office of chief or councillor of a band becomes vacant when

(a) the person who holds that office

(i) is convicted of an indictable offence,

(ii) dies or resigns his office, or

(iii) is or becomes ineligible to hold office by virtue of this Act; or

(b) the Minister declares that in his opinion the person who holds that office

(i) is unfit to continue in office by reason of his having been convicted of an offence,

(ii) has been absent from three consecutive meetings of the council without being authorized to do so, or

(iii) was guilty, in connection with an election, of corrupt practice, accepting a bribe, dishonesty or malfeasance.

Secret du vote

(2) Les règlements pris sous le régime de l'alinéa (1)c) contiennent des dispositions assurant le secret du vote.

S.R., ch. I-6, art. 76.

Qualités exigées des électeurs au poste de chef

77 (1) Un membre d'une bande, qui a au moins dix-huit ans et réside ordinairement sur la réserve, a qualité pour voter en faveur d'une personne présentée comme candidat au poste de chef de la bande et, lorsque la réserve, aux fins d'élection, ne comprend qu'une section électorale, pour voter en faveur de personnes présentées aux postes de conseillers.

Conseiller

(2) Un membre d'une bande, qui a dix-huit ans et réside ordinairement dans une section électorale établie aux fins d'élection, a qualité pour voter en faveur d'une personne présentée au poste de conseiller pour représenter cette section.

L.R. (1985), ch. I-5, art. 77; L.R. (1985), ch. 32 (1er suppl.), art. 14.

Mandat

78 (1) Sous réserve des autres dispositions du présent article, les chef et conseillers d'une bande occupent leur poste pendant deux années.

Vacance

(2) Le poste de chef ou de conseiller d'une bande devient vacant dans les cas suivants :

a) le titulaire, selon le cas :

(i) est déclaré coupable d'un acte criminel,

(ii) meurt ou démissionne,

(iii) est ou devient inhabile à détenir le poste aux termes de la présente loi;

b) le ministre déclare qu'à son avis le titulaire, selon le cas :

(i) est inapte à demeurer en fonctions parce qu'il a été déclaré coupable d'une infraction,

(ii) a, sans autorisation, manqué les réunions du conseil trois fois consécutives,

(iii) à l'occasion d'une élection, s'est rendu coupable de manœuvres frauduleuses, de malhonnêteté ou de méfaits, ou a accepté des pots-de-vin.

Indian
Elections of Chiefs and Band Councils
Sections 78-81

Indiens
Élection des chefs et des conseils de bande
Articles 78-81

Disqualification

(3) The Minister may declare a person who ceases to hold office by virtue of subparagraph (2)(b)(iii) to be ineligible to be a candidate for chief or councillor of a band for a period not exceeding six years.

Special election

(4) Where the office of chief or councillor of a band becomes vacant more than three months before the date when another election would ordinarily be held, a special election may be held in accordance with this Act to fill the vacancy.

R.S., c. I-6, s. 78.

Governor in Council may set aside election

79 The Governor in Council may set aside the election of a chief or councillor of a band on the report of the Minister that he is satisfied that

(a) there was corrupt practice in connection with the election;

(b) there was a contravention of this Act that might have affected the result of the election; or

(c) a person nominated to be a candidate in the election was ineligible to be a candidate.

R.S., c. I-6, s. 79.

Regulations respecting band and council meetings

80 The Governor in Council may make regulations with respect to band meetings and council meetings and, without restricting the generality of the foregoing, may make regulations with respect to

(a) presiding officers at such meetings;

(b) notice of such meetings;

(c) the duties of any representative of the Minister at such meetings; and

(d) the number of persons required at such meetings to constitute a quorum.

R.S., c. I-6, s. 80.

Powers of the Council

By-laws

81 (1) The council of a band may make by-laws not inconsistent with this Act or with any regulation made by the Governor in Council or the Minister, for any or all of the following purposes, namely,

Privation du droit d'être candidat

(3) Le ministre peut déclarer un individu, qui cesse d'occuper ses fonctions en raison du sous-alinéa (2)b)(iii), inhabile à être candidat au poste de chef ou de conseiller d'une bande durant une période maximale de six ans.

Élection spéciale

(4) Lorsque le poste de chef ou de conseiller devient vacant plus de trois mois avant la date de la tenue ordinaire de nouvelles élections, une élection spéciale peut avoir lieu en conformité avec la présente loi afin de remplir cette vacance.

S.R., ch. I-6, art. 78.

Le gouverneur en conseil peut annuler une élection

79 Le gouverneur en conseil peut rejeter l'élection du chef ou d'un des conseillers d'une bande sur le rapport du ministre où ce dernier se dit convaincu, selon le cas :

a) qu'il y a eu des manœuvres frauduleuses à l'égard de cette élection;

b) qu'il s'est produit une infraction à la présente loi pouvant influer sur le résultat de l'élection;

c) qu'une personne présentée comme candidat à l'élection ne possédait pas les qualités requises.

S.R., ch. I-6, art. 79.

Règlements sur les assemblées de la bande et du conseil

80 Le gouverneur en conseil peut prendre des règlements sur les assemblées de la bande et du conseil et, notamment, des règlements concernant :

a) les présidents de ces assemblées;

b) les avis de ces assemblées;

c) les fonctions de tout représentant du ministre à ces assemblées;

d) le nombre de personnes requis à ces assemblées pour constituer un quorum.

S.R., ch. I-6, art. 80.

Pouvoirs du conseil

Règlements administratifs

81 (1) Le conseil d'une bande peut prendre des règlements administratifs, non incompatibles avec la présente loi ou avec un règlement pris par le gouverneur en

Indian
Powers of the Council
Section 81

Indiens
Pouvoirs du conseil
Article 81

(a) to provide for the health of residents on the reserve and to prevent the spreading of contagious and infectious diseases;

(b) the regulation of traffic;

(c) the observance of law and order;

(d) the prevention of disorderly conduct and nuisances;

(e) the protection against and prevention of trespass by cattle and other domestic animals, the establishment of pounds, the appointment of pound-keepers, the regulation of their duties and the provision for fees and charges for their services;

(f) the construction and maintenance of watercourses, roads, bridges, ditches, fences and other local works;

(g) the dividing of the reserve or a portion thereof into zones and the prohibition of the construction or maintenance of any class of buildings or the carrying on of any class of business, trade or calling in any zone;

(h) the regulation of the construction, repair and use of buildings, whether owned by the band or by individual members of the band;

(i) the survey and allotment of reserve lands among the members of the band and the establishment of a register of Certificates of Possession and Certificates of Occupation relating to allotments and the setting apart of reserve lands for common use, if authority therefor has been granted under section 60;

(j) the destruction and control of noxious weeds;

(k) the regulation of bee-keeping and poultry raising;

(l) the construction and regulation of the use of public wells, cisterns, reservoirs and other water supplies;

(m) the control or prohibition of public games, sports, races, athletic contests and other amusements;

(n) the regulation of the conduct and activities of hawkers, peddlers or others who enter the reserve to buy, sell or otherwise deal in wares or merchandise;

(o) the preservation, protection and management of fur-bearing animals, fish and other game on the reserve;

(p) the removal and punishment of persons trespassing on the reserve or frequenting the reserve for prohibited purposes;

conseil ou par le ministre, pour l'une ou l'ensemble des fins suivantes :

a) l'adoption de mesures relatives à la santé des habitants de la réserve et les précautions à prendre contre la propagation des maladies contagieuses et infectieuses;

b) la réglementation de la circulation;

c) l'observation de la loi et le maintien de l'ordre;

d) la répression de l'inconduite et des incommodités;

e) la protection et les précautions à prendre contre les empiétements des bestiaux et autres animaux domestiques, l'établissement de fourrières, la nomination de gardes-fourrières, la réglementation de leurs fonctions et la constitution de droits et redevances pour leurs services;

f) l'établissement et l'entretien de cours d'eau, routes, ponts, fossés, clôtures et autres ouvrages locaux;

g) la division de la réserve ou d'une de ses parties en zones, et l'interdiction de construire ou d'entretenir une catégorie de bâtiments ou d'exercer une catégorie d'entreprises, de métiers ou de professions dans une telle zone;

h) la réglementation de la construction, de la réparation et de l'usage des bâtiments, qu'ils appartiennent à la bande ou à des membres de la bande pris individuellement;

i) l'arpentage des terres de la réserve et leur répartition entre les membres de la bande, et l'établissement d'un registre de certificats de possession et de certificats d'occupation concernant les attributions, et la mise à part de terres de la réserve pour usage commun, si l'autorisation à cet égard a été accordée aux termes de l'article 60;

j) la destruction et le contrôle des herbes nuisibles;

k) la réglementation de l'apiculture et de l'aviculture;

l) l'établissement de puits, citernes et réservoirs publics et autres services d'eau du même genre, ainsi que la réglementation de leur usage;

m) la réglementation ou l'interdiction de jeux, sports, courses et concours athlétiques d'ordre public et autres amusements du même genre;

Indian
Powers of the Council
Section 81

Indiens
Pouvoirs du conseil
Article 81

(p.1) the residence of band members and other persons on the reserve;

(p.2) to provide for the rights of spouses or common-law partners and children who reside with members of the band on the reserve with respect to any matter in relation to which the council may make by-laws in respect of members of the band;

(p.3) to authorize the Minister to make payments out of capital or revenue moneys to persons whose names were deleted from the Band List of the band;

(p.4) to bring subsection 10(3) or 64.1(2) into effect in respect of the band;

(q) with respect to any matter arising out of or ancillary to the exercise of powers under this section; and

(r) the imposition on summary conviction of a fine not exceeding one thousand dollars or imprisonment for a term not exceeding thirty days, or both, for violation of a by-law made under this section.

n) la réglementation de la conduite et des opérations des marchands ambulants, colporteurs ou autres personnes qui pénètrent dans la réserve pour acheter ou vendre des produits ou marchandises, ou en faire un autre commerce;

o) la conservation, la protection et la régie des animaux à fourrure, du poisson et du gibier de toute sorte dans la réserve;

p) l'expulsion et la punition des personnes qui pénètrent sans droit ni autorisation dans la réserve ou la fréquentent pour des fins interdites;

p.1) la résidence des membres de la bande ou des autres personnes sur la réserve;

p.2) l'adoption de mesures relatives aux droits des époux ou conjoints de fait ou des enfants qui résident avec des membres de la bande dans une réserve pour toute matière au sujet de laquelle le conseil peut établir des règlements administratifs à l'égard des membres de la bande;

p.3) l'autorisation du ministre à effectuer des paiements sur des sommes d'argent au compte de capital ou des sommes d'argent de revenu aux personnes dont les noms ont été retranchés de la liste de la bande;

p.4) la mise en vigueur des paragraphes 10(3) ou 64.1(2) à l'égard de la bande;

q) toute question qui découle de l'exercice des pouvoirs prévus par le présent article, ou qui y est accessoire;

r) l'imposition, sur déclaration de culpabilité par procédure sommaire, d'une amende maximale de mille dollars et d'un emprisonnement maximal de trente jours, ou de l'une de ces peines, pour violation d'un règlement administratif pris aux termes du présent article.

Power to restrain by order where conviction entered

(2) Where any by-law of a band is contravened and a conviction entered, in addition to any other remedy and to any penalty imposed by the by-law, the court in which the conviction has been entered, and any court of competent jurisdiction thereafter, may make an order prohibiting the continuation or repetition of the offence by the person convicted.

Pouvoir de rendre une ordonnance

(2) Lorsqu'un règlement administratif d'une bande est violé et qu'une déclaration de culpabilité est prononcée, le tribunal ayant prononcé la déclaration de culpabilité et tout tribunal compétent par la suite peuvent, en plus de toute autre réparation et de toute peine imposée par le règlement administratif, rendre une ordonnance interdisant la continuation ou la répétition de l'infraction par la personne déclarée coupable.

Power to restrain by court action

(3) Where any by-law of a band passed is contravened, in addition to any other remedy and to any penalty imposed

Pouvoir d'intenter une action en justice

(3) La violation d'un règlement administratif d'une bande peut, sans préjudice de toute autre réparation et

Indian
Powers of the Council
Sections 81-83

Indiens
Pouvoirs du conseil
Articles 81-83

by the by-law, such contravention may be restrained by court action at the instance of the band council.

R.S., 1985, c. I-5, s. 81; R.S., 1985, c. 32 (1st Supp.), s. 15; 2000, c. 12, s. 152.

82 [Repealed, 2014, c. 38, s. 7]

Money by-laws

83 (1) Without prejudice to the powers conferred by section 81, the council of a band may, subject to the approval of the Minister, make by-laws for any or all of the following purposes, namely,

(a) subject to subsections (2) and (3), taxation for local purposes of land, or interests in land, in the reserve, including rights to occupy, possess or use land in the reserve;

(a.1) the licensing of businesses, callings, trades and occupations;

(b) the appropriation and expenditure of moneys of the band to defray band expenses;

(c) the appointment of officials to conduct the business of the council, prescribing their duties and providing for their remuneration out of any moneys raised pursuant to paragraph (a);

(d) the payment of remuneration, in such amount as may be approved by the Minister, to chiefs and councillors, out of any moneys raised pursuant to paragraph (a);

(e) the enforcement of payment of amounts that are payable pursuant to this section, including arrears and interest;

(e.1) the imposition and recovery of interest on amounts that are payable pursuant to this section, where those amounts are not paid before they are due, and the calculation of that interest;

(f) the raising of money from band members to support band projects; and

(g) with respect to any matter arising out of or ancillary to the exercise of powers under this section.

Restriction on expenditures

(2) An expenditure made out of moneys raised pursuant to subsection (1) must be so made under the authority of a by-law of the council of the band.

de toute peine imposée par celui-ci, être refrénée par une action en justice à la demande du conseil de bande.

L.R. (1985), ch. I-5, art. 81; L.R. (1985), ch. 32 (1er suppl.), art. 15; 2000, ch. 12, art. 152.

82 [Abrogé, 2014, ch. 38, art. 7]

Règlements administratifs

83 (1) Sans préjudice des pouvoirs que confère l'article 81, le conseil de la bande peut, sous réserve de l'approbation du ministre, prendre des règlements administratifs dans les domaines suivants :

a) sous réserve des paragraphes (2) et (3), l'imposition de taxes à des fins locales, sur les immeubles situés dans la réserve, ainsi que sur les droits sur ceux-ci, et notamment sur les droits d'occupation, de possession et d'usage;

a.1) la délivrance de permis, de licences ou d'agréments aux entreprises, professions, métiers et occupations;

b) l'affectation et le déboursement de l'argent de la bande pour couvrir les dépenses de cette dernière;

c) la nomination de fonctionnaires chargés de diriger les affaires du conseil, en établissant leurs fonctions et prévoyant leur rétribution sur les fonds prélevés en vertu de l'alinéa a);

d) le versement d'une rémunération, pour le montant que le ministre peut approuver, aux chefs et conseillers, sur les fonds prélevés en vertu de l'alinéa a);

e) les mesures d'exécution forcée visant le recouvrement de tout montant qui peut être perçu en application du présent article, arrérages et intérêts compris;

e.1) l'imposition, pour non-paiement de tout montant qui peut être perçu en application du présent article, d'intérêts et la fixation, par tarif ou autrement, de ces intérêts;

f) la réunion de fonds provenant des membres de la bande et destinés à supporter des entreprises de la bande;

g) toute question qui découle de l'exercice des pouvoirs prévus par le présent article, ou qui y est accessoire.

Restriction

(2) Toute dépense à faire sur les fonds prélevés en application du paragraphe (1) doit l'être sous l'autorité d'un règlement administratif pris par le conseil de la bande.

Indian
Powers of the Council
Sections 83-85.1

Indiens
Pouvoirs du conseil
Articles 83-85.1

Appeals

(3) A by-law made under paragraph (1)(a) must provide an appeal procedure in respect of assessments made for the purposes of taxation under that paragraph.

Précision

(3) Les règlements administratifs pris en application de l'alinéa (1)a) doivent prévoir la procédure de contestation de l'évaluation en matière de taxation.

Minister's approval

(4) The Minister may approve the whole or a part only of a by-law made under subsection (1).

Approbation

(4) Le ministre peut approuver la totalité d'un règlement administratif visé au paragraphe (1) ou une partie seulement de celui-ci.

Regulations re by-laws

(5) The Governor in Council may make regulations respecting the exercise of the by-law making powers of bands under this section.

Règlement relatif au pouvoir réglementaire

(5) Le gouverneur en conseil peut, par règlement, régir l'exercice du pouvoir réglementaire de la bande prévu au présent article.

By-laws must be consistent with regulations

(6) A by-law made under this section remains in force only to the extent that it is consistent with the regulations made under subsection (5).

R.S., 1985, c. I-5, s. 83; R.S., 1985, c. 17 (4th Supp.), s. 10.

Maintien des règlements administratifs

(6) Les règlements administratifs pris en application du présent article ne demeurent en vigueur que dans la mesure de leur compatibilité avec les règlements pris en application du paragraphe (5).

L.R. (1985), ch. I-5, art. 83; L.R. (1985), ch. 17 (4e suppl.), art. 10.

Recovery of taxes

84 Where a tax that is imposed on an Indian by or under the authority of a by-law made under section 83 is not paid in accordance with the by-law, the Minister may pay the amount owing together with an amount equal to one-half of one per cent thereof out of moneys payable out of the funds of the band to the Indian.

R.S., c. I-6, s. 84.

Recouvrement d'impôts

84 Lorsqu'un impôt frappant un Indien en vertu ou sous l'autorité d'un règlement administratif pris en vertu de l'article 83 n'est pas acquitté conformément au règlement administratif, le ministre peut payer le montant dû ainsi qu'une somme égale à un demi pour cent dudit montant sur l'argent payable à l'Indien sur les fonds de la bande.

S.R., ch. I-6, art. 84.

85 [Repealed, R.S., 1985, c. 17 (4th Supp.), s. 11]

85 [Abrogé, L.R. (1985), ch. 17 (4e suppl.), art. 11]

By-laws relating to intoxicants

85.1 (1) Subject to subsection (2), the council of a band may make by-laws

(a) prohibiting the sale, barter, supply or manufacture of intoxicants on the reserve of the band;

(b) prohibiting any person from being intoxicated on the reserve;

(c) prohibiting any person from having intoxicants in his possession on the reserve; and

(d) providing for exceptions to any of the prohibitions established pursuant to paragraph (b) or (c).

Règlements administratifs sur les boissons alcoolisées

85.1 (1) Sous réserve du paragraphe (2), le conseil d'une bande peut prendre des règlements administratifs en vue :

a) d'interdire la vente, le troc, la fourniture ou la fabrication de boissons alcoolisées sur la réserve de la bande;

b) d'interdire à toute personne d'être en état d'ivresse sur la réserve;

c) d'interdire à toute personne d'avoir en sa possession des boissons alcoolisées sur la réserve;

d) de prévoir des exceptions aux interdictions visées aux alinéas b) ou c).

Indian
Powers of the Council
Sections 85.1-86

Indiens
Pouvoirs du conseil
Articles 85.1-86

Consent of electors

(2) A by-law may not be made under this section unless it is first assented to by a majority of the electors of the band who voted at a special meeting of the band called by the council of the band for the purpose of considering the by-law.

(3) [Repealed, 2014, c. 38, s. 8]

Offence

(4) Every person who contravenes a by-law made under this section is guilty of an offence and liable on summary conviction

(a) in the case of a by-law made under paragraph (1)(a), to a fine of not more than one thousand dollars or to imprisonment for a term not exceeding six months or to both; and

(b) in the case of a by-law made under paragraph (1)(b) or (c), to a fine of not more than one hundred dollars or to imprisonment for a term not exceeding three months or to both.

R.S., 1985, c. 32 (1st Supp.), s. 16; 2014, c. 38, s. 8.

Publication of by-laws

86 (1) The council of a band shall publish a copy of every by-law made by the council under this Act on an Internet site, in the *First Nations Gazette* or in a newspaper that has general circulation on the reserve of the band, whichever the council considers appropriate in the circumstances.

Copies of by-laws

(2) The council of a band shall, on request by any person, provide to the person a copy of a by-law made by the council.

For greater certainty

(3) For greater certainty, publishing a by-law on an Internet site in accordance with subsection (1) does not discharge the council of a band from its obligation under subsection (2) to provide a copy of the by-law to any person who requests one.

Coming into force

(4) A by-law made by the council of a band under this Act comes into force on the day on which it is first published under subsection (1) or on any later day specified in the by-law.

Consentement des électeurs

(2) Les règlements administratifs prévus au présent article ne peuvent être pris qu'avec le consentement préalable de la majorité des électeurs de la bande ayant voté à l'assemblée spéciale de la bande convoquée par le conseil de cette dernière pour l'étude de ces règlements.

(3) [Abrogé, 2014, ch. 38, art. 8]

Infraction

(4) Quiconque contrevient à un règlement administratif pris en vertu du présent article commet une infraction et encourt, sur déclaration de culpabilité par procédure sommaire :

a) dans le cas d'un règlement pris en vertu de l'alinéa (1)a), une amende maximale de mille dollars et un emprisonnement maximal de six mois, ou l'une de ces peines;

b) dans le cas d'un règlement pris en vertu des alinéas (1)b) ou c), une amende maximale de cent dollars et un emprisonnement maximal de trois mois, ou l'une de ces peines.

L.R. (1985), ch. 32 (1er suppl.), art. 16; 2014, ch. 38, art. 8.

Publication des règlements administratifs

86 (1) Le conseil d'une bande est tenu de publier tout règlement administratif qu'il a pris sous le régime de la présente loi sur un site Internet, dans la *Gazette des premières nations* ou dans un journal largement diffusé sur la réserve de la bande, selon ce qu'il estime approprié dans les circonstances.

Copies des règlements administratifs

(2) Le conseil d'une bande est tenu de fournir à toute personne qui en fait la demande une copie de tout règlement administratif qu'il a pris.

Précision

(3) Il est entendu que le fait de publier un règlement administratif sur un site Internet en conformité avec le paragraphe (1) ne libère pas le conseil de l'obligation prévue au paragraphe (2) de fournir des copies du règlement aux personnes qui en font la demande.

Entrée en vigueur

(4) Les règlements administratifs pris par le conseil d'une bande sous le régime de la présente loi entrent en vigueur à la date de leur publication initiale en application du paragraphe (1) ou à la date ultérieure qu'ils fixent.

Indian
Powers of the Council
Sections 86-88

Indiens
Pouvoirs du conseil
Articles 86-88

Duration of publication — Internet site

(5) A by-law that is published on an Internet site under subsection (1) must remain accessible in that manner for the period during which it is in force.

R.S., 1985, c. I-5, s. 86; 2014, c. 38, s. 9.

Durée de la publication : site Internet

(5) Les règlements administratifs publiés sur un site Internet en application du paragraphe (1) doivent demeurer accessibles sur un tel site jusqu'à ce qu'ils cessent d'être en vigueur.

L.R. (1985), ch. I-5, art. 86; 2014, ch. 38, art. 9.

Taxation

Taxation

Property exempt from taxation

87 (1) Notwithstanding any other Act of Parliament or any Act of the legislature of a province, but subject to section 83 and section 5 of the *First Nations Fiscal Management Act*, the following property is exempt from taxation:

(a) the interest of an Indian or a band in reserve lands or surrendered lands; and

(b) the personal property of an Indian or a band situated on a reserve.

Biens exempts de taxation

87 (1) Nonobstant toute autre loi fédérale ou provinciale, mais sous réserve de l'article 83 et de l'article 5 de la *Loi sur la gestion financière des premières nations*, les biens suivants sont exemptés de taxation :

a) le droit d'un Indien ou d'une bande sur une réserve ou des terres cédées;

b) les biens meubles d'un Indien ou d'une bande situés sur une réserve.

Idem

(2) No Indian or band is subject to taxation in respect of the ownership, occupation, possession or use of any property mentioned in paragraph (1)(a) or (b) or is otherwise subject to taxation in respect of any such property.

Idem

(2) Nul Indien ou bande n'est assujetti à une taxation concernant la propriété, l'occupation, la possession ou l'usage d'un bien mentionné aux alinéas (1)a) ou b) ni autrement soumis à une taxation quant à l'un de ces biens.

Idem

(3) No succession duty, inheritance tax or estate duty is payable on the death of any Indian in respect of any property mentioned in paragraphs (1)(a) or (b) or the succession thereto if the property passes to an Indian, nor shall any such property be taken into account in determining the duty payable under the *Dominion Succession Duty Act*, chapter 89 of the Revised Statutes of Canada, 1952, or the tax payable under the *Estate Tax Act*, chapter E-9 of the Revised Statutes of Canada, 1970, on or in respect of other property passing to an Indian.

R.S., 1985, c. I-5, s. 87; 2005, c. 9, s. 150; 2012, c. 19, s. 677.

Idem

(3) Aucun impôt sur les successions, taxe d'héritage ou droit de succession n'est exigible à la mort d'un Indien en ce qui concerne un bien de cette nature ou la succession visant un tel bien, si ce dernier est transmis à un Indien, et il ne sera tenu compte d'aucun bien de cette nature en déterminant le droit payable, en vertu de la *Loi fédérale sur les droits successoraux*, chapitre 89 des Statuts revisés du Canada de 1952, ou l'impôt payable, en vertu de la *Loi de l'impôt sur les biens transmis par décès*, chapitre E-9 des Statuts revisés du Canada de 1970, sur d'autres biens transmis à un Indien ou à l'égard de ces autres biens.

L.R. (1985), ch. I-5, art. 87; 2005, ch. 9, art. 150; 2012, ch. 19, art. 677.

Legal Rights

Droits légaux

General provincial laws applicable to Indians

88 Subject to the terms of any treaty and any other Act of Parliament, all laws of general application from time to time in force in any province are applicable to and in respect of Indians in the province, except to the extent that those laws are inconsistent with this Act or the *First Nations Fiscal Management Act*, or with any order, rule,

Lois provinciales d'ordre général applicables aux Indiens

88 Sous réserve des dispositions de quelque traité et de quelque autre loi fédérale, toutes les lois d'application générale et en vigueur dans une province sont applicables aux Indiens qui s'y trouvent et à leur égard, sauf dans la mesure où ces lois sont incompatibles avec la présente loi ou la *Loi sur la gestion financière des premières nations*

Indian
Legal Rights
Sections 88-90

Indiens
Droits légaux
Articles 88-90

regulation or law of a band made under those Acts, and except to the extent that those provincial laws make provision for any matter for which provision is made by or under those Acts.

R.S., 1985, c. I-5, s. 88; 2005, c. 9, s. 151; 2012, c. 19, s. 678.

Restriction on mortgage, seizure, etc., of property on reserve

89 (1) Subject to this Act, the real and personal property of an Indian or a band situated on a reserve is not subject to charge, pledge, mortgage, attachment, levy, seizure, distress or execution in favour or at the instance of any person other than an Indian or a band.

Exception

(1.1) Notwithstanding subsection (1), a leasehold interest in designated lands is subject to charge, pledge, mortgage, attachment, levy, seizure, distress and execution.

Conditional sales

(2) A person who sells to a band or a member of a band a chattel under an agreement whereby the right of property or right of possession thereto remains wholly or in part in the seller may exercise his rights under the agreement notwithstanding that the chattel is situated on a reserve.

R.S., 1985, c. I-5, s. 89; R.S., 1985, c. 17 (4th Supp.), s. 12.

Property deemed situated on reserve

90 (1) For the purposes of sections 87 and 89, personal property that was

(a) purchased by Her Majesty with Indian moneys or moneys appropriated by Parliament for the use and benefit of Indians or bands, or

(b) given to Indians or to a band under a treaty or agreement between a band and Her Majesty,

shall be deemed always to be situated on a reserve.

Restriction on transfer

(2) Every transaction purporting to pass title to any property that is by this section deemed to be situated on a reserve, or any interest in such property, is void unless the transaction is entered into with the consent of the Minister or is entered into between members of a band or between the band and a member thereof.

---

ou quelque arrêté, ordonnance, règle, règlement ou texte législatif d'une bande pris sous leur régime, et sauf dans la mesure où ces lois provinciales contiennent des dispositions sur toute question prévue par la présente loi ou la *Loi sur la gestion financière des premières nations* ou sous leur régime.

L.R. (1985), ch. I-5, art. 88; 2005, ch. 9, art. 151; 2012, ch. 19, art. 678.

Inaliénabilité des biens situés sur une réserve

89 (1) Sous réserve des autres dispositions de la présente loi, les biens d'un Indien ou d'une bande situés sur une réserve ne peuvent pas faire l'objet d'un privilège, d'un nantissement, d'une hypothèque, d'une opposition, d'une réquisition, d'une saisie ou d'une exécution en faveur ou à la demande d'une personne autre qu'un Indien ou une bande.

Dérogation

(1.1) Par dérogation au paragraphe (1), les droits découlant d'un bail sur une terre désignée peuvent faire l'objet d'un privilège, d'un nantissement, d'une hypothèque, d'une opposition, d'une réquisition, d'une saisie ou d'une exécution.

Ventes conditionnelles

(2) Une personne, qui vend à une bande ou à un membre d'une bande un bien meuble en vertu d'une entente selon laquelle le droit de propriété ou le droit de possession demeure acquis en tout ou en partie au vendeur, peut exercer ses droits aux termes de l'entente, même si le bien meuble est situé sur une réserve.

L.R. (1985), ch. I-5, art. 89; L.R. (1985), ch. 17 (4ᵉ suppl.), art. 12.

Biens considérés comme situés sur une réserve

90 (1) Pour l'application des articles 87 et 89, les biens meubles qui ont été :

a) soit achetés par Sa Majesté avec l'argent des Indiens ou des fonds votés par le Parlement à l'usage et au profit d'Indiens ou de bandes;

b) soit donnés aux Indiens ou à une bande en vertu d'un traité ou accord entre une bande et Sa Majesté,

sont toujours réputés situés sur une réserve.

Restriction sur le transfert

(2) Toute opération visant à transférer la propriété d'un bien réputé, en vertu du présent article, situé sur une réserve, ou un droit sur un tel bien, est nulle à moins qu'elle n'ait lieu avec le consentement du ministre ou ne soit conclue entre des membres d'une bande ou entre une bande et l'un de ses membres.

Indian
Legal Rights
Sections 90-92

Indiens
Droits légaux
Articles 90-92

Destruction of property

(3) Every person who enters into any transaction that is void by virtue of subsection (2) is guilty of an offence, and every person who, without the written consent of the Minister, destroys personal property that is by this section deemed to be situated on a reserve is guilty of an offence.

R.S., c. I-6, s. 90.

Trading with Indians

Certain property on a reserve may not be acquired

91 (1) No person may, without the written consent of the Minister, acquire title to any of the following property situated on a reserve, namely,

(a) an Indian grave house;

(b) a carved grave pole;

(c) a totem pole;

(d) a carved house post; or

(e) a rock embellished with paintings or carvings.

Saving

(2) Subsection (1) does not apply to chattels referred to therein that are manufactured for sale by Indians.

Removal, destruction, etc.

(3) No person shall remove, take away, mutilate, disfigure, deface or destroy any chattel referred to in subsection (1) without the written consent of the Minister.

Punishment

(4) A person who contravenes this section is guilty of an offence and liable on summary conviction to a fine not exceeding two hundred dollars or to imprisonment for a term not exceeding three months.

R.S., c. I-6, s. 91.

92 [Repealed, 2014, c. 38, s. 10]

Destruction de biens

(3) Quiconque conclut une opération déclarée nulle par le paragraphe (2) commet une infraction; commet aussi une infraction quiconque détruit, sans le consentement écrit du ministre, un bien meuble réputé, en vertu du présent article, situé sur une réserve.

S.R., ch. I-6, art. 90.

Commerce avec les indiens

Interdiction d'acquérir certains biens situés sur une réserve

91 (1) Nul ne peut, sans le consentement écrit du ministre, acquérir la propriété de l'un des biens suivants, situés sur une réserve :

a) une maison funéraire indienne;

b) un monument funéraire sculpté;

c) un poteau totémique;

d) un poteau sculpté de maison;

e) une roche ornée d'images gravées ou peintes.

Exception

(2) Le paragraphe (1) ne s'applique pas aux biens meubles y mentionnés qui sont fabriqués en vue de la vente par des Indiens.

Enlèvement, destruction, etc.

(3) Nul ne peut enlever, emporter, mutiler, défigurer, détériorer ou détruire un bien meuble mentionné au paragraphe (1), sans le consentement écrit du ministre.

Peine

(4) Quiconque contrevient au présent article commet une infraction et encourt, sur déclaration de culpabilité par procédure sommaire, une amende maximale de deux cents dollars ou un emprisonnement maximal de trois mois.

S.R., ch. I-6, art. 91.

92 [Abrogé, 2014, ch. 38, art. 10]

Indian
Removal of Materials from Reserves
Sections 93-102

Indiens
Enlèvement d'objets sur les réserves
Articles 93-102

Removal of Materials from Reserves

Enlèvement d'objets sur les réserves

Removal of material from reserve

93 A person who, without the written permission of the Minister or his duly authorized representative,

(a) removes or permits anyone to remove from a reserve

(i) minerals, stone, sand, gravel, clay or soil, or

(ii) trees, saplings, shrubs, underbrush, timber, cordwood or hay, or

(b) has in his possession anything removed from a reserve contrary to this section,

is guilty of an offence and liable on summary conviction to a fine not exceeding five hundred dollars or to imprisonment for a term not exceeding three months or to both.

R.S., c. I-6, s. 93.

Enlèvement d'objets sur la réserve

93 Une personne qui, sans la permission écrite du ministre ou de son représentant dûment autorisé :

a) soit enlève ou permet à quelqu'un d'enlever d'une réserve :

(i) des minéraux, des pierres, du sable, du gravier, de la glaise, ou de la terre,

(ii) des arbres, de jeunes arbres, des arbrisseaux, des broussailles, du bois de service, du bois de corde ou du foin;

b) soit a en sa possession une chose enlevée d'une réserve contrairement au présent article,

commet une infraction et encourt, sur déclaration de culpabilité par procédure sommaire, une amende maximale de cinq cents dollars et un emprisonnement maximal de trois mois, ou l'une de ces peines.

S.R., ch. I-6, art. 93.

Offences, Punishment and Enforcement

Infractions, peines et contrôle d'application

94 to 100 [Repealed, R.S., 1985, c. 32 (1st Supp.), s. 17]

94 à 100 [Abrogés, L.R. (1985), ch. 32 (1er suppl.), art. 17]

Certificate of analysis is evidence

101 In every prosecution under this Act a certificate of analysis furnished by an analyst employed by the Government of Canada or by a province shall be accepted as evidence of the facts stated therein and of the authority of the person giving or issuing the certificate, without proof of the signature of the person appearing to have signed the certificate or his official character, and without further proof thereof.

R.S., c. I-6, s. 101.

Le certificat de l'analyse constitue une preuve

101 Dans toute poursuite intentée sous le régime de la présente loi, un certificat d'analyse fourni par un analyste à l'emploi du gouvernement du Canada ou d'une province doit être accepté comme preuve des faits qu'il énonce et de l'autorité de la personne qui délivre le certificat, sans qu'il soit nécessaire de prouver l'authenticité de la signature qui y est apposée ou la qualité officielle du signataire et sans autre preuve à cet égard.

S.R., ch. I-6, art. 101.

Penalty where no other provided

102 Every person who is guilty of an offence against any provision of this Act or any regulation made by the Governor in Council or the Minister for which a penalty is not provided elsewhere in this Act or the regulations is liable on summary conviction to a fine not exceeding two hundred dollars or to imprisonment for a term not exceeding three months or to both.

R.S., c. I-6, s. 102.

Peine lorsque la loi n'en établit pas d'autre

102 Toute personne coupable d'une infraction à une disposition de la présente loi ou d'un règlement pris par le gouverneur en conseil ou le ministre, et pour laquelle aucune peine n'est prévue ailleurs dans la présente loi ou les règlements, encourt, sur déclaration de culpabilité par procédure sommaire, une amende maximale de deux cents dollars et un emprisonnement maximal de trois mois, ou l'une de ces peines.

S.R., ch. I-6, art. 102.

Indian
Offences, Punishment and Enforcement
Sections 103-104

Indiens
Infractions, peines et contrôle d'application
Articles 103-104

Seizure of goods

103 (1) Whenever a peace officer, a superintendent or a person authorized by the Minister believes on reasonable grounds that a by-law made under subsection 81(1) or 85.1(1) has been contravened or an offence against section 90 or 93 has been committed, he may seize all goods and chattels by means of or in relation to which he believes on reasonable grounds the by-law was contravened or the offence was committed.

Detention

(2) All goods and chattels seized pursuant to subsection (1) may be detained for a period of three months following the day of seizure unless during that period proceedings are undertaken under this Act in respect of the offence, in which case the goods and chattels may be further detained until the proceedings are finally concluded.

Forfeiture

(3) Where a person is convicted of an offence against the sections mentioned in subsection (1), the convicting court or judge may order that the goods and chattels by means of or in relation to which the offence was committed, in addition to any penalty imposed, are forfeited to Her Majesty and may be disposed of as the Minister directs.

Search

(4) A justice who is satisfied by information on oath that there is reasonable ground to believe that there are in a reserve or in any building, receptacle or place any goods or chattels by means of or in relation to which an offence against any of the sections mentioned in subsection (1) has been, is being or is about to be committed may at any time issue a warrant under his hand authorizing a person named therein or a peace officer at any time to search the reserve, building, receptacle or place for any of those goods or chattels.

R.S., 1985, c. I-5, s. 103; R.S., 1985, c. 32 (1st Supp.), s. 19; 2014, c. 38, s. 11.

Disposition of fines

104 (1) Subject to subsection (2), every fine, penalty or forfeiture imposed under this Act belongs to Her Majesty for the benefit of the band, or of one or more members of the band, with respect to which the offence was committed or to which the offender, if an Indian, belongs.

Saisie des marchandises

103 (1) Chaque fois qu'un agent de la paix, un surintendant ou une autre personne autorisée par le ministre a des motifs raisonnables de croire qu'une infraction à un règlement administratif pris en vertu des paragraphes 81(1) ou 85.1(1) ou aux articles 90 ou 93 a été commise, il peut saisir toutes les marchandises et tous les biens meubles au moyen ou à l'égard desquels il a des motifs raisonnables de croire que l'infraction a été commise.

Détention

(2) Toutes les marchandises et tous les biens meubles saisis conformément au paragraphe (1) peuvent être détenus pendant une période de trois mois à compter du jour de la saisie, à moins que, dans cette période, on n'engage des poursuites en vertu de la présente loi à l'égard de cette infraction, auquel cas les marchandises et biens meubles peuvent être détenus jusqu'à la conclusion définitive des poursuites.

Confiscation

(3) Dans le cas où une personne est déclarée coupable d'une infraction aux articles mentionnés au paragraphe (1), le tribunal ou le juge qui la déclare coupable peut ordonner, en sus de toute peine infligée, que les marchandises et les biens meubles au moyen ou à l'égard desquels l'infraction a été commise soient confisqués au profit de Sa Majesté, et qu'il en soit disposé conformément aux instructions du ministre.

Perquisition

(4) Un juge de paix convaincu, après dénonciation sous serment, qu'il existe un motif raisonnable de croire que, sur une réserve ou dans un bâtiment, contenant ou lieu, se trouvent des marchandises ou des biens meubles au moyen ou à l'égard desquels une infraction à l'un des articles mentionnés au paragraphe (1) a été commise, se commet ou est sur le point de se commettre, peut lancer un mandat sous son seing, autorisant une personne y nommée ou un agent de la paix à faire, en tout temps, une perquisition dans la réserve, le bâtiment, contenant ou lieu, pour rechercher ces marchandises ou biens meubles.

L.R. (1985), ch. I-5, art. 103; L.R. (1985), ch. 32 (1er suppl.), art. 19; 2014, ch. 38, art. 11.

Emploi des amendes

104 (1) Sous réserve du paragraphe (2), toute amende, peine ou confiscation infligée en vertu de la présente loi appartient à Sa Majesté au bénéfice de la bande — ou d'un ou de plusieurs de ses membres — à l'égard de laquelle l'infraction a été commise, ou dont le délinquant, si c'est un Indien, fait partie.

Indian
Offences, Punishment and Enforcement
Sections 104-108

Indiens
Infractions, peines et contrôle d'application
Articles 104-108

Exception

(2) The Governor in Council may from time to time direct that a fine, penalty or forfeiture described in subsection (1) shall be paid to a provincial, municipal or local authority that bears in whole or in part the expense of administering the law under which the fine, penalty or forfeiture is imposed, or that the fine, penalty or forfeiture shall be applied in the manner that he considers will best promote the purposes of the law under which the fine, penalty or forfeiture is imposed, or the administration of that law.

Disposition of fines imposed under by-laws

(3) If a fine is imposed under a by-law made by the council of a band under this Act, it belongs to the band and subsections (1) and (2) do not apply.

R.S., 1985, c. I-5, s. 104; 2014, c. 38, s. 12.

105 [Repealed, 2014, c. 38, s. 13]

Jurisdiction of provincial court judges

106 A provincial court judge has, with respect to matters arising under this Act, jurisdiction over the whole county, union of counties or judicial district in which the city, town or other place for which he is appointed or in which he has jurisdiction under provincial laws is situated.

R.S., 1985, c. I-5, s. 106; R.S., 1985, c. 27 (1st Supp.), s. 203.

Appointment of justices

107 The Governor in Council may appoint persons to be, for the purposes of this Act, justices of the peace and those persons have the powers and authority of two justices of the peace with regard to

(a) any offence under this Act; and

(b) any offence under the *Criminal Code* relating to cruelty to animals, common assault, breaking and entering and vagrancy, where the offence is committed by an Indian or relates to the person or property of an Indian.

R.S., c. I-6, s. 107.

Commissioners for taking oaths

108 For the purposes of this Act or any matter relating to Indian affairs

(a) persons appointed by the Minister for the purpose,

(b) superintendents, and

Exception

(2) Le gouverneur en conseil peut ordonner que le montant de l'amende, de la peine ou de la confiscation soit versé à une autorité provinciale, municipale ou locale qui supporte, en totalité ou en partie, les frais d'application de la loi aux termes de laquelle l'amende, la peine ou la confiscation est infligée, ou que l'amende, la peine ou la confiscation soit employée de la manière qui, à son avis, favorisera le mieux les fins de la loi selon laquelle l'amende, la peine ou la confiscation est infligée, ou l'application de cette loi.

Emploi des amendes infligées en vertu des règlements administratifs

(3) Dans le cas où l'amende est infligée en vertu d'un règlement administratif pris par le conseil d'une bande sous le régime de la présente loi, elle appartient à la bande et les paragraphes (1) et (2) ne s'appliquent pas.

L.R. (1985), ch. I-5, art. 104; 2014, ch. 38, art. 12.

105 [Abrogé, 2014, ch. 38, art. 13]

Juridiction des juges de la cour provinciale

106 Un juge de la cour provinciale a compétence, à l'égard de toutes questions découlant de la présente loi, dans tout le comté, tous les comtés unis ou tout le district judiciaire où se trouve la ville ou autre endroit pour lequel il a été nommé ou dans lequel il a compétence aux termes de la législation provinciale.

L.R. (1985), ch. I-5, art. 106; L.R. (1985), ch. 27 (1er suppl.), art. 203.

Nomination de juges de paix

107 Le gouverneur en conseil peut nommer des personnes qui seront chargées, pour l'application de la présente loi, de remplir les fonctions de juge de paix, et ces personnes ont la compétence de deux juges de paix à l'égard :

a) des infractions visées par la présente loi;

b) de toute infraction aux dispositions du *Code criminel* sur la cruauté envers les animaux, les voies de fait simples, l'introduction par effraction et le vagabondage, lorsqu'elle est commise par un Indien ou se rattache à la personne ou aux biens d'un Indien.

S.R., ch. I-6, art. 107.

Commissaires aux serments

108 Aux fins de la présente loi ou de toute question concernant les affaires indiennes, les personnes suivantes sont des commissaires aux serments :

a) les personnes nommées à cet effet par le ministre;

b) les surintendants;

Indian
Offences, Punishment and Enforcement
Sections 108-116

Indiens
Infractions, peines et contrôle d'application
Articles 108-116

(c) the Minister and the Deputy Minister of Indigenous Services,

are commissioners for the taking of oaths.

R.S., 1985, c. I-5, s. 108; 2019, c. 29, s. 358.

Enfranchisement

109 to 113 [Repealed, R.S., 1985, c. 32 (1st Supp.), s. 20]

Schools

Agreements with provinces, etc.

114 (1) The Governor in Council may authorize the Minister, in accordance with this Act, to enter into agreements on behalf of Her Majesty for the education in accordance with this Act of Indian children, with

(a) the government of a province;

(b) the Commissioner of Yukon;

(c) the Commissioner of the Northwest Territories;

(c.1) the Commissioner of Nunavut; and

(d) a public or separate school board.

(e) [Repealed, 2014, c. 38, s. 14]

Schools

(2) The Minister may, in accordance with this Act, establish, operate and maintain schools for Indian children.

R.S., 1985, c. I-5, s. 114; 1993, c. 28, s. 78; 2002, c. 7, s. 184; 2014, c. 38, s. 14.

Regulations

115 The Minister may

(a) provide for and make regulations with respect to standards for buildings, equipment, teaching, education, inspection and discipline in connection with schools; and

(b) provide for the transportation of children to and from school.

(c) and (d) [Repealed, 2014, c. 38, s. 15]

R.S., 1985, c. I-5, s. 115; 2014, c. 38, s. 15.

Attendance

116 (1) Subject to section 117, every Indian child who has attained the age of seven years shall attend school.

---

c) le ministre et le sous-ministre des Services aux Autochtones.

L.R. (1985), ch. I-5, art. 108; 2019, ch. 29, art. 358.

Émancipation

109 à 113 [Abrogés, L.R. (1985), ch. 32 (1er suppl.), art. 20]

Écoles

Accords avec les provinces, etc.

114 (1) Le gouverneur en conseil peut, en conformité avec la présente loi, autoriser le ministre à conclure, au nom de Sa Majesté et pour l'instruction des enfants indiens conformément à la présente loi, des accords avec :

a) le gouvernement d'une province;

b) le commissaire du Yukon;

c) le commissaire des Territoires du Nord-Ouest;

c.1) le commissaire du territoire du Nunavut;

d) une commission d'écoles publiques ou séparées.

e) [Abrogé, 2014, ch. 38, art. 14]

Écoles

(2) Le ministre peut, en conformité avec la présente loi, établir, diriger et entretenir des écoles pour les enfants indiens.

L.R. (1985), ch. I-5, art. 114; 1993, ch. 28, art. 78; 2002, ch. 7, art. 184; 2014, ch. 38, art. 14.

Règlements

115 Le ministre peut :

a) pourvoir à des normes de construction, d'installation, d'enseignement, d'inspection et de discipline relativement aux écoles, et prendre des règlements à cet égard;

b) assurer le transport, aller et retour, des enfants à l'école.

c) et d) [Abrogés, 2014, ch. 38, art. 15]

L.R. (1985), ch. I-5, art. 115; 2014, ch. 38, art. 15.

Fréquentation scolaire

116 (1) Sous réserve de l'article 117, tout enfant indien qui a atteint l'âge de sept ans doit fréquenter l'école.

Indian
Schools
Sections 116-122

Indiens
Écoles
Articles 116-122

Idem

(2) The Minister may

(a) require an Indian who has attained the age of six years to attend school; and

(b) require an Indian who becomes sixteen years of age during the school term to continue to attend school until the end of that term.

(c) [Repealed, 2014, c. 38, s. 16]

R.S., 1985, c. I-5, s. 116; 2014, c. 38, s. 16.

When attendance not required

117 An Indian child is not required to attend school if the child

(a) is, by reason of sickness or other unavoidable cause that is reported promptly to the principal, unable to attend school; or

(b) is under efficient instruction at home or elsewhere.

R.S., 1985, c. I-5, s. 117; 2014, c. 38, s. 17.

118 [Repealed, 2014, c. 38, s. 17]

119 [Repealed, 2014, c. 38, s. 17]

120 [Repealed, 2014, c. 38, s. 17]

121 [Repealed, 2014, c. 38, s. 17]

Definitions

122 The following definitions apply in sections 114 to 117.

child means an Indian who has attained the age of six years but has not attained the age of sixteen years, and a person who is required by the Minister to attend school; (*enfant*)

school includes a day school, technical school and high school. (*école*)

truant officer [Repealed, 2014, c. 38, s. 18]

R.S., 1985, c. I-5, s. 123; 2014, c. 38, s. 18.

Idem

(2) Le ministre peut :

a) enjoindre à un Indien qui a atteint l'âge de six ans de fréquenter l'école;

b) exiger qu'un Indien qui atteint l'âge de seize ans pendant une période scolaire continue à fréquenter l'école jusqu'à la fin de cette période.

c) [Abrogé, 2014, ch. 38, art. 16]

L.R. (1985), ch. I-5, art. 116; 2014, ch. 38, art. 16.

Cas où la fréquentation scolaire n'est pas requise

117 Un enfant indien n'est pas tenu de fréquenter l'école dans l'un ou l'autre des cas suivants :

a) il est incapable de le faire par suite de maladie ou pour une autre cause inévitable, qui est promptement signalée au principal;

b) il reçoit une instruction suffisante à la maison ou ailleurs.

L.R. (1985), ch. I-5, art. 117; 2014, ch. 38, art. 17.

118 [Abrogé, 2014, ch. 38, art. 17]

119 [Abrogé, 2014, ch. 38, art. 17]

120 [Abrogé, 2014, ch. 38, art. 17]

121 [Abrogé, 2014, ch. 38, art. 17]

Définitions

122 Les définitions qui suivent s'appliquent aux articles 114 à 117.

agent de surveillance [Abrogée, 2014, ch. 38, art. 18]

école Sont assimilés à une école un externat, une école technique et une école secondaire. (*school*)

enfant Indien qui a atteint l'âge de six ans mais n'a pas atteint l'âge de seize ans, ainsi qu'une personne que le ministre oblige à fréquenter l'école. (*child*)

L.R. (1985), ch. I-5, art. 123; 2014, ch. 38, art. 18.

RELATED PROVISIONS

— R.S., 1985, c. 32 (1st Supp.), s. 22

Saving from liability

22 For greater certainty, no claim lies against Her Majesty in right of Canada, the Minister, any band, council of a band or member of a band or any other person or body in relation to the omission or deletion of the name of a person from the Indian Register in the circumstances set out in paragraph 6(1)(c), (d) or (e) of the *Indian Act*.

— R.S., 1985, c. 32 (1st Supp.), s. 23

Report of Minister to Parliament

23 (1) The Minister shall cause to be laid before each House of Parliament, not later than two years after this Act is assented to, a report on the implementation of the amendments to the *Indian Act*, as enacted by this Act, which report shall include detailed information on

(a) the number of persons who have been registered under section 6 of the *Indian Act*, and the number entered on each Band List under subsection 11(1) of that Act, since April 17, 1985;

(b) the names and number of bands that have assumed control of their own membership under section 10 of the *Indian Act*; and

(c) the impact of the amendments on the lands and resources of Indian bands.

Review by Parliamentary committee

(2) Such committee of Parliament as may be designated or established for the purposes of this subsection shall, forthwith after the report of the Minister is tabled under subsection (1), review that report and may, in the course of that review, undertake a review of any provision of the *Indian Act* enacted by this Act.

— R.S., 1985, c. 27 (2nd Supp.), s. 11

Transitional: proceedings

11 Proceedings to which any of the provisions amended by the schedule apply that were commenced before the coming into force of section 10 shall be continued in accordance with those amended provisions without any further formality.

DISPOSITIONS CONNEXES

— L.R. (1985), ch. 32 (1er suppl.), art. 22

Aucune réclamation

22 Il demeure entendu qu'il ne peut être présenté aucune réclamation contre Sa Majesté du chef du Canada, le ministre, une bande, un conseil de bande, un membre d'une bande ou autre personne ou organisme relativement à l'omission ou au retranchement du nom d'une personne du registre des Indiens dans les circonstances prévues aux alinéas 6(1)c), d) ou e) de la *Loi sur les Indiens*.

— L.R. (1985), ch. 32 (1er suppl.), art. 23

Rapport du ministre au Parlement

23 (1) Au plus tard deux ans après la date de sanction de la présente loi, le ministre fait déposer devant chaque chambre du Parlement un rapport sur l'application des modifications de la *Loi sur les Indiens* prévues dans la présente loi. Le rapport contient des renseignements détaillés sur :

a) le nombre de personnes inscrites en vertu de l'article 6 de la *Loi sur les Indiens* et le nombre de personnes dont le nom a été consigné dans une liste de bande en vertu du paragraphe 11(1) de cette loi, depuis le 17 avril 1985;

b) les noms et le nombre des bandes qui décident de l'appartenance à leurs effectifs en vertu de l'article 10 de la *Loi sur les Indiens*;

c) l'effet des modifications sur les terres et les ressources des bandes d'Indiens.

Examen par un comité parlementaire

(2) Le comité parlementaire désigné ou constitué pour l'application du présent paragraphe examine sans délai après son dépôt par le ministre le rapport visé au paragraphe (1). Il peut, dans le cadre de cet examen, procéder à la révision de toute disposition de la *Loi sur les Indiens* édictée par la présente loi.

— L.R. (1985), ch. 27 (2e suppl.), art. 11

Disposition transitoire : procédure

11 Les procédures intentées en vertu des dispositions modifiées en annexe avant l'entrée en vigueur de l'article 10 se poursuivent en conformité avec les nouvelles dispositions sans autres formalités.

— R.S., 1985, c. 17 (4th Supp.), s. 7(2)

Transitional

7 (2) The Surrendered Lands Register kept in the Department before the coming into force of this Act constitutes, on the coming into force of this Act, the Surrendered and Designated Lands Register.

— 1990, c. 16, s. 24(1)

Transitional: proceedings

24 (1) Every proceeding commenced before the coming into force of this subsection and in respect of which any provision amended by this Act applies shall be taken up and continued under and in conformity with that amended provision without any further formality.

— 1990, c. 17, s. 45(1)

Transitional: proceedings

45 (1) Every proceeding commenced before the coming into force of this subsection and in respect of which any provision amended by this Act applies shall be taken up and continued under and in conformity with that amended provision without any further formality.

— 1998, c. 30, s. 10

Transitional — proceedings

10 Every proceeding commenced before the coming into force of this section and in respect of which any provision amended by sections 12 to 16 applies shall be taken up and continued under and in conformity with that amended provision without any further formality.

— 2005, c. 9, s. 145

Continuation of existing by-laws

145 (1) By-laws made by a first nation under paragraph 83(1)(a), or any of paragraphs 83(1)(d) to (g), of the *Indian Act* that are in force on the day on which the name of the first nation is added to the schedule are deemed to be laws made under section 5 or 9, as the case may be, to the extent that they are not inconsistent with section 5 or 9, and remain in force until they are repealed or replaced.

Amendment of existing by-laws

(2) For greater certainty, subsections 5(2) to (7) apply to amendments of by-laws referred to in subsection (1).

— L.R. (1985), ch. 17 (4ᵉ suppl.), par. 7(2)

Disposition transitoire

7 (2) Le registre appelé avant l'entrée en vigueur de la présente loi Registre des terres cédées devient, à compter de celle-ci, le Registre des terres cédées ou désignées.

— 1990, ch. 16, par. 24(1)

Disposition transitoire : procédures

24 (1) Les procédures intentées avant l'entrée en vigueur du présent paragraphe et auxquelles des dispositions visées par la présente loi s'appliquent se poursuivent sans autres formalités en conformité avec ces dispositions dans leur forme modifiée.

— 1990, ch. 17, par. 45(1)

Disposition transitoire : procédures

45 (1) Les procédures intentées avant l'entrée en vigueur du présent paragraphe et auxquelles s'appliquent des dispositions visées par la présente loi se poursuivent sans autres formalités en conformité avec ces dispositions dans leur forme modifiée.

— 1998, ch. 30, art. 10

Procédures

10 Les procédures intentées avant l'entrée en vigueur du présent article et auxquelles s'appliquent des dispositions visées par les articles 12 à 16 se poursuivent sans autres formalités en conformité avec ces dispositions dans leur forme modifiée.

— 2005, ch. 9, art. 145

Maintien des règlements administratifs existants

145 (1) Les règlements administratifs pris par une première nation en vertu de l'alinéa 83(1)a), ou de l'un des alinéas 83(1)d) à g), de la *Loi sur les Indiens* et qui sont en vigueur à la date à laquelle le nom de celle-ci est inscrit à l'annexe sont réputés être des textes législatifs pris en vertu des articles 5 ou 9, selon le cas, dans la mesure où ils ne sont pas incompatibles avec ces articles, et demeurent en vigueur tant qu'ils ne sont pas remplacés ou abrogés.

Modification des règlements administratifs existants

(2) Il est entendu que les paragraphes 5(2) à (7) s'appliquent à la modification des règlements administratifs visés au paragraphe (1).

— 2008, c. 32, s. 21

Existing interests — *Indian Act*

21 (1) Despite section 12, if an interest in land in the Former Tsawwassen Reserve was granted or approved under the *Indian Act* and exists on the effective date of the Agreement, the interest continues in effect in accordance with its terms and conditions unless a replacement interest is issued in accordance with Chapter 4 of the Agreement.

Transfer of rights and obligations

(2) On the effective date of the Agreement, the rights and obligations of Her Majesty in right of Canada as grantor in respect of such an interest are transferred to the Tsawwassen First Nation, which assumes those rights and obligations in accordance with the interest's terms and conditions.

— 2008, c. 32, s. 25

Documents in land registries

25 As of the effective date of the Agreement, registrations or records affecting Tsawwassen Lands that are registered or recorded in a land registry under the *Indian Act* or the *First Nations Land Management Act* have no effect.

— 2010, c. 18, s. 3.1

Report

3.1 (1) The Minister of Indian Affairs and Northern Development shall cause to be laid before each House of Parliament, not later than two years after this Act comes into force, a report on the provisions and implementation of this Act.

Review by committee

(2) Such committee of Parliament as may be designated or established for the purposes of this subsection shall, forthwith after the report of the Minister is tabled under subsection (1), review that report and shall, in the course of that review, undertake a review of any provision of this Act.

— 2010, c. 18, s. 4, as amended by 2015, c. 3, s. 98

Definitions

4 In sections 5 to 9, ***band***, ***Band List***, ***council of a band***, ***registered*** and ***Registrar*** have the same meaning as in subsection 2(1) of the *Indian Act*.

— 2008, ch. 32, art. 21

Droits existants : *Loi sur les Indiens*

21 (1) Malgré l'article 12, les droits sur les terres de l'ancienne réserve de Tsawwassen accordés ou approuvés sous le régime de la *Loi sur les Indiens* et existants à la date d'entrée en vigueur de l'accord sont maintenus, ainsi que les conditions dont ils sont assortis, à moins qu'un intérêt de remplacement soit accordé conformément au chapitre 4 de l'accord.

Transfert des droits et obligations

(2) Les droits et obligations qui incombent à Sa Majesté du chef du Canada à l'égard de ces droits sur les terres sont, à la date d'entrée en vigueur de l'accord, transférés à la Première Nation de Tsawwassen qui s'en acquitte conformément aux conditions dont ceux-ci sont assortis.

— 2008, ch. 32, art. 25

Registres des terres

25 À compter de la date d'entrée en vigueur de l'accord, les inscriptions et dossiers relatifs aux terres tsawwassennes figurant dans tout registre des terres en vertu de la *Loi sur les Indiens* ou de la *Loi sur la gestion des terres des premières nations* sont sans effet.

— 2010, ch. 18, art. 3.1

Rapport

3.1 (1) Au plus tard deux ans après la date d'entrée en vigueur de la présente loi, le ministre des Affaires indiennes et du Nord canadien fait déposer devant chaque chambre du Parlement un rapport sur les dispositions de la présente loi et sa mise en œuvre.

Examen par le comité

(2) Le comité parlementaire désigné ou constitué pour l'application du présent paragraphe examine sans délai le rapport visé au paragraphe (1) après son dépôt. Dans le cadre de l'examen, le comité procède à la révision des dispositions de la présente loi.

— 2010, ch. 18, art. 4, modifié par 2015, ch. 3, art. 98

Définitions

4 Aux articles 5 à 9, ***bande***, ***conseil de bande***, ***inscrit***, ***liste de bande*** et ***registraire*** s'entendent au sens du paragraphe 2(1) de la *Loi sur les Indiens*.

— 2010, c. 18, s. 5

Registration continued

5 For greater certainty, subject to any deletions made by the Registrar under subsection 5(3) of the *Indian Act*, any person who was, immediately before the day on which this Act comes into force, registered and entitled to be registered under paragraph 6(1)(a) or (c) of the *Indian Act* continues to be registered.

— 2010, c. 18, s. 6

Registration entitlements recognized

6 For greater certainty, for the purposes of paragraph 6(1)(f) and subsection 6(2) of the *Indian Act*, the Registrar must recognize any entitlements to be registered that existed under paragraph 6(1)(a) or (c) of that Act immediately before the day on which this Act comes into force.

— 2010, c. 18, s. 7

Membership maintained — paragraphs 6(1)(a) and (c)

7 For greater certainty, subject to any membership rules established by a band, any person who, immediately before the day on which this Act comes into force, was entitled to be registered under paragraph 6(1)(a) or (c) of the *Indian Act* and had the right to have their name entered in the Band List maintained by that band continues to have that right.

— 2010, c. 18, s. 8

Membership maintained — paragraph 6(1)(c.1)

8 For greater certainty, subject to any membership rules established by a band on or after the day on which this Act comes into force, any person who is entitled to be registered under paragraph 6(1)(c.1) of the *Indian Act*, as enacted by subsection 2(3), and who had, immediately before that day, the right to have their name entered in the Band List maintained by that band continues to have that right.

— 2010, c. 18, s. 9

No liability

9 For greater certainty, no person or body has a right to claim or receive any compensation, damages or indemnity from Her Majesty in right of Canada, any employee or agent of Her Majesty, or a council of a band, for anything done or omitted to be done in good faith in the exercise of their powers or the performance of their duties, only because

— 2010, ch. 18, art. 5

Inscription maintenue

5 Il est entendu que, sous réserve de tout retranchement effectué par le registraire en vertu du paragraphe 5(3) de la *Loi sur les Indiens*, toute personne qui, à l'entrée en vigueur de la présente loi, était inscrite et avait le droit de l'être en vertu des alinéas 6(1)a) ou c) de la *Loi sur les Indiens* le demeure.

— 2010, ch. 18, art. 6

Droit à l'inscription maintenu

6 Il est entendu que, pour l'application de l'alinéa 6(1)f) et du paragraphe 6(2) de la *Loi sur les Indiens*, le registraire est tenu de reconnaître tout droit d'être inscrit qui existait en vertu des alinéas 6(1)a) ou c) de cette loi à l'entrée en vigueur de la présente loi.

— 2010, ch. 18, art. 7

Appartenance maintenue : alinéas 6(1)a) et c)

7 Il est entendu que, sous réserve des règles d'appartenance fixées par la bande, toute personne qui, à l'entrée en vigueur de la présente loi, avait le droit d'être inscrite en vertu des alinéas 6(1)a) ou c) de la *Loi sur les Indiens* et avait droit à ce que son nom soit consigné dans la liste de bande tenue par celle-ci conserve le droit à ce que son nom y soit consigné.

— 2010, ch. 18, art. 8

Appartenance maintenue : alinéa 6(1)c.1)

8 Il est entendu que, sous réserve des règles d'appartenance fixées par la bande à compter de la date d'entrée en vigueur de la présente loi, toute personne qui a le droit d'être inscrite en vertu de l'alinéa 6(1)c.1) de la *Loi sur les Indiens*, édicté par le paragraphe 2(3), et qui, à cette date, avait droit à ce que son nom soit consigné dans la liste de bande tenue par celle-ci conserve le droit à ce que son nom y soit consigné.

— 2010, ch. 18, art. 9

Absence de responsabilité

9 Il est entendu qu'aucune personne ni aucun organisme ne peut réclamer ou recevoir une compensation, des dommages-intérêts ou une indemnité de l'État, de ses préposés ou mandataires ou d'un conseil de bande en ce qui concerne les faits — actes ou omissions — accomplis de bonne foi dans l'exercice de leurs attributions, du seul fait qu'une personne n'était pas inscrite — ou que le nom d'une personne n'était pas consigné dans une liste de bande — à l'entrée en vigueur de la présente loi et que

(a) a person was not registered, or did not have their name entered in a Band List, immediately before the day on which this Act comes into force; and

(b) one of the person's parents is entitled to be registered under paragraph 6(1)(c.1) of the *Indian Act*, as enacted by subsection 2(3).

— 2017, c. 25, s. 4

Definition of *declaration*

4 (1) In sections 5 to 8 and 15, ***declaration*** means the declaration made on August 3, 2015 by the Superior Court of Quebec in *Descheneaux c. Canada (Procureur général)*, 2015 QCCS 3555, that paragraphs 6(1)(a), (c) and (f) and subsection 6(2) of the *Indian Act* are inoperative.

Same meaning

(2) Words and expressions used in sections 5 to 10.1 have the same meaning as in the *Indian Act*.

— 2017, c. 25, s. 5

Application

5 Sections 6 to 8 apply if the suspension of the declaration expires before the day on which the order referred to in subsection 15(1) is made.

— 2017, c. 25, s. 6

Registration continued

6 For greater certainty, subject to any deletions made by the Registrar under subsection 5(3) of the *Indian Act*, any person who was, immediately before the suspension of the declaration expires, registered and entitled to be registered under paragraph 6(1)(a), (c) or (f) or subsection 6(2) of that Act continues to be registered.

— 2017, c. 25, s. 7

Registration entitlements recognized

7 For greater certainty, subject to any deletions made by the Registrar under subsection 5(3) of the *Indian Act*, for the purposes of paragraph 6(1)(f) and subsection 6(2) of that Act, the Registrar must, in respect of the period beginning on the day after the day on which the suspension of the declaration expires and ending on the day on which the order referred to in subsection 15(1) is made, recognize any entitlements to be registered that existed under paragraph 6(1)(a), (c) or (f) or subsection 6(2) of the *Indian Act* immediately before the suspension of the declaration expires.

l'un de ses parents a le droit d'être inscrit en vertu de l'alinéa 6(1)c.1) de la *Loi sur les Indiens*, édicté par le paragraphe 2(3).

— 2017, ch. 25, art. 4

Définition de *déclaration*

4 (1) Aux articles 5 à 8 et 15, ***déclaration*** s'entend de la déclaration d'inopérabilité relative aux alinéas 6(1)a), c) et f) et au paragraphe 6(2) de la *Loi sur les Indiens* rendue le 3 août 2015 par la Cour supérieure du Québec dans l'affaire *Descheneaux c. Canada (Procureur général)*, 2015 QCCS 3555.

Terminologie

(2) Les termes des articles 5 à 10.1 s'entendent au sens de la *Loi sur les Indiens*.

— 2017, ch. 25, art. 5

Application

5 Les articles 6 à 8 s'appliquent si l'expiration de la suspension de la déclaration survient avant la date de la prise du décret visé au paragraphe 15(1).

— 2017, ch. 25, art. 6

Inscription maintenue

6 Il est entendu que, sous réserve de tout retranchement effectué par le registraire en vertu du paragraphe 5(3) de la *Loi sur les Indiens*, toute personne qui, à l'expiration de la suspension de la déclaration, était inscrite et avait le droit de l'être en vertu des alinéas 6(1)a), c) ou f) ou du paragraphe 6(2) de cette loi demeure inscrite.

— 2017, ch. 25, art. 7

Droit à l'inscription reconnu

7 Il est entendu que, sous réserve de tout retranchement effectué par le registraire en vertu du paragraphe 5(3) de la *Loi sur les Indiens*, pour l'application de l'alinéa 6(1)f) et du paragraphe 6(2) de cette loi — et pour la période commençant le lendemain de la date d'expiration de la suspension de la déclaration et se terminant à la date de la prise du décret visé au paragraphe 15(1) — le registraire est tenu de reconnaître tout droit d'être inscrit qui existait, en vertu des alinéas 6(1)a), c) ou f) ou du paragraphe 6(2) de cette loi, à l'expiration de la suspension de la déclaration.

— 2017, c. 25, s. 8

Membership continued

8 For greater certainty, any person whose name appeared immediately before the expiry of the suspension of the declaration on a Band List maintained in the Department is not deprived of the right to have their name entered on that Band List by reason only of the declaration.

— 2017, c. 25, s. 9

Construction

9 The provisions of the *Indian Act* that are amended by this Act are to be liberally construed and interpreted so as to remedy any disadvantage to a woman, or her descendants, born before April 17, 1985, with respect to registration under the *Indian Act* as it read on April 17, 1985, and to enhance the equal treatment of women and men and their descendants under the *Indian Act*.

— 2017, c. 25, s. 10

No liability

10 For greater certainty, no person or body has a right to claim or receive any compensation, damages or indemnity from Her Majesty in right of Canada, any employee or agent of Her Majesty in right of Canada, or a council of a band, for anything done or omitted to be done in good faith in the exercise of their powers or the performance of their duties, only because

(a) a person was not registered, or did not have their name entered in a Band List, immediately before the day on which this section comes into force; and

(b) one of the person's parents is entitled to be registered under paragraph 6(1)(c.01) or (c.02) or any of paragraphs 6(1)(c.2) to (c.6) of the *Indian Act*.

— 2017, c. 25, s. 10.1

No liability

10.1 For greater certainty, no person or body has a right to claim or receive any compensation, damages or indemnity from Her Majesty in right of Canada, any employee or agent of Her Majesty in right of Canada, or a council of a band, for anything done or omitted to be done in good faith in the exercise of their powers or the performance of their duties, only because

— 2017, ch. 25, art. 8

Appartenance maintenue

8 Il est entendu que la déclaration à elle seule ne peut priver quiconque dont le nom apparaît, à l'expiration de celle-ci, sur la liste de bande tenue au ministère du droit à ce que son nom y soit consigné.

— 2017, ch. 25, art. 9

Règle d'interprétation

9 Les dispositions de la *Loi sur les Indiens* qui sont modifiées par la présente loi s'interprètent de façon large afin de remédier à tout désavantage qu'ont subi les femmes ou leurs descendants nés avant le 17 avril 1985 en ce qui a trait à l'inscription au titre de la *Loi sur les Indiens* dans sa version du 17 avril 1985 et afin de parvenir à un traitement égal, sous le régime de la *Loi sur les Indiens*, des femmes et des hommes et de leurs descendants.

— 2017, ch. 25, art. 10

Absence de responsabilité

10 Il est entendu qu'aucune personne ni aucun organisme ne peut réclamer ou recevoir une compensation, des dommages-intérêts ou une indemnité de l'État, de ses préposés ou mandataires ou d'un conseil de bande en ce qui concerne les faits — actes ou omissions — accomplis de bonne foi dans l'exercice de leurs attributions, du seul fait qu'une personne n'était pas inscrite — ou que le nom d'une personne n'était pas consigné dans une liste de bande — à la date d'entrée en vigueur du présent article et que l'un de ses parents a le droit d'être inscrit en vertu des alinéas 6(1)c.01), c.02), ou c.2) à c.6) de la *Loi sur les Indiens*.

— 2017, ch. 25, art. 10.1

Absence de responsabilité

10.1 Il est entendu qu'aucune personne ni aucun organisme ne peut réclamer ou recevoir une compensation, des dommages-intérêts ou une indemnité de l'État, de ses préposés ou mandataires ou d'un conseil de bande en ce qui concerne les faits — actes ou omissions — accomplis de bonne foi dans l'exercice de leurs attributions, du seul fait qu'une personne n'était pas inscrite — ou que le nom d'une personne n'était pas consigné dans une liste de bande — à la date d'entrée en vigueur du présent

(a) a person was not registered, or did not have their name entered in a Band List, immediately before the day on which this section comes into force; and

(b) that person or one of the person's parents, grandparents or other ancestors is entitled to be registered under paragraph 6(1)(a.1), (a.2) or (a.3) of the *Indian Act*.

— 2017, c. 25, s. 11

Consultations by Minister

11 (1) The Minister must, within six months after the day on which this Act receives royal assent, initiate consultations with First Nations and other interested parties in order to address, in collaboration with those First Nations and other parties, issues raised by the provisions of the *Indian Act* related to registration and band membership, including consultations on

(a) issues relating to adoption;

(b) the 1951 cut-off date for entitlement to registration;

(c) the second-generation cut-off rule;

(d) unknown or unstated paternity;

(e) enfranchisement;

(f) the continued federal government role in determining Indian status and band membership; and

(g) First Nations' authorities to determine band membership.

Requirement

(2) The Minister, the First Nations and the other interested parties must, during the consultations, consider the impact of the *Canadian Charter of Rights and Freedoms*, of the United Nations Declaration on the Rights of Indigenous Peoples and, if applicable, of the *Canadian Human Rights Act*, in regard to those issues.

Report to Parliament — design of consultation process

(3) The Minister must cause to be laid before each House of Parliament, within five months after the day on which this Act receives royal assent, a report on the design of a process by which the Minister is to carry out the consultations described to in subsection (1).

article et que la personne ou l'un de ses parents ou un autre de ses ascendants a le droit d'être inscrit en vertu de l'un des alinéas 6(1)a.1), a.2) ou a.3) de la *Loi sur les Indiens*.

— 2017, ch. 25, art. 11

Consultations par le ministre

11 (1) Le ministre, dans les six mois suivant la date de la sanction de la présente loi, débute les consultations et la collaboration avec les Premières Nations et les autres parties intéressées en vue d'apporter des solutions aux questions soulevées à l'égard des dispositions de la *Loi sur les Indiens* concernant l'inscription et l'appartenance à une bande, notamment des consultations à l'égard :

a) de questions relatives à l'adoption;

b) de la date limite de 1951 relativement au droit à l'inscription;

c) de l'exclusion après la deuxième génération;

d) de la paternité inconnue ou non déclarée;

e) de l'émancipation;

f) du rôle continu de l'administration fédérale dans la détermination du statut d'Indien et de l'appartenance à une bande;

g) des pouvoirs des Premières Nations en vue de la détermination de l'appartenance à une bande.

Obligation

(2) Le ministre, les Premières Nations et les autres parties intéressées doivent, lors des consultations, tenir compte des effets de la *Charte canadienne des droits et libertés*, de la Déclaration des Nations Unies sur les droits des peuples autochtones et, si elle est applicable, de la *Loi canadienne sur les droits de la personne* relativement aux questions soulevées.

Rapport au Parlement — plan du processus de consultation

(3) Le ministre fait déposer devant chaque chambre du Parlement, dans les cinq mois suivant la date de la sanction de la présente loi, un rapport sur le plan du processus par lequel il procédera aux consultations prévues au paragraphe (1).

Report to Parliament — results of consultations

(4) The Minister must cause to be laid before each House of Parliament, within 12 months after the day on which the consultations begin, a report on the progress made as a result of the consultations and collaboration. The report must set out details as to the consultations carried out, including details related to

(a) issues relating to adoption;

(b) the 1951 cut-off date for entitlement to registration;

(c) the second-generation cut-off rule;

(d) unknown or unstated paternity;

(e) enfranchisement;

(f) the continued federal government role in determining Indian status and band membership; and

(g) First Nations' authorities to determine band membership.

Referral to committee

(5) Each report stands referred to any committee of the Senate, of the House of Commons or of both Houses of Parliament that is designated or established to review matters related to Aboriginal affairs.

— 2017, c. 25, s. 12

Report to Parliament

12 (1) The Minister must, within three years after the day on which this Act receives royal assent,

(a) undertake the following reviews:

(i) a review of the provisions of section 6 of the *Indian Act* that are enacted by this Act in order to determine whether all of the sex-based inequities have been eliminated with respect to those provisions, and

(ii) a review of the operation of the provisions of the *Indian Act* that are enacted by this Act; and

(b) cause to be laid before each House of Parliament a report on those reviews that includes, if he or she determines that any sex-based inequities still exist with respect to the provisions of section 6 of the *Indian Act* that are enacted by this Act, a statement of any changes to the *Indian Act* that he or she recommends

Rapport au Parlement — résultats des consultations

(4) Le ministre fait déposer devant chaque chambre du Parlement, dans les douze mois suivant la date du début des consultations, un rapport sur les progrès réalisés à la suite des consultations et de la collaboration. Le rapport contient des détails concernant les consultations qui ont eu lieu, notamment des détails à l'égard :

a) de questions relatives à l'adoption;

b) de la date limite de 1951 relativement au droit à l'inscription;

c) de l'exclusion après la deuxième génération;

d) de la paternité inconnue ou non déclarée;

e) de l'émancipation;

f) du rôle continu de l'administration fédérale dans la détermination du statut d'Indien et de l'appartenance à une bande;

g) des pouvoirs des Premières Nations en vue de la détermination de l'appartenance à une bande.

Renvoi en comité

(5) Sont saisis d'office de ces rapports tout comité du Sénat, tout comité de la Chambre des communes et tout comité mixte désignés ou constitués pour étudier les questions relatives aux affaires autochtones.

— 2017, ch. 25, art. 12

Rapport au Parlement

12 (1) Dans les trois ans suivant la date de sanction de la présente loi, le ministre :

a) procède à l'examen :

(i) des dispositions de l'article 6 de la *Loi sur les Indiens* édictées par la présente loi pour déterminer si toutes les iniquités fondées sur le sexe à l'égard de ces dispositions ont été éliminées,

(ii) de l'application des dispositions de la *Loi sur les Indiens* édictées par la présente loi;

b) fait déposer devant chaque chambre du Parlement un rapport portant sur l'examen visé à l'alinéa a), lequel fait état notamment — s'il conclut qu'il existe toujours des iniquités fondées sur le sexe à l'égard des dispositions de cet article 6 de la *Loi sur les Indiens* édictées par la présente loi — des modifications qu'il recommande d'apporter à la *Loi sur les Indiens* pour réduire ou éliminer ces iniquités.

in order to reduce or eliminate those sex-based inequities.

Referral to committee

(2) The report stands referred to any committee of the Senate, of the House of Commons or of both Houses of Parliament that is designated or established to review matters related to Aboriginal affairs.

— 2017, c. 25, s. 13

Publication

13 The Minister must publish every report laid before Parliament under sections 11 and 12 on the Department's website immediately after their tabling.

— 2017, c. 25, s. 14

Same meaning

14 Words and expressions used in sections 11 to 13 have the same meaning as in the *Indian Act*.

— 2023, c. 16, s. 62

By-laws approved

62 All by-laws made under subsection 83(1) of the *Indian Act* from July 15, 2019 to May 16, 2020 that received approval, in whole or in part, from the Minister of Crown-Indigenous Relations during that time are deemed to have received it instead from the Minister of Indigenous Services.

Renvoi en comité

(2) Sont saisis d'office de ce rapport tout comité du Sénat, tout comité de la Chambre des communes et tout comité mixte désignés ou constitués pour étudier les questions relatives aux affaires autochtones.

— 2017, ch. 25, art. 13

Publication

13 Le ministre publie les rapports déposés au Parlement en application des articles 11 et 12 sur le site Web de son ministère immédiatement après leur dépôt.

— 2017, ch. 25, art. 14

Terminologie

14 Les termes des articles 11 à 13 s'entendent au sens de la *Loi sur les Indiens*.

— 2023, ch. 16, art. 62

Règlements administratifs approuvés

62 Les règlements administratifs qui ont été pris en vertu du paragraphe 83(1) de la *Loi sur les Indiens* entre le 15 juillet 2019 et le 16 mai 2020, inclusivement, et qui ont reçu l'approbation, en tout ou en partie, du ministre des Relations Couronne-Autochtones au cours de cette période, sont réputés l'avoir reçue du ministre des Services aux Autochtones.

Appendix E

Sections of Constitution Act

E.0.1 CONSTITUTION ACT, 1867
30 & 31 Victoria, c. 3 (U.K.)

Equality Rights

Equality before and under law and equal protection and benefit of
law
* 15 (1) Every individual is equal before and under the law and has
the right to the equal protection and equal benefit of the law without
discrimination and, in particular, without discrimination based on
race, national or ethnic origin, colour, religion, sex, age or mental or
physical disability.

General

Aboriginal rights and freedoms not affected by Charter
25 The guarantee in this Charter of certain rights and freedoms shall
not be construed so as to abrogate or derogate from any aboriginal,
treaty or other rights or freedoms that pertain to the aboriginal peoples of Canada including
* (a) any rights or freedoms that have been recognized by the Royal
Proclamation of October 7, 1763; and
* (b) any rights or freedoms that now exist by way of land claims
agreements or may be so acquired.(95)

PART II Rights of the Aboriginal Peoples of Canada

Recognition of existing aboriginal and treaty rights

* 35 (1) The existing aboriginal and treaty rights of the aboriginal peoples of Canada are hereby recognized and affirmed.
* Definition of aboriginal peoples of Canada
(2) In this Act, aboriginal peoples of Canada includes the Indian, Inuit and Métis peoples of Canada.
* Land claims agreements
(3) For greater certainty, in subsection (1) treaty rights includes rights that now exist by way of land claims agreements or may be so acquired.
* Aboriginal and treaty rights are guaranteed equally to both sexes
(4) Notwithstanding any other provision of this Act, the aboriginal and treaty rights referred to in subsection (1) are guaranteed equally to male and female persons.(97) Commitment to participation in constitutional conference
35.1 The government of Canada and the provincial governments are committed to the principle that, before any amendment is made to Class 24 of section 91 of the Constitution Act, 1867, to section 25 of this Act or to this Part,
* (a) a constitutional conference that includes in its agenda an item relating to the proposed amendment, composed of the Prime Minister of Canada and the first ministers of the provinces, will be convened by the Prime Minister of Canada; and
* (b) the Prime Minister of Canada will invite representatives of the aboriginal peoples of Canada to participate in the discussions on that item.(98)

www.ingramcontent.com/pod-product-compliance
Lightning Source LLC
Chambersburg PA
CBHW080415270326

41929CB00018B/3032